Set Me Free

Brian Gallagher needs little introduction to spiritual directors. His leadership in the ministry of spiritual direction and the formation of spiritual directors, which I was fortunate to share, has inspired and supported spiritual directors locally and internationally. Spiritual directors and those involved in the formation of spiritual directors will find Brian's writing insightful, practically helpful, and personally challenging. This is especially true of his teaching on discernment of spirits, which I find all the more valuable because it is clearly based on his own practice and learning over many years. All people who are sincere in their listening to the invitation of God's Spirit in their lives and in the lives of those to whom they minister will be helped by this book. I recommend it highly.

Sue Richardson pbvm
Co-founder of the Siloam formation program for spiritual directors

Brian Gallagher has shown a life-time commitment to deep listening and discernment. *Set me Free* explores the heart journey required to come to a place of liberation and consolation. The work is a testament to the programs in which he has collaborated to form spiritual directors as authentic accompaniers to others seeking peace, confidence and freedom. I recommend *Set me Free* to all formation programs and libraries dedicated to quality spiritual direction, facilitation and supervision.

Tim Moloney cfc
National Chair, Conference of Spiritual Directors, Australia

In *Set me Free: Spiritual Direction and Discernment of Spirits*, Brian Gallagher offers a remarkably clear and rigorous account of the practice of spiritual direction. The book is thorough, well researched and well written. The author describes the pastoral practice that is at the heart of spiritual direction: a spiritual director discerning their inner movements while contemplatively listening to the one being directed. The sacred ministry of spiritual direction will come to nothing without a discerning heart.

Importantly, he distils the core insights of others and integrates them with his own wisdom born of fifty years' experience as a spiritual director. The book is filled with psychological, theological and spiritual insight. If you are a beginning spiritual director or an experienced practitioner, or one who provides formation and ongoing supervision in the discipline of spiritual direction, your ministry will be enhanced by reading and re-reading this book.

Michael Smith sj
International Director of Mission and Identity,
Jesuit Refugee Service, Rome.

SET ME FREE

SPIRITUAL DIRECTION & DISCERNMENT OF SPIRITS

BRIAN GALLAGHER MSC

COVENTRY PRESS

Published in Australia by

Coventry Press
33 Scoresby Road
Bayswater Vic. 3153
Australia

ISBN 9780987643100

Copyright © Brian Gallagher 2019

All rights reserved. Other than for the purposes and subject to the conditions prescribed under the *Copyright Act*, no part of this publication may be reproduced, stored in a retrieval system, or transmitted in any form or by any means, electronic, mechanical, photocopying, recording or otherwise, without the prior permission of the publisher.

Scripture quotations are from the *New Revised Standard Version Bible*, copyright 1989, Division of Christian Education of the National Council of the Churches of Christ in the United States of America. Used by permission. All rights reserved.

Cataloguing-in-Publication entry is available from the National Library of Australia http://catalogue.nla.gov.au/.

Cover design by Ian James - www.jgd.com.au
Text by Megan Low, Film Shot Graphics

Printed in Australia

Contents

Foreword 9

Introduction 13

1. God's Spirit in our Lives............................. 22

2. The Tradition of Spiritual Direction 41

3. Learning from Experience 69

4. Discernment: Consolation and Desolation 88

5. The Ways of the Spirit 122

6. Discernment of Spirits in Spiritual Direction 159

7. Discernment of Spirits in Christian Decision Making .. 202

8. Becoming discerning: the Gift of Freedom 222

9. Becoming discerning: Growth in inner freedom 254

10. Formation of Spiritual Directors 286

Conclusion 318

Appendix The Formation Program *Siloam* 321

Recommended Reading 330

You looked with love upon me,
and deep within, your eyes imprinted grace.
This mercy set me free,
held in your love's embrace,
to lift my eyes adoring to your face.

John of the Cross

from *The Spiritual Canticle*

Foreword

With his comprehensive, *Set Me Free: Spiritual Direction and Discernment of Spirits*, Dr Brian Gallagher msc has given us an inspiring and practical resource for the formation of those involved in spiritual direction. His text reaches deeply into the theological and pastoral meaning of the matter. This might be expected of one whose reflections emerge from a wide and long experience of the realities involved and of the people engaged in spiritual direction, so as to assist others to be more responsive to ways of the Spirit and more courageously committed to "the one thing necessary".

In this respect, I could not but be impressed by the way the author insists that spiritual direction is essentially not merely a pastoral skill, nor even a form of psychological and self-realisation therapy, but most radically the way of directing people to God. Touched and attracted by the infinite and all merciful Other, the director and the directee are drawn out of themselves to adore the Living God, and to leave behind self-destructive demons and the idols that oppress the human spirit. *Set Me Free* is indeed a document of spiritual freedom and a capacious and critical way of thinking about it—and helping others to do the same! The book's references to Teresa of Avila, John of the Cross, and Ignatius Loyola, and theologians such as Karl Rahner, Denis Edwards, Elizabeth Johnson and many others indicate something of the scope and erudition of this volume.

This is not to be wondered at, since Brian Gallagher has been a Missionary of the Sacred Heart (MSC) for much of his life. A blend of pastoral engagement, creative reflection and lively communication is characteristic of his religious order, centred as it is on the Sacred Heart. The concern to structure and inform an adequate spiritual direction has its origins here, as "heart speaks to heart" in order to ensure that all our efforts to speak of God really touch the heart. In other words, *Set Me Free* has its origins in a great tradition of commitment and Christian experience, characterised by deep sensitivity to the humanity of God amongst us—and the ways the heart of God draws us toward the fulness of life.

Subtitle of this text. *Spiritual Direction and Discernment of Spirits*, suggests how this text is earthed in experience, and in the skilful assessment of what can happen in the heights and depths of that experience. The great tradition embodied in the theory and practice of this study calls for new applications and new contemporary relevance. Never have new forms of spiritual direction and discernment been more urgent. Our culture has become very irritable and intolerant of differences. There might be many reasons for this spiritual unease, each awaiting its adequate interpretation. Such as the very meaning of "spirituality": is it an excuse for evading all precise commitments? Has it been taken over by forms of (profitable) consumerism? At a time when, in the words of WB Yeats, the "centre cannot hold", "when the best lack all conviction", "when the worst are filled with passionate intensity", the soul must practise deep breathing if it is to survive in a conflict-riven atmosphere, poisoned by advertising and ever-agitated by the media. What is real? What is truth? What is real life? These are far from being metaphysical questions, for they have become urgent matters in the authentic conduct of contemporary life, and even in living out the sexual polarity of male/ female .

What is the way of discernment that can withstand the ubiquitous nonsense of political correctness and the like? There is much to be done, but there are also rich resources. Brian Gallagher's *Set Me Free* is a splendid example of the wisdom of the past and the promise of the future—if we are to be "set free" to surrender to the infinities of God and recognise the God-given potential, so often hidden, of our human existence.

Tony Kelly, CSsR
Australian Catholic University

Introduction

This book is written primarily for spiritual directors, pastoral ministers, ministry supervisors and educators. The sections on living a discerning way of life may also be of interest to a wider readership.

My initial formation as a spiritual director was in 1976/77 at the Centre for Religious Development and Weston School of Theology, at that time in Cambridge MA, and the Jesuit Retreat Centre in Gloucester MA. I was privileged to study with and be mentored by Jesuit priests William Barry and William Connolly who were prominent in the revival of the ministry of spiritual direction in the 1970s. Their classic work, *The Practice of Spiritual Direction,* is widely accepted as a basic text for the ministry.[1] Barry and Connolly define spiritual direction as:

> the help given by one Christian to another which enables that person to pay attention to God's personal communication to him/her, to respond to this personally communicating God, and to live out the consequences of the relationship.[2]

They are at pains to stress that the focus of spiritual direction is *relationship* with God:

---

1   William A. Barry and William J. Connolly, *The Practice of Spiritual Direction* (San Francisco, CA: Harper & Row, 1982). Barry and Connolly, Jesuit priests, founded the Centre for Religious Development in Cambridge, MA and began their program for the formation of spiritual directors in 1971. Connolly died in 2013.
2   Ibid., 8.

> Spiritual direction is concerned with helping a person directly with his or her relationship with God.
>
> Religious experience is to spiritual direction what foodstuff is to cooking. Without religious experience (any experience of the mysterious Other whom we call God), there can be no spiritual direction.[3]

Those who come for spiritual direction use a wide variety of experience and language to describe why they come, what they hope for, and what they choose to talk about. Spiritual directors have found that whatever the language used, the deep desire is almost always for more intimate relationship with God. The spiritual director listens for signs of God's presence and God's invitation in whatever experience the directee chooses to bring. The phrase 'a contemplative, discerning approach' to spiritual direction describes this way of listening. It is the phrase commonly used to capture the ministry of the spiritual director.[4]

I have learned that, for the sake of accurate discernment, spiritual directors do well to notice also the movements of the spirits in themselves, when they listen to their directees in this contemplative way. Discernment is defined as:

> the process by which we examine, in the light of faith and in the connaturality of love, the nature

---

3 Ibid., 5 & 8.
4 'Spiritual Direction' is the traditional term for this ministry, though it is sometimes referred to as 'spiritual accompaniment' or 'mentoring'. Usually spiritual direction is conducted in face-to-face situations. Exceptions are spiritual direction by correspondence (for example, Francis de Sales' direction of Jane Francis de Chantal and John Chapman's direction of a wide variety of people who wrote seeking his guidance.) As well, in more recent times, some spiritual directors conduct their ministry electronically.

of the spiritual states we experience in ourselves and in others. The purpose of such examination is to decide as far as possible which of the movements we experience lead to the Lord and to a more perfect service of him and our brothers, and which deflect us from this goal.[5]

In other words:

> Discernment of spirits involves chiefly an interpretive sorting out in faith of inner, affective experiences, so that, through dealing properly with the experiences, one can find and be with God in every situation and moment of life.'[6]

For 'to live as a Christian means to live in communion with the Spirit of God.'[7]

The term 'discernment' is derived from the Greek *diakrisis*, literally *to separate* or *to sort out*. In more contemporary thinking and practice, discernment is seen as the process of separating or sifting one's inner 'movements', the felt needs and desires, the spontaneous impulses and affective habits, the thoughts, imaginings, emotions, attractions and repulsions in one's experience of life. The sifting involves being sensitive to these movements, recognising and naming the movements, then understanding where they come from and where they lead.

---

[5] Edward Malatesta, "Introduction to Discernment of Spirits," in *Discernment of Spirits* (Collegeville, MN: The Liturgical Press, 1970), 9. Malatesta uses exclusive language, as common at that time. I have left all quotations in their original language.

[6] George Aschenbrenner, "Currents in Spirituality: The Past Decade," *Review for Religious* 39, no. 2 (1980): 198.

[7] Malatesta, "Introduction to Discernment of Spirits," in *Discernment of Spirits*, 9.

This separation is captured well by the symbol for discernment in Hindu religions: the white swan. The Hindu myth is that the swan, given a mixture of milk and water to drink, will drink the milk and leave the water. Hence:

> ... the art of discernment is called in Sanskrit 'the science of the water and the milk', and why the white swan, pure and majestic and aloof in the clear waters, is its symbol and its model. The soul itself is called 'the swan' and the highest type of religious ascetic is called 'the supreme swan'.[8]

This symbol highlights the gift of discernment, the integrated and spontaneous ability to separate opposing attractions in the 'mixture' that is everyone's everyday experience.

In the process of this separating, 'the fundamental principle is that the best guide to the discernment of interior movements is the discovery of the direction in which they lead.'[9] God's Spirit is alluring, always drawing towards God. (Hosea 2:14) And so, the movements that come from the Spirit of God lead to life, to personal freedom, to relationship and to community, ultimately to God:

> The fruit of the Spirit is love, joy, peace, patience, kindness, generosity, faithfulness, gentleness and self-control. (Galatians 5:22-23)

---

8 Carlos G. Valles, *The Art of Choosing* (New York: Doubleday, 1989), 99.
9 Ernest E. Larkin, "What to Know About Discernment," *Review for Religious* 60, no. 2 (2001): 163.
Denis Edwards, *Breath of Life: A Theology of the Creator Spirit* (Maryknoll, NY: Orbis Books, 2004), 162.
Denis Edwards, "Discernment of the Holy Spirit," *Presence* 13, no. 4 (2007): 21-29.

Introduction

> For you were called to freedom, brothers and sisters – only do not use your freedom as an opportunity for self-indulgence... (Galatians 5:13)

> Now the Lord is the Spirit, and where the Spirit of the Lord is, there is freedom. (2 Corinthians 3:17)

Thomas Dubay develops the scriptural signs further under three headings: moral behaviour, doctrinal criteria and communal criteria. The signs that Dubay lists under moral behaviour are God-directedness, new love, cross-asceticism, frugality, uncluttered freedom or detachment. Under doctrinal criteria, he names sound doctrine and being at odds with the prevailing spirit of the world. Under communal criteria, Dubay's signs are unity and obedience freely given.[10] Dubay sees humility as the under-pining of all these signs.

Further, the apostle Paul says that the Spirit of God is 'for building up the Body of Christ' (Ephesians 4:12).[11] The gifts of the Spirit are given for the common good: because one moved by the Spirit of God becomes more loving, God's Spirit is seen to promote relationships, to build community (1 Corinthians 12:7 and 14:4,12) and to work towards wholeness. Jacques Guillet summarises: 'Love is a direct and privileged gift of the Spirit.'[12]

God's Spirit is experienced in a movement of love or desire for God, a sense of being at peace with God, with others, and with oneself. The emphasis is on relationships and on building community. The personal experience of the Spirit of God shows

---

[10] Thomas Dubay, *Authenticity: A Biblical Theology of Discernment* (San Francisco, CA: Ignatius Press, 1977, updated 1997), 143-81.
[11] God's Spirit is said to be 'edifying', taken from the Latin word *aedificare*: to build.
[12] Jacques Guillet, "Sacred Scripture in Discernment of Spirits," in *Discernment of Spirits* (Collegeville, MN: The Liturgical Press, 1970), 47.

itself in more loving relationships. The Spirit of God is relational: while given to an individual, others reap the fruit. This is the way in which God's Spirit works in human experience.

These fruits of following the Spirit of God are manifest in faith in Jesus:

> By this you know the Spirit of God: every spirit that confesses that Jesus Christ has come in the flesh has come from God, and every spirit that does not confess Jesus is not from God. (1 John 4:2-3)

For Jesus is the first gift of God's love. Jesus, the Christ, is the 'head of the body', in whom 'all things hold together' (Colossians 1:17-18). Community builds on Jesus Christ:

> For in him, all the fullness of God was pleased to dwell; and through him, God was pleased to reconcile to himself all things, whether on earth or in heaven, by making peace through the blood of his cross. (Colossians 1:19-20)

On the other hand, movements prompted by some spirit not-of-God lead to non-life, to isolation and loss of one's inner freedom.[13] In the same Galatians text (5:22-23), Paul lists 'quarrels, dissensions, factions', the very opposite of the fruit of the good Spirit. These fruits of the different spirits are developed in chapter 4.

Discernment comes into play because:

> ... these criteria are not exactly measurable. Each of them can be mistaken for other reactions...

---

13   I use the term 'spirits not-of-God' where other commentators refer to 'evil spirits', 'bad spirits', 'counter spirits'.

Introduction

> Mere relief at having made a decision can look like the peace of the Spirit, for example. Witless enthusiasm can look like joy. Apathy sometimes resembles patience. Peace can mean a quiet sense of inner freedom that results from openness to God and willingness to respond to God... but it can also mean no more than the absence of strong feeling.[14]

This necessary process of sifting or 'recognising and admitting differences'[15] asks for a contemplative listening to the inner movements in one's self, both to recognise the movements and to come to understand their significance. Barbara Albrecht stresses that one's listening is not only with the ear. In listing the 'spiritual senses', she speaks of 'a nose for the things of God' needed 'to differentiate between good and evil, between true and false.[16] Following St Benedict, Mary Margaret Funk calls this 'listening with the ear of the heart.'[17] David Stendl-Rast says simply 'a listening heart.'[18]

Numerous studies of discernment exist: some are theological,[19] some scriptural,[20] some more exegetical studies of the writings of Ignatius Loyola.[21] In contrast, my approach is

---

14   Barry and Connolly, *The Practice of Spiritual Direction*, 106, 09.
15   Ibid., 102.
16   Barbara Albrecht, "Discernment of Spirits," *Review for Religious* 38, no. 3 (1979): 388-89.
17   Mary Margaret Funk, *Discernment Matters* (Collegeville, MN: Liturgical Press, 2013), 3, 71. Timothy Fry, ed. *The Rule of Saint Benedict* (Collegeville, MN: Liturgical Press, 1981), Prologue, verse 1.
18   David Stendl-Rast, *A Listening Heart* (New York: Crossroad, 1999), 1-7.
19   For example, Mark A. McIntosh, *Discernment and Truth* (New York: Crossroad Publishing Co., 2004).
20   For example, Dubay, *Authenticity*.
21   For example, Jules J. Toner, *A Commentary on St. Ignatius' Rules for the Discernment of Spirits* (St. Louis, MO: Institute of Jesuit Sources, 1982).

decidedly experiential. This book offers a practical theology of discernment of spirits in the ministry of spiritual direction. As well, I develop implications for the formation of discerning spiritual directors. I quote the formation program *Siloam* at the Heart of Life Spirituality Centre in Melbourne as an illustration of a formation program for spiritual directors that is grounded in discernment of spirits. Some detail of this program is included in appendices.

I have ministered as a spiritual director for lay and religious men and women for almost fifty years – in religious formation, in formation for ministry, in retreat settings and in both informal and more formal situations of ongoing spiritual guidance. In 1979, I began the formation program for spiritual directors called *Siloam* at the Heart of Life Centre, supervising other spiritual directors, leading seminars and lecturing in spirituality and formation for thirty years. I have been supervised in my ministry, personally and in peer supervision and I have attended the annual conferences of the professional body, the Conference of Spiritual Directors, Australia. I have had rich opportunity to reflect on and learn from experience in collaboration with other spiritual directors and other supervisors.

With this background, I am able to call upon my own experience as both spiritual director and supervisor of other spiritual directors and the experience of many other spiritual directors. I am convinced that discernment is integral to the practice of spiritual direction. Growth in inner freedom and becoming more discerning is critical in the personal lives of spiritual directors and in their ministry of supporting others. I illustrate this with numerous stories that I have constructed from my experience. The stories capture experience frequently heard in

Introduction

spiritual direction, but they are not about any one person: real experience, but not real people. Names and descriptive details are fictitious. Many people will identify with the experiences described, but no one will identify with the individuals named. The examples are based on my own experience and my listening to other people as a spiritual director.

Two points of clarification are in order. I believe that relationship with God, not decision making, is primary in discernment. Noticing the ways of the spirits in one's whole life is basic to the subsequent making of good decisions, sometimes referred to as discernment of God's Will. My concern, then, is for growth in relationships, particularly relationship with God. And secondly, I recognise that discernment of spirits is frequently associated with the teaching of Ignatius Loyola. While I acknowledge the significant contribution of the *Spiritual Exercises* of Ignatius Loyola to any contemporary study of discernment, I situate the practice of discernment many centuries prior to Ignatius. I base my understanding and my approach on the human experience of the spirits, on human values and on values embedded in the Sacred Scriptures.

1

God's Spirit in our Lives

Come, Holy Spirit
fill the hearts of your faithful
and enkindle in them the fire of your love.
Send forth your Spirit
and they shall be created
and you shall renew the face of the earth[1]

Foundational to my faith and my ministry is the conviction that:

> God's love has been poured into our hearts through the Holy Spirit that has been given to us. (Romans 5:5)

In prayer, this is expressed as *Your breath is my breath*. This has been my personal prayer mantra for many years. Deep down, I know God's gift of the Spirit, breathing in me, in all people and in all creation, sustaining all life, and holding together all of creation (Psalm 33:6). I believe this is gift of God's very self. For God is a self-giving God. This is who God is. As Catherine LaCugna says, '[God's] self-revelation or self-communication is nothing less than what God is as God.'[2] With Karl Rahner and

---

1   Traditional hymn to the Holy Spirit, based on Psalm 104.
2   Catherine Mowry LaCugna, *God for Us: The Trinity and Christian Life* (New York: HarperOne, 1991 (Copyright 1973)), 209.

Denis Edwards, I call this 'God's self-bestowal'. God's action in creation is 'a Trinitarian act of self-bestowal.'[3] God's loving self-bestowal grounds my theology of the Holy Spirit.

A central insight in Karl Rahner's theology, developed by Denis Edwards, is that God's action in creation, in incarnation and in the life of grace is the one act of God, grounded in the unity of the divine being.[4] From the beginning, God creates a world in which the Word is made flesh and the Spirit is poured out. The incarnation does not come about as a remedy for sin, as some theologies claim, but is central to God's creative act. The sending of the Spirit, often associated only with Pentecost, is central to God's creative act. 'Creation, redemption, and consummation are (thus) anchored in God's eternity.'[5] All are gifts of God's very self.

In Sacred Scripture, the Holy Spirit is revealed as *Ruah,* the breath of God breathing life into all creation. (Genesis 1:2, 2:7). The Scriptures depict the Spirit as ever-present and all-pervading: 'Your immortal Spirit is in all things.' (Wisdom 12:1). 'Where can I go from your Spirit?' (Psalm 139:7) The Psalms also link Word and Spirit in creation: 'By the Word of the Lord, the heavens were made, and all their host by the breath of his mouth.' (Psalm 33:6). God's gift of the Spirit is present and sustains all life from the beginning of creation. Scriptural passages such as these grounded the teaching of the early Church.

For example, Basil of Caesarea, bishop and theologian (330-379) stresses the communion of the Trinity and the equal divinity of the Holy Spirit. Ambrose, bishop of Milan (340-387) argued that with the Father and the Son, the Spirit is the creator of all

---

3   Denis Edwards, *How God Acts: Creation, Redemption and Special Divine Action* (Hindmarsh, SA: ATF Theology, 2010), 39.
4   Ibid., 39-42.
5   LaCugna, *God for Us: The Trinity and Christian Life,* 209.

things.⁶ In 381, the equal divinity of the Spirit is affirmed in the Nicene-Constantinopolitan creed: I believe in the Holy Spirit, who with the Father and the Son is co-worshipped and co-glorified. God's very being is communion. This is the tradition of the Church's teaching, the basis of the subsequent development of Trinitarian theology. The reference to God as 'persons-in-communion' flows from this foundational tradition.⁷

Even with this tradition, for centuries, much theological discourse and teaching treated the incarnation and the gift of the Spirit as quite separate doctrines from a theology of God. God was often considered in isolation, the mystery of God in Godself, remote and unapproachable. In more recent times, the fullness of the tradition has begun to be reclaimed and developed.

Dominican theologian Yves Congar wrote his theology of the Holy Spirit in a major work entitled *I believe in the Holy Spirit*. Congar argues that the gift of the Spirit is present from the beginning of creation, penetrating all creation, and that the Word and the Spirit of God work together.⁸ Moreover, he says that 'it is important to remember that no action can be attributed to the Holy Spirit independently of the Father and the Son.'⁹ Congar insists that these statements are 'absolutely biblical' and are found also in the writings of the Church Fathers and medieval theologians.

---

6   See, for example, Edwards, *Breath of Life*, 41-2. Edwards describes the theology of Basil of Caesarea, in particular: ibid. 17-30
7   ibid., 24-5.
8   Yves Congar, *I Believe in the Holy Spirit* (New York: Crossroad Publishing Company, 1997), II, 67.
9   Ibid., II, 85. Edwards follows a similar argument, speaking of the 'reciprocal relationship of God's Word and God's Spirit': Edwards, *Breath of Life*, 38, 159.

Congar was an advisor to the Vatican Council II. Some years after the Council, Pope John Paul II wrote his encyclical, *Dominum et Vivificantem,* translated as *The Holy Spirit in the Life of the Church and in the World.*[10] The Pope emphasises the divine equality of Father, Son and Holy Spirit and speaks of 'the action of the Holy Spirit... from the beginning, throughout the world, exercised in every place and every time, indeed in every individual, and closely linked with the mystery of incarnation and redemption.'[11] Trinitarian theologians continue to develop this conviction.

For example, Edwards, writing in dialogue with emerging cosmological discoveries, argues:

> The history of the Spirit... is coextensive with the *total* life of the universe. God's Spirit has been breathing life into the processes of the evolving universe from the very first... The Spirit of God was present in the very emergence of the human... embracing early humans in self-offering love.[12]

Similarly, Stephen Bevans argues in his theology of mission that 'the Spirit is the way God as Holy Mystery is present to the world from the first nanosecond of creation – giving life, courage, wisdom, prophecy, healing...'[13] From the first moment of creation, God gives Godself in Word and Spirit.

This gift of Godself to creation implies a communion lived also in all people and in all creation. 'If divine being is communion,

---

10   John Paul II, *Dominum et Vivificantem* (Homebush NSW: St Pauls Publications, 1986), #22.
11   Ibid., #53.
12   Edwards, *Breath of Life,* 33, 51.
13   Stephen Bevans, "The Mission Has a Church, the Mission Has Ministers," *Compass* 43, no. 3 (2009): 4.

then created being too exists only in and from communion... being in relationship is of the essence of things.'¹⁴ For this reason, Trinitarian theology speaks also of God's life in humanity and in creation, God's intimate relationship with humanity and all creation, and the ways in which humanity and creation are drawn into relationship with God, sharing in the divine communion.[15]

People report in spiritual direction that a noticeable fruit of prayer with the mantra, *Your breath is my breath*, is that even while the prayer is usually quite empty – 'a painful awareness of God's otherness' said one person – sometimes there are glimpses of God's breath, God's Spirit, breathing in all people and all creation, not only in the one praying. In such experience, these people are sensing a bonding with creation. In Wisdom literature, this is expressed as 'Wisdom... pervades and penetrates all things.' (Wisdom 7:24) Indeed, the communion in God of all humanity and all creation broadens what had become a too narrow focus in the ministry of spiritual direction.

Centuries later, John of the Cross captured the experience beautifully in his poetry:

> *Your fragrant breathing stills me*
> *Your grace, your glory, fills me*
> *so tenderly, your love becomes my own.*[16]

---

14   Edwards, *Breath of Life*, 26.
15   See, for example, Catherine LaCugna's discussion of Karl Rahner's theology of the Trinity: LaCugna, *God for Us: The Trinity and Christian Life*, passim. Karl Rahner, *The Trinity*, trans. Joseph Donceel (New York: Crossroad, 1997).
16   John's poem *The Living Flame*: John of the Cross, *Centered on Love: The Poems of Saint John of the Cross*, trans. Marjorie Flower (Varroville NSW: The Carmelite Nuns, 1983, reprinted 2002), 23.

I recognise this Spirit-gifted communion of all creation, too, in the unmistakable signs of the Spirit at work in the movements of our times: the movement towards justice and peace for the oppressed, the feminist movement seeking the full equality of women, and the ecological movement calling for a renewed relationship with the earth.

When an appreciation of God's giving Godself in Word and in Spirit is lost, relationships suffer and creation is divided. I identify with Elizabeth Johnson's thesis that the 'major taproot of the crisis' in both ecology and sexism is a 'hierarchical dualism' that divides reality into two separate and opposing spheres, assigning higher value to one over the other. Johnson notes that 'humanity is detached from and more important than nature, man is separate from and more valuable than woman, God is disconnected from the world, utterly and simply transcendent over it.'[17] She argues that 'these predicaments are intrinsically related to forgetting the Creator Spirit who pervades the world in the dance of life.'[18]

Johnson calls the Spirit 'the vivifier, the one who quickens, animates, stirs, enlivens, gives life even now...'[19] She sees the ongoing gift of the Spirit as the 'unceasing dynamic flow of divine power that sustains the universe, bringing forth life.'[20] The Spirit is the life-giver, dwelling in all creation: 'Your immortal Spirit is in all things." (Wisdom 12:1)

---

17 Elizabeth A. Johnson, *Woman, Earth and Creator Spirit* (New York: Paulist, 1993), 10-1. Anne Clifford shares this view and develops 'kinship' or 'the web of life' as alternative models: Anne M. Clifford, *Introducing Feminist Theology* (Maryknoll, NY: Orbis Books, 2001), 224.

18 Johnson, *Woman, Earth and Creator Spirit*, 2.

19 Elizabeth A. Johnson, *Ask the Beasts: Darwin and the God of Love* (London: Bloomsbury, 2014), 128.

20 Johnson, *Woman, Earth and Creator Spirit*, 42.

Both feminist theology, emphasising the fullness of humanity in all people, and ecological theology, emphasising the integrity of all creation, offer a corrective to the dualism Johnson describes. I discuss each briefly, noting especially their emphasis on relationships.

Feminist Theology

In response to a heightened global awareness of the oppression of women, feminist theology aims to recover the full humanity and equality of women: 'God created them, male and female.' (Genesis 1:26-27) Before God, women and men are equal, both created 'in the image of God' and both imbued with the Spirit of God.

Johnson's thorough and compassionate outline of the origins and rationale of feminist theology stresses the liberation of women 'as genuine human persons in communities of mutuality.'[21] Johnson argues that most language about God is 'both humanly oppressive and religiously idolatrous.'[22] Both the images used and the concepts accompanying them reflect the experience of men in charge within a patriarchal system.

Rosemary Radford Ruether argues similarly, noting that in Judeo-Christian cultures 'male monotheism reinforces the social hierarchy of patriarchal rule through its religious system in a way that was not the case with paired images of God and Goddess', as in all previous human consciousness.[23] Ruether

---

21 Elizabeth A. Johnson, *She Who Is: The Mystery of God in Feminist Theological Discourse* (New York: Crossroad, 1993), 32.
22 Ibid., 18.
23 Rosemary Radford Ruether, *Sexism and God-Talk* (London: SCM Press, 1983), 53.

quotes Isaiah (42:13-14, 16-17) to illustrate the mixture of male and female images of God.[24] Elizabeth Schussler Fiorenza also gives detailed Scriptural background to feminist theology.[25] A considerable body of work to the present day has developed these beginnings.

While many theologians, liturgists, spiritual directors and formators of spiritual directors, opt to use the word 'God' consistently, thus avoiding male images and pronouns for God, Johnson argues that such usage still 'prevents the insight into holy mystery that might occur were female symbols set free to give rise to thought.'[26] In speaking of God, Johnson calls upon the fullness of female humanity, as well as of male humanity and of cosmic reality, all seen as divine symbols in equivalent ways. She argues that, since both male and female are created in the divine image, 'either can equally well be used as metaphor to point to divine mystery.'[27] Indeed, 'as verily as God is our Father, so verily is God our Mother.'[28]

I emphasise that both female and male images of the divine are representation of the fullness of God, not mere aspects of God. Johnson advocates the equivalent usage of both female and male symbolism to represent God, rather than the limited understanding of the Spirit as the 'feminine dimension' of God, as is common in much Church practice. Feminist theology recovers a vision of God – 'I am who I am' (Exodus 3:14) – that

---

24   Ibid., 56.
25   Elizabeth Schussler Fiorenza, *In Memory of Her: A Feminist Theological Reconstruction of Christian Origins* (New York: Crossroad, 1983).
26   Johnson, *She Who Is: The Mystery of God in Feminist Theological Discourse*, 44.
27   Ibid., 55.
28   Julian of Norwich, *Revelations of Divine Love* (Melbourne: Penguin Books, 1998), chapter 59. Julian of Norwich lived in C14.

had been lost in patriarchal language and practice. In fact, both female and male images are needed. Neither alone is adequate to represent God.

The mutual relationships between all people and all creation, inherent to the Trinitarian theology outlined, take shape in feminist theology. For example, Kathleen Fischer summarises that feminism emphasises 'inclusion rather than exclusion, connectedness rather than separateness, and mutuality in relationships rather than dominance and submission.'[29]

Ecological Theology

The same emphasis on the inter-connectedness and inter-dependence of all creation is found in ecological theology and ecological practice: relationships in creation exist in mutual relationship. Edwards argues that 'the theological insight that God's being is relational can provide a basis for a vision of the fundamental reality of the universe as relational.'[30] Thus he refers to 'Trinitarian relationships of mutual love'. The experience of both caring for and depending upon one's environment is to share in the communion of God.

Pope Francis stresses relationships in his encyclical on 'our common home', *Laudato Si,* interpreting the creation accounts in the book of Genesis to suggest that human life is grounded in three fundamental and closely intertwined relationships:

---

29 Kathleen Fischer, *Women at the Well: Feminist Perspectives on Spiritual Direction* (New York: Paulist, 1988), 2.

30 Denis Edwards, *Ecology at the Heart of Faith* (Maryknoll, NY: Orbis Books, 2006), 79-80.

with God, with neighbour and with the earth itself.[31] The Pope writes that 'no creature is self-sufficient... creatures exist only in dependence on each other, to complete each other, in the service of each other.'[32] God's vivifying Spirit in creation unites all creation in the communion of God's life.

Arguably, much of the present ecological crisis throughout the world – the exploitation of the earth's resources, the denudation of forests, the pollution of the earth and the atmosphere – has come about through a presumption that human beings dominate the rest of creation. The presumption has been that creation exists for the sake of humanity, the dualism described by Johnson above. Much of humanity has lost any sense of dependence on creation. Gerald May believes that this attitude originates in the concept of 'stewardship', for 'no matter how benevolent they are, (stewards) forever remain apart from that which they care for.'[33]

Pope Francis is clear in his rejection of the concept of human dominion over creation, calling for 'a relationship of mutual responsibility between human beings and nature.'[34] We are called to care for creation, but not from a position of superiority or domination, but one of 'kinship',[35] honouring the communion of all people and all creation – and honouring the Spirit of God.

---

31   Francis, *Laudato Si* (Strathfield NSW: St. Pauls Publications, 2015), #66.
32   Ibid., #86.
33   Gerald G. May, *The Wisdom of the Wilderness: Experiencing the Healing Power of Nature* (San Francisco: HarperOne, 2006).
34   Francis, *Laudato Si*, #67.
35   See, for example, Clifford, *Introducing Feminist Theology*, 224. Edwards, *Ecology at the Heart of Faith*, 22. The kinship model is favoured by many theologians of ecology. Edwards bases his description on the Canticle of Creation of Francis of Assisi.

My experience suggests that not all people have absorbed the dualistic attitude described by Johnson, and that many who have are not aware that they have. The attitude shows itself in a presumed remoteness of God, seen as utterly transcendent and untouchable, a presumption, in fact, that defeats its own purpose. The surprising paradox is that one is gifted with awareness of God's otherness only by living in the tangible concreteness of one's humanity and one's environment. Experience of God becomes possible only in living one's humanity fully, not in putting it aside, as though God were separate.

I discuss the influence of these theological developments on the practice of spiritual direction in the following chapter. Johnson believes that the emphasis on mutual relationships with all people and with all creation has revolutionised theology.[36] This revolution has a profound effect on the ministry of spiritual direction and formation of spiritual directors – as did the former theology where God was seen as aloof and uninvolved, and the Spirit of God as mere periphery. In many formation programs, however, any change has been quite slow.[37]

A Trinitarian Theology of the Holy Spirit

Trinitarian theology of the Holy Spirit grounds all that follows in this book. The same theology permeates the teaching and the approach to formation in the program *Siloam* which I describe

---

36 Johnson, *She Who Is: The Mystery of God in Feminist Theological Discourse*, 32.

37 Other factors, theological, psychological and cultural, contribute to this. For example, the behaviour of a person who tends to relate to others from a position of superiority is as likely to flow from unconscious psychological needs as any theological position. I discuss these influences in chapters 5 and 8.

in detail in chapter 10, though it was undeveloped and not clearly articulated in the early years of the program. Indeed, as I have outlined, major developments in Trinitarian theology have come about since that time.

The presence of God's Spirit, permeating all life and all creation from the very beginning is the essential framework for my ministry of spiritual direction:

> You spare all things, for they are yours, O Lord, you who love the living. For your immortal Spirit is in all things. (Wisdom 11:26 to 12:1)

> The Spirit who is both one and transcendent is able to penetrate all things without violating or doing violence to them... The Spirit is unique and present everywhere, transcendent and inside all things, subtle and sovereign, able to respect freedom and to inspire it. The Spirit can further God's plan...[38]

To be fully present to all humanity and to all creation, to listen to the Spirit of God in all voices, invites quite significant inner conversion for many people. For example, one's first recognition of common humanity before differences – to see *people*, human people, before foreigners, or black skins, or refugees – can be a powerful point of conversion. The risk involved in focusing solely on differences is that it breeds separateness and comparisons. Whereas the recognition of relatedness in uniqueness leads to genuine compassion. At the same time, acceptance of unique differences amongst people can be a point of conversion for others. Listening truly to voices quite different

---

38   Congar, *I Believe in the Holy Spirit*, II, 17.

from one's own, as in ecumenical dialogue, can be a powerful point of conversion.

Similarly, people experience the invitation to conversion in their relationship with the environment, the community of creation which they both care for and depend upon. All creation is sacred, made so in the very moment of creation, confirmed by Jesus shedding his blood over the earth and the ever-present Spirit of love holding creation as one. Such conversion is doubtless ongoing, as one is drawn into solidarity or oneness with all creatures.

My theology of Spirit recognises the Spirit of God in the equality of all people and the wholeness of all creation. This theology overcomes any hint of dualism and leads to a realisation of the sacredness of the earth and the full and equal humanity of women and men. Being attuned to this Spirit is the focus of the ministry of spiritual direction and discernment of spirits.

Within this theology of the Holy Spirit, I now consider the question: can human beings experience the Spirit of God? The question is basic to my approach to discernment of spirits. Edwards names the same question a 'fundamental question for theology'.[39]

The human experience of the Spirit of God

Vatican Council II teaches that 'the People of God believes that it is led by the Spirit of the Lord who fills the whole world.'[40]

---

39   Edwards, *Breath of Life*, 51-4.
40   Vatican II, "Gaudium et Spes (Constitution on the Church in the Modern World)," in *Vatican Council II: The Basic Sixteen Documents*, ed. Austin Flannery (Northport, NJ: Costello Publishing Company, 1996), #11.

My question about the human experience of God's Spirit is an immediate consequence.

In my experience as a spiritual director, I hear many examples of experiences of transcendence: someone's experience of being captivated by an especially beautiful sunset or the blessing of a chance meeting with a long-lost dear one, or maybe the experience of being held by an unexpected, creative inspiration to compose a piece of music. Such experiences take one outside of oneself. They are experiences of transcendence, which I understand to be experiences of God's Spirit.

Theologically, such openness to the Spirit of God transcending our limited experience can be understood as God's grace at work. Rahner points out that 'alongside the experience of transcendence in ordinary knowing and loving, there are also particular moments when this ever-present experience of the Spirit is brought more clearly to the forefront of conscious experience. These are moments that are commonly thought of as religious experience.'[41] The examples referred to above fit Rahner's description of religious experience as experiences of God's Spirit.

Other spiritual directors write of the same experience. In responding to my question, Edwards initially acknowledges the risks of self-deception and delusion in interpreting experience. He then uses Rahner's argument for an experience of Spirit 'in ordinary human experience.' Edwards refers to experiences of transcendence that go beyond the ordinary but happen *in* the ordinary. His examples are the restless searching for answers to one's questions and the never-fulfilled human desire for

---

41   Edwards, *Breath of Life*, 53-4. See Karl Rahner, "Experience of the Holy Spirit," in *Theological Investigations* (New York: Seabury, 1983), 196-7.

love. One does find some answers and does experience love, but one is always drawn deeper. He sees these experiences of transcendence as experiences of the Spirit of God.

Rahner's approach to the question of the human experience of God is found also in his 'Reflections on the Experience of Grace', written some years earlier.[42] Rahner distinguishes between the experience of grace permeating or seasoning our earthly lives and everyday experience, and the different experience of grace that he called the Spirit 'in its proper transcendence'. Rahner asks questions to help the reader reflect on personal experience. For example:

> Have we ever kept quiet, even though we wanted to defend ourselves when we had been unfairly treated? Have we ever forgiven someone even though we got no thanks and our silent forgiveness was taken for granted?...

Rahner argues that, if we are able to answer yes to these questions, then we have experienced something 'of eternity', an experience that the Spirit is 'more than merely part of this temporal world.' He calls such an experience 'a taste of pure Spirit'.[43] I notice in spiritual direction that many people do answer 'yes' to one or other of Rahner's questions, but usually a tentative 'yes'. They say, understandably, that the experience is not what they imagined an experience of God would be like. There is no felt consolation. On the other hand, the experience is clearly gift, not something of one's own making. Rahner insists that this is an experience of 'pure Spirit'.

---

42 Karl Rahner, "Reflections on the Experience of Grace," in *Theological Investigations* (New York: Seabury, 1967), III, 86-9.

43 Ibid., 89. Rahner reflects on the same questions in Karl Rahner, *The Mystical Way in Everyday Life* (Maryknoll, NY: Orbis Books, 2010), 185.

Later, writing in the persona of Ignatius Loyola, as though Ignatius himself were speaking, Rahner speaks of his own experience of God as confirmation of his argument that one can and does experience God:

> All I am saying is this: I have experienced God, the nameless and unfathomable one, the silent and yet near one, in the trinity of his love for me... God himself, truly, God himself I experienced, and not simply human words about him...[44]

Congar's answer to the question about the human experience of God's Spirit is found is what he calls 'practical evidence' of God's presence in one's life. He quotes Augustine: 'ask your inward parts: if they are full of charity, you have the Spirit of God.'[45]

Rahner and Congar both affirm my conclusion that one can and does experience the Spirit of God, consistent with my earlier argument that the very nature of God is self-communicating and self-giving, and broadening my focus on religious experience. In that gift, God's vivifying Spirit dwells in all creation and all people.

Barry adds a slight nuance to the question when he queries the very legitimacy of spiritual direction's focus on experience. I identify with Barry's statement that 'experience... seems problematic to many people... By its very nature, experience seems a purely subjective thing.'[46] Barry acknowledges the 'well-founded criticism' of the earlier work of Connolly and himself

---

44 Karl Rahner, *Ignatius of Loyola Speaks*, trans. Annemarie S Kidder (South Bend, IN: St. Augustine's Press, 2013), 6, 9, 18.
45 Congar, *I Believe in the Holy Spirit*, II, 82.
46 William A. Barry, *Spiritual Direction and the Encounter with God* (New York: Paulist, 2004), 3.

that the theology of their approach to the ministry 'presupposes that God acts in our world in such a way that we can experience God's action'.[47] In response, Barry wrote *Spiritual Direction and the Encounter with God*, developing a theology to validate the earlier presupposition.

My own question to Barry concerned his sole focus on a person's experience in prayer when writing of the experience of God.[48] In his later writing, however, Barry argues that 'directors and directees need not confine themselves to discussions of formal prayer'. He argues rather that 'any experience can be examined to discover the mysterious Other whom we call God'.[49] This shift in his thinking came from his theology of human experience and the possibility of religious experience. Barry argues that all human experience has a religious dimension. The believer will recognise the religious dimension of any experience.[50] This, too, is consistent with my theology that the Spirit of God permeates all life and all creation. I develop this point in chapter 6.

Barry concludes that experience of God is indeed accessible to human people: 'Because of God's immanence, God is always encounterable'. This is the gift of God's ever-present Spirit. Clearly, this does not mean that one can always be aware of the Spirit, but one can become more and more attuned to God's presence in one's life.

I note Edwards' earlier reminder of the risk of self-deception and Barry's caution that one needs to be wary of 'mindless credulity' towards one's experience, even while believing that God's desire

---

47 Ibid., 2.
48 This was the case in the earlier writing of Barry and Connolly, *The Practice of Spiritual Direction*.
49 Barry, *Spiritual Direction and the Encounter with God*, 35.
50 Ibid., 21.

will show itself in experience.[51] I discuss the risk of self-deception in reflecting on one's experience in chapter 3, where the steps of interpreting and verifying one's reflection are seen as essential in any process of discernment. Self-deception becomes less a risk as one grows in inner freedom. My subsequent discussion clarifies how discernment takes this risk of self-deception into account.

In summary, I believe that we can and do experience the Spirit of God. The work of the spiritual director is to focus on and listen to this Spirit in the experience of those who come for spiritual direction. The difficulty for the spiritual director is that, even when a person wishes to 'be guided by the Spirit' (Galatians 5:25), there are also other spirits at work, working against God's Spirit. I consider the experience of these spirits in what follows.

The human experience of spirits not-of-God

Both the spiritual director and the directee are invited to confront any spirits not-of-God:

> Be strong in the Lord and the strength of his power. Put on the whole armour of God, so that you may be able to stand against the wiles of the devil. (Ephesians 6:10-12)

Spirits not-of-God work against the Spirit of God. Jesus knew the experience of conflicting spirits when tempted in the desert (Matthew 4:1-11). I note many similar examples of conflicting spirits in chapter 4. And in chapter 5, I develop an understanding of the ways in which God's Spirit and spirits not-of-God attract a

---

51   William A. Barry, "Towards a Theology of Discernment," *The Way Supplement* 64, no. Spring (1989): 136. Barry, *Spiritual Direction and the Encounter with God*, 82.

person, based on my theology and psychology of the experience of human freedom.

Unfreedoms, often quite unconscious, block any response to the call to be free.[52] Traditional teaching in spirituality recognises this experience and uses the term 'attachments' to describe those areas of one's inner life that are not only unfree, but are imagined to be non-negotiable. Psychologically, attachments are called 'compulsions' or 'inner needs'. I discuss these *unfreedoms* more fully and consider their role in discernment in subsequent chapters.

---

52   My term 'unfreedom' is intended to capture the human experience of one's limited freedom. The experience is developed in chapter 8 in terms of a person's inner attachments or needs.

2
The Tradition of Spiritual Direction

Give me a word for my soul.[1]

The development of Spiritual Direction practice

Discipleship and listening to wise elders is mentioned frequently in the sacred scriptures, but the actual ministry of spiritual direction is thought to have begun with the desert mothers and fathers of the third and fourth centuries. Thomas Merton argues that the ministry actually became necessary at that time precisely because men and women had removed themselves from community and local church to live as solitaries in the desert. Prior to that time, most people received spiritual support and guidance from their bishop or pastor.

> But when the first solitaries retired to the desert, they separated themselves from the Christian community... They lived solitary and dangerous lives far from any church and rarely participating even in the mystery of the Eucharist. Yet they had gone into the wilderness to seek Christ...

---

[1] Traditional request attributed to the Desert Mothers and Fathers.

Hence the need for 'discernment of spirits' and a [spiritual] director.[2]

And so these men and women sought out a 'spiritual father' or 'spiritual mother'.

From these beginnings, the ministry has had a rather chequered history.

Though the personal experience of God is the traditional focus of spiritual direction, this focus was lost for some centuries.[3] This was due, in part, to the Rule of St Benedict that accompanied the beginnings of monasticism in the sixth century. The Rule encouraged 'manifestation of thoughts' privately and confidentially to the abbot or a wise elder.[4] Though this was not considered to be sacramental, the practice seems more akin to confession than to spiritual direction. Indeed, many believe that 'the practice of sacramental confession gradually began to merge with the direction relationship'.[5] Effectively, there was no spiritual direction, in the traditional sense. Benedictine scholar Jean Leclerq, in fact, argues that spiritual guidance has not been strong in Benedictine practice, even to the present day. Most often, 'guidance was given to the whole community via preaching and good example'.[6] In such an approach, personal experience of God is overlooked. Leclerq summarises that

---

2 Thomas Merton, *Spiritual Direction and Meditation* (Collegeville, MN: Liturgical Press, 1960), 3-4.
3 This was roughly the same time period in which the tradition of the Church's theology of the communion of God and the equal divinity of Father, Son and Holy Spirit, was also lost, as outlined in my chapter 1.
4 Fry, *The Rule of Saint Benedict*, chapter VII, verse 44.
5 Janet Ruffing, *Uncovering Stories of Faith: Spiritual Direction and Narrative* (New York: Paulist, 1989), 7.
6 Jean Leclerq, "Traditions in Spiritual Guidance: Spiritual Direction in the Benedictine Tradition," *The Way* 27, no. January (1987): 56.

'spiritual guidance has not been a favourite theme of Benedictine spiritual literature'.[7]

The link between sacramental confession and spiritual guidance turned the focus more towards a person's behaviour and the external practices of living a good life. Though there were notable exceptions, this more authoritarian and clerical approach prevailed for centuries. The exceptions are the charismatic spiritual directors of 'the golden age of spiritual direction'[8]: Julian of Norwich,[9] Ignatius Loyola,[10] Teresa of Avila[11] and John of the Cross,[12] Francis de Sales[13] and Augustine Baker.[14]

---

7   Ibid., 54.
8   Ibid., 59-60.
9   Julian of Norwich (1342-1416): see Julian of Norwich, *Revelations of Divine Love*.
10   Ignatius Loyola (1491-1556): see Ignatius Loyola, *The Spiritual Exercises of St. Ignatius Loyola*, ed. George E. Gans (Chicago, IL: Loyola University Press, 1998). Ignatius founded the Society of Jesus in 1534, approved by Rome in 1540. He is thought to have written *The Spiritual Exercises* during the years 1525-1540 after significant conversion experiences, described in my chapter 4.
11   Teresa of Avila (1515-1582): see, for example, Teresa of Avila, "The Way of Perfection," in *The Collected Works of St. Teresa of Avila*, ed. Kieran Kavamagh and Otilio Rodriguez (Washington, DC: Institute of Carmelite Studies, 1963).
12   John of the Cross (1542-1591): see, for example, John of the Cross, "The Ascent of Mount Carmel," in *The Collected Works of St. John of the Cross*, ed. Kieran Kavamagh and Otilio Rodriguez (Washington, DC: Institute of Carmelite Studies, 1973). Several others of John of the Cross' works are cited in this thesis.
13   Francis de Sales (1567-1622): see Francis de Sales, *Selected Letters*, trans. Elisabeth Stopp (London: Faber and Faber, 1960). Francis was Bishop of Geneva (1602-1622), ministering as spiritual director for many people. His spiritual direction of Jane Frances de Chantal, mainly in letters, is best known.
14   Augustine Baker (1575-1641): see Norbert Sweeny, ed. *Holy Wisdom: Directions for the Prayer of Contemplation (Extracted out of More Than Forty Treatises by the Venerable Father Augustine Baker)* (London: Burns, Oates and Washbourne, Ltd., edited in 1876). Baker was an early English Benedictine.

What I consider to be a revival of the ministry happened barely fifty years ago, since Vatican Council II. Aided by a study of the tradition and a return to early sources, the approach in spiritual direction practice focused again on the religious experience of the one asking for guidance. In these recent times, the revival has given rise to numbers of new formation programs for spiritual directors, particularly in the United States, and a plethora of books and articles on spiritual direction.

Initial examples of this study of the tradition are the works of Jean Laplace in France[15] and Kenneth Leech in the United Kingdom.[16] In a time when ministry was practically confined to the ordained clergy, these men were involved in face-to-face ministries which were not primarily spiritual direction as we know it today. They wrote mainly for clergy and, in keeping with their time, in exclusive language. Thus Laplace describes the spiritual director as a 'spiritual father', the essence of which description is accurate still:

> As fatherhood does in man, it calls on the most intimate components of our human and spiritual natures... it opens out, in the disinterestedness of a love that asks no return, all the capacities for giving that there are in a man...
>
> In the disinterestedness with which a spiritual father undertakes, for no advantage except for love, to commit himself to the service of another in order to help him on his way to God, there is a

---

15   Jean Laplace, *Preparing for Spiritual Direction* (Chicago, IL: OFM Herald Press, 1975). Laplace was a French pastor.
16   Kenneth Leech, *Soul Friend: The Practice of Christian Spirituality* (London: Sheldon Press, 1977). Leech was an Anglican priest who worked in a wide variety of ministries in London.

dynamism which, if we could perceive its source, would seem to spring from the depths of divine compassion.[17]

John English also wrote around the same time, reflecting on his ministry of directing the *Spiritual Exercises* of Ignatius Loyola.[18] English acknowledges 'the considerable difference between the (spiritual) direction one receives when going through the thirty-day Exercises and the direction one should give or receive outside that experience'.[19] English develops his learnings from his direction of the *Spiritual* Exercises, often called 'spiritual counselling'.

A few years later, spiritual directors tended to write more on what they were actually doing as spiritual directors. Tilden Edwards,[20] Katherine Dyckman and Patrick Carroll,[21] and Carolyn Gratton[22] all wrote books that included quite practical approaches to spiritual direction and their learnings from their experience. A concern to clarify how spiritual direction differed from psychological counselling was uppermost in these writings. Gratton summarises:

---

17   Laplace, *Preparing for Spiritual Direction*, 91-2.
18   John J. English, *Spiritual Freedom* (Guelph, Ontario: Loyola House, 1973). Jesuit priest John English was director of Loyola House retreat centre in Guelph, Ontario, Canada.
19   Ibid., 14.
20   Tilden Edwards, *Spiritual Friend* (New York: Paulist, 1980). Edwards was the director of the *Shalem* Institute for Spiritual Formation in Washington DC.
21   Katherine Marie Dyckman and L. Patrick Carroll, *Inviting the Mystic, Supporting the Prophet: An Introduction to Spiritual Direction* (New York: Paulist, 1981). These authors shared ministry in the program called *Resources for Spiritual Leadership* in the Archdiocese of Seattle.
22   Carolyn Gratton, *Gidelines for Spiritual Direction* (Denville, NJ: Dimension Books, 1980). Carolyn Gratton, *The Art of Spiritual Guidance* (New York: Crossroad, 1992). Gratton was a teacher, later professor of spirituality, at the Institute of Formative Spirituality, Duquesne University, Pittsburg, PA.

Directors focus on the heart's need for transformation, for metanoia, on its need for mercy and forgiveness, for salvation and humility, for truth and self-acceptance. They are interested more in internal meanings and motivations, in the heart's desire for reconciliation and solidarity with Christ and neighbour.[23]

The next development was even more significant. The careful empirical approach of several experienced spiritual directors led to their writing not only what they were doing as spiritual directors, but also what was actually happening in their direction of others. William Barry and William Connolly,[24] Francis Vanderwall[25] and Alan Jones[26] were fore-runners in this development. By listening for what actually happens in spiritual direction, these spiritual directors were reclaiming the ministry's focus on God's work and on people's experience of God in their lives. This shift in focus has numerous implications for spiritual direction practice. Such a focus is central to my approach to the ministry.

The writings of Barry and Connolly have had lasting influence on the ministry of spiritual directors. Both wrote numerous articles on spiritual direction in *Review for Religious* during those early years, and Barry has continued his ministry with several books and articles in *Human Development* and *The Way*

---

23 Gratton, *Gidelines for Spiritual Direction*, 193.
24 Barry and Connolly, *The Practice of Spiritual Direction*.
25 Francis Vanderwall, *Spiritual Direction: An Invitation to an Abundant Life* (New York: Paulist, 1981).
26 Alan Jones, *Exploring Spiritual Direction: An Essay on Christian Friendship* (Minneapolis, MN: Seabury Press, 1982). Jones was from the Episcopal Centre for Christian Spirituality, General Theological Seminary, New York.

Supplement. Most recently, writing what he called a 'retrospective reflection', Barry reiterated and recommitted himself to the principles enunciated in the very first book written by Connolly and himself.[27]

This is the definition of spiritual direction quoted from Barry and Connolly's first writing:

> ... the help given by one Christian to another which enables that person to pay attention to God's personal communication to him/her, to respond to this personally communicating God, and to live out the consequences of the relationship.

Barry and Connolly describe relationship with God in terms of *experience* of God or *religious experience*: 'spiritual direction is concerned with helping a person directly with his or her relationship with God'.[28] Barry and Connolly include a chapter *Fostering the Contemplative Attitude,* Jones has a chapter *Spiritual Direction as a work of Contemplation* and Vanderwall treats sensitivity to God's Spirit, all insisting that such listening needs to be contemplative:

> Contemplation is simple attentiveness to what is there... For the Christian, contemplation is based on an act of faith that what is really there will reveal itself... Contemplation is very humbling because it is not an activity in which I do anything...[29]

Two later books emphasise this same way of listening: Josef Sudbrack concludes his study with a chapter entitled *Spiritual*

---

27 William A. Barry, "What Is Spiritual Direction: A Retrospective Reflection," *Presence* 21, no. 2 (2015): 31.
28 Barry and Connolly, *The Practice of Spiritual Direction*, 8. Jones, *Spiritual Direction*, 103-4.
29 Jones, *Spiritual Direction*, 103-4.

Guidance through God's Spirit,[30] Francis Nemeck and Marie Theresa Coombs include a chapter on *Spiritual Direction as Listening*,[31] both books approaching the ministry in a contemplative way. These writings have been collated by Kevin Culligan[32] and in two short articles that I wrote about the same time.[33]

Since that time, two major theological developments – in feminist theology and ecological theology – have impacted profoundly on the ministry of spiritual direction. I discussed these theologies in chapter 1. I consider their influence on spiritual direction now. The emphasis on mutual and equal relationships amongst all people and with all creation affects both the understanding and the experience of God that people bring to spiritual direction and the focus of the spiritual director's listening.

Spiritual directors intentionally focus on the unique experience of each directee. This is true for both female and male directees. At the same time, Janet Ruffing notes from her experience that women and men relate their experience differently. Women tend to tell their stories in a 'multi-dimensional' manner, including all detail, whereas men tend rather to speak uni-dimensionally, often more succinctly, without detail.[34] Ruffing and Theresa

---

30 Joseph Sudbrack, *Spiritual Guidance* (New York: Paulist, 1983).
31 Francis Kelly Nemeck and Marie Theresa Coombs, *The Way of Spiritual Direction* (Wilmington, Del: Michael Glazier, 1983). Coombs lived a strict eremitical life in Texas; Nemeck was the director of an eremitical house of prayer, also in southern Texas.
32 Kevin G. Culligan, ed. *Spiritual Direction: Contemporary Readings* (Locust Valley, NY: Living Flame Press, 1983).
33 Brian Gallagher, "Spiritual Direction: God's Work," *Compass* 17, no. 2 (1983): 39-40. Brian Gallagher, "Writings in Spiritual Direction," *Compass* 18, no. 4 (1984): 21-3.
34 Janet Ruffing, *Uncovering Stories of Faith*, 123-6

Moser develop this, emphasising 'the differences in the ways women and men experience themselves and construct their world'.[35] Agreeing with Johnson's argument (chapter 1), they write of the risk that some of the key metaphors and scriptural texts used in the Spiritual Exercises of Ignatius Loyola, for example, may alienate, disempower, or 'positively oppress' some women:

> Since all of these texts were produced within patriarchal cultures, it is necessary to make the patriarchal layer explicit – that which is anti-woman... [then] women can experience something liberating, affirming and inviting of themselves.[36]

Dyckman, Garvin and Liebert also reflect on Ignatius' *Spiritual Exercises*, initially acknowledging the difficulties they have encountered in women's experience – the symbolism, Ignatius' unswerving obedience to the church, and the centrality of Christ, the male saviour[37] – and then summarising some of the 'liberating possibilities' in a non-hierarchical, dynamic, cyclic, process-oriented reading of the *Exercises*.[38]

Other feminist writings that have been influential include Elizabeth Tetlow's translation of Ignatius' Rules for Discernment into inclusive language[39] and Joann Wolski Conn's 'revision' of the descriptions of consolation and desolation. Conn's work, in

---

35 Janet Ruffing and Theresa Moser, "An Option for Women?," *The Way Supplement* 74, no. Summer (1992): 96.
36 Ibid.
37 Katherine Marie Dyckman, Mary Garvin, and Elizabeth Liebert, *The Spiritual Exercises Reclaimed: Uncovering Liberating Possibilities for Women* (New York: Paulist, 2001), 3.
38 Ibid., 80.
39 Elizabeth Tetlow, *An Inclusive Language translation of the Ignatian Rules for Discernment* in Joann Wolski Conn, ed. *Women's Spirituality: Resources for Christian Development* (New York: Paulist Press, 1986), 219-25.

particular, serves to remind spiritual directors to be particularly attentive to differences in women's experience:

> Consolation, as Ignatius defines it, is a trustworthy measure for women's self-transcendence. What actually leads one toward God – not merely what feels comfortable, secure or 'consoling' – is the consolation characteristic of God's Spirit. If women's awkwardness in learning to care for their interests results in a freer relationship with God, then this discomfort is not desolation... The direction it manifests – a mature relationship to God – shows it is consolation. If women's frustration expressed in anger and resentment, even anger at God, can result in a more candid, adult response to God, then its direction reveals it to be consolation.[40]

Conn's examples of consolation and desolation from women's experience, defined by the direction in which the movements lead, are consistent with my experience. Much of this discussion on discernment in the *Spiritual Exercises* applies equally to the ministry of ongoing spiritual direction.

Guenther uses feminine images to describe the ministry of spiritual direction: she speaks of a spiritual director as 'mother', 'maternal listener', and 'midwife':[41]

> Good mothering enables the child to develop his capabilities, grow to maturity, and move away from reliance on the mother. My Virginia neighbours,

---

[40] Joann Wolski Conn, *Revisioning Ignatian Rules for Discernment* in ibid., 315.

[41] Margaret Guenther, *Holy Listening: The Art of Spiritual Direction* (Boston, MA: Cowley Publications, 1992). chapters 3, 4

the black bears, are competent mothers: the cubs are nurtured as long as necessary, and then briskly on their way.[42]

'Good mothering' is a helpful image for both female and male spiritual directors, but I stress that such imagery is intended to capture the fullness of the ministry, not merely some feminine aspect of being a spiritual director.

In relation to ecological theology, care for the earth was seen to be the fruit of one's awareness of creation's inter-connectedness. In his first Encyclical teaching, Pope John Paul II wrote that human beings frequently seem 'to see no other meaning in their natural environment than what serves for immediate use and consumption'.[43] Subsequently he called for an 'ecological conversion', meaning an experience of oneself as intimately united with all that exists. Pope Francis repeated the call to conversion in his encyclical *Laudato Si*.[44] This terminology is now used widely in ecology and appears frequently in spiritual direction.

For example, people bring to spiritual direction experience where they have been powerfully moved by images of the human destruction of rain forests and the extinction of numerous species of animals, or experience where they have been brought to their knees by sudden awareness of the immense vastness of the skies or the unexpected vision of a shooting star. Less dramatically, directees speak of their awareness of the beauty of a sunset or their delight in gardening. As spiritual directors help their directees to fill out such experiences and hear the

---

42 Ibid., 121.
43 John Paul II, *Redemptor Hominis* (Homebush, NSW: St Pauls Publications, 1979), #15.
44 Francis, *Laudato Si*, #218.

invitation of God's Spirit, I notice that these experiences are frequently openings to ecological conversion.[45]

Numerous writers point out that 'nature is God's first and primary revelation'.[46] Indeed, many directees come to God in and through the natural world. Terrence Moran believes that for many people 'the natural world is itself the spiritual director'.[47] Over and above the experiences with nature that directees bring to spiritual direction, these authors argue that one cannot minister as a spiritual director today without some awareness of the wider context of ecology. This is true in my experience.

In all of the commentators cited, the understanding that God's Spirit is the true spiritual director is paramount. From his psychological starting point, Gerald May writes:

> When we examine the most destructive aberrations that have occurred in the name of religion throughout history, we see the recurrent phenomenon of spiritual leaders taking destiny upon themselves, playing God, substituting personal mastery for surrender to divine will.[48]

---

45 Edwards lists a number of experiences that he sees as inherent to 'the mysticism of ecological praxis', akin to experiences that are often encountered in spiritual direction: Edwards, *Ecology at the Heart of Faith*, 118.

46 For example, Yvonne R. Prowse, "Spiritual Direction and the Call to Ecological Conversion," *Presence* 22, no. 4 (2016): 18. Christine Valters Painter, "Earth as Soul Care Matrix," *Presence* 23, no.2 (2017: 7

47 Terrence J. Moran, "Spiritual Direction and the New Cosmology," *Presence* 15, no. 3 (2009): 7.

48 Gerald G. May, *Care of Mind, Care of Spirit* (San Francisco, CA: Harper & Row, 1982), 16. Gerald May was a practising psychiatrist, a spiritual director and a formator of spiritual directors. He was based at the *Shalem Institute* Institute for Spiritual Formation, Washington, DC till his death in 2005.

The Tradition of Spiritual Direction

This insistence is utterly consistent with the tradition of spiritual direction. Merton captures the tradition in a quotation from Augustine Baker:

> The director is not to teach his own way, nor indeed any determinate way of prayer... in a word, he is only God's usher, and must lead souls in God's way, not his own.[49]

Both Ignatius Loyola and John of the Cross insist on the same point:

> There can be no greater mistake... than to want to mould others to one's own image.[50]

> Directors should reflect that they themselves are not the chief agent, guide, and mover of souls, but that the principal guide is the Holy Spirit, who is never neglectful of souls.[51]

Margaret Guenther summarises her reflections with the one sentence: 'For spiritual directors, the Holy Spirit is the true director'.[52]

Psychological factors in Spiritual Direction

Two implications of the stated focus on religious experience are the need to be aware of the psychological factors that can influence a directee's noticing and interpreting their experience,

---

49 Merton, *Spiritual Direction and Meditation*, 12.
50 This is taken from the diary of Luis Gonzalez de Camara, the scribe of Ignatius Loyola's biography. (see below) De Camara is quoting Ignatius. The sentence is cited in Philip Sheldrake, "Traditions in Spiritual Guidance: St Ignatius and Spiritual Direction," *The Way* 24, no. October (1984): 314.
51 John of the Cross, "The Living Flame of Love," in *The Collected Works of St. John of the Cross*, 3.46.
52 Guenther, *Holy Listening*, 112.

and the need for discernment of spirits in listening to the directee's experience.

Building on the early literature, Gerald May has made a significant contribution in his writings on psychology and spiritual direction.[53] May is precise in describing the different approaches of the two disciplines of his experience – psychiatry and spiritual direction – even while stressing their complementarity:

> It is the function of therapists to help patients solve problems. But, although spiritual directors may be called upon to help solve various problems... their most fundamental role is to attend to God's power, love and grace...[54]

From this conviction, May shows how a spiritual director can learn from the psychological sciences, noting that they are 'different approaches to a common reality'.[55] May suggests further that the two disciplines support one another and work side-by-side in a contemplative approach, as captured in his subtitle *A Contemplative Psychology*. He stresses that this is not to be confused with a psychology of contemplation. Rather, the opposite:

> If we could relinquish our attachment to self-supremacy and open our hearts to the awesome simplicity of spiritual truth, all of our endeavours, including the giving and receiving of psychological

---

53 For example, May, *Care of Mind, Care of Spirit*. Gerald G. May, *Will and Spirit: A Contemplative Psychology* (San Francisco, CA: Harper & Row, 1982). Gerald G. May, *Addiction and Grace* (San Francisco, CA: HarperSanFrancisco, 1988).
54 May, *Care of Mind, Care of Spirit*, 48.
55 Gerald G. May, *Pilgrimage Home* (New York: Paulist, 1979), 66.

help and understanding, could be deeply spiritual acts.[56]

This 'relinquishing attachment', May calls 'willingness' or openness to mystery, in contrast to 'wilfulness', the effort to master or control one's destiny. Indeed, he sees most traditional psychologies characterised more by wilfulness than willingness. Elsewhere, May uses the psychological term 'addiction' to describe one's 'attachment to self-supremacy'. To define it directly, 'addiction is a state of compulsion, obsession or preoccupation that enslaves a person's will and desire'.[57] The importance for spiritual directors of this distinction between willingness and wilfulness is that any wilfulness – hidden agendas, conscious or unconscious inner attachments, risks of manipulating a directee's experience – will result in the director mis-reading the signs of the spirits in the other's experience, as described in chapter 6.

Barry considers the same unconscious dynamics in his writing on one's 'default image of God'.[58] He uses the psychoanalytic terminology of 'schemata' or psychic patterns to describe ingrained ways of relating to other people and to God. These patterns in the way a person relates are often deeply rooted in one's psyche, explained by early childhood experiences. This is relevant to Luigi Rulla's treatment of attachments or *unfreedoms* in a person's make-up, which I discuss in chapter 8. Their importance for spiritual directors is precisely what May has described.

---

56 May, *Will and Spirit*, 21.
57 May, *Addiction and Grace*, 13-4.
58 William A. Barry, "Changing the Default Image of God," *Human Development* 26, no. 1 (2005): 28-33.

Discernment in daily life

Ignatius Loyola (1491-1556) wrote his pioneering work on discernment in his Spiritual Exercises during the years 1525-1540.[59] Ignatius' work is a primary source for any study of discernment. Extensive writing on the subject has built on the initial work of Ignatius Loyola and his twenty-two 'rules for discernment'. In surveying that writing, I emphasise the *experience* of God's Spirit and spirits not-of-God, on which any theory of discernment is built. Ignatius is quite clear in his autobiography that he is speaking of his own experience:

> [Ignatius] answered that he had not made up the Exercises all at once, but when he found that some things were helpful to his soul, he thought they might also be helpful to others, and so he put them in writing...[60]

Karl Rahner confirms this in his *Ignatius of Loyola Speaks*. He writes as Ignatius:

> This was my personal experience, beginning with my very own and first exercises at Manresa, where the eyes of my spirit were opened and I could see everything as in God. This is the experience that I wanted to convey to others by the giving of the exercises.[61]

---

59 Ignatius Loyola, *The Spiritual Exercises of St. Ignatius*, ed. Louis J. Puhl (Chicago, IL: Loyola University Press, 1951).
60 Ignatius Loyola, *The Autobiography of St. Ignatius Loyola*, ed. John C. Olin, trans. Joseph F O'Callaghan (New York: Fordham University Press, 1992), 92. Ignatius narrated his biography in answer to questions from a scribe, Luis Gonzalez de Camara, who wrote it for him, in the third person.
61 Rahner, *Ignatius of Loyola Speaks*, 16.

Reflecting on his own and others' experience, Ignatius developed a systematic teaching on discernment. Hugo Rahner argues that Ignatius simply codified the tradition developed earlier, a tradition particularly in John Cassian (c 360-435), John Climacus (c 579-649) and the Desert Mothers and Fathers.[62] Similarly, Michael Buckley asserts:

> [Ignatius' rules] are formal codifications of insights and responses which have arisen and justified themselves in Ignatius' own religious practice... Ignatius' rules do have a patristic heritage... but Ignatius' work, though situated within this ecclesiastical tradition, seems strangely innocent of it.[63]

The tradition of discernment, in fact, pre-existed Ignatius by many centuries, beginning as early as Origen (184-253) and Antony of Egypt (251-356).[64]

Offering an early description of the God's Spirit at work, Origen wrote

> We learn to discern clearly when a soul is moved by the presence of a spirit of a better kind, namely when it suffers no mental disturbance or aberration whatsoever, as a result of the

---

62 see Ernest E. Larkin, *Silent Presence* (Denville NJ: Dimension Books, 1981), 8.
63 Michael J. Buckley, "The Structure of the Rules for Discernment of Spirits," *The Way Supplement* 20, no. Autumn (1973): 26.
64 For example, Benedicta Ward, "Discernment: A Rare Bird," *The Way Supplement* 64 (1989): 10-7. Danny E. Morris and Charles M. Olsen, *Discerning God's Will Together* (Nashville, TN: Upper Room Books, 1997). McIntosh, *Discernment and Truth*, 32-42. Joseph T. Lienhard, "On Discernment of Spirits in the Early Church," *Theological Studies* 41, no. 3 (1980).

immediate inspiration and does not lose the free judgement of the will...⁶⁵

In his commentary on Origen, Leinhard says that 'the good Spirit is recognised by the fact that the soul's tranquillity is undisturbed and its freedom is respected'.⁶⁶

Antony, too, is said to have spoken of the ways of God's Spirit and other spirits to the monks who had followed him into the desert:

> The vision of the holy ones ... comes so quietly and gently that immediately joy, gladness and courage arise in the soul. For the Lord who is our joy is with them ... The thoughts of the soul remain unruffled and undisturbed, for the love of what is divine... possesses it. But the inroad and display of the evil spirits is fraught with confusion, with din, with sounds and cryings... from which arise fear in the heart, tumult, confusion of thought... disregard of virtue and unsettled habits...⁶⁷

Though he was 'strangely innocent' of this tradition, Ignatius would write very similar words twelve centuries later, illustrating Hugo Rahner's argument that Ignatius codified the earlier tradition. At the same time, if Ignatius had not read these earlier works, such strikingly similar descriptions of the ways of the spirits in two quite independent authors, centuries apart, gives added credibility to their understanding of the spirits.

---

65   Origen, *The Writings of Origen*, trans. Frederick Crombie, vol. X, *Ante-Nicene Christian Library* (Edinburgh: T. & T. Clark, 1869), Book III, Chapter II. Lienhard, "On Discernment of Spirits in the Early Church," 512.
66   Lienhard, "On Discernment of Spirits in the Early Church," 512.
67   Athanasius, *The Life of Antony*, trans. Robert T Meyer, vol. 10, *Ancient Christian Writers* (New York: Newman Press, 1950), #36. Lienhard, "On Discernment of Spirits in the Early Church," 515-6.

Both Antony and Ignatius were writing from their personal experience of the spirits. My writing, too, will build on the human experience of God's Spirit and spirits not-of-God, studying how these spirits can attract and the different directions in which they lead. My methodology uses such experience as starting point, equivalently discovering 'rules for discernment' in one's own experience. In this approach, I agree with Maureen Conroy:

> Without the lively experiencing of God, the rules remain an archaic description, a skeleton of experience. Our personal relationship with God is what moves a *past description* into a *personal experience.*[68]

Jules Toner has written extensively on discernment – what he calls 'Ignatian discernment' – in two commentaries and two books of case studies.[69] The titles of his books establish a clear distinction between 'Discernment of Spirits' and 'Discernment of God's Will'. The latter is about Christian decision making, the former, which underpins decision making, is about the ways of the spirits in one's life. Though I will have subsequent points of disagreement with Toner, I see this distinction as essential to any approach to discernment.

I argue that discernment is primarily about relationship with God, not about decision making. It is in relationship with God and with all God's creation, with oneself and with others, that the unique invitation of the Spirit of God becomes clear.

---

68 Maureen Conroy, *The Discerning Heart* (Chicago, IL: Loyola Press, 1993), 61.

69 Toner, *Discernment of Spirits*. Jules J. Toner, *Discerning God's Will* (St. Louis, MO: Institute of Jesuit Sources, 1991). Jules J. Toner, *Spirit of Light or Darkness* (St. Louis, MO: Institute of Jesuit Sources, 1995). Jules J. Toner, *What Is Your Will, O God* (St. Louis, MO: Institute of Jesuit Sources, 1995).

Though not all commentators make the distinction between discernment of spirits and discernment of God's Will, many do focus on relationship with God as the basis of discernment:

> ... (decision making) is a call to be in relationship with the Lord, a call to respond to the Spirit who speaks in our hearts and in our lives...[70]
>
> ... Christian discernment is not the same as decision making. Reaching a decision can be straight forward: we consider our goals and options; maybe we list the pros and cons of each possible choice; and then we choose the action that meets our goal most effectively. Discernment, on the other hand, is about listening and responding to that place within us where our deepest desires align with God's desire.[71]

Similarly, Sheldrake argues that discernment 'is a matter of attitude and of relationships – the quality of how we relate to our own self, to other people, to created reality, to God.'[72] Jim Manney says that 'discernment and decision making are not synonymous in the Ignatian tradition'[73] and Roger Haight summarises that 'discernment of spirits is linked to the decision making process... but is distinct from it'.[74]

---

70 Mary Benet McKinney, *Sharing Wisdom: A Process for Group Decision Making* (Allen, Texas: Tabor Publishing, 1987), 16.

71 Michael J. Christensen and Rebecca J. Laird, eds., *Discernment: Reading the Signs of Daily Life* (London: SPCK, 2013), xvii. The Foreword to Henri Nouwen's writings was written by Robert A Jonas.

72 Philip Sheldrake, *Befriending Our Desires* (London: Darton, Longman & Todd, 2001), 105.

73 Jim Manney, *What Do You Really Want?* (Huntington, IN: Our Sunday Visitor, 2015), 112.

74 Roger Haight, *Christian Spirituality for Seekers: Reflections on the Spiritual Exercises of Ignatius Loyola* (Maryknoll, NY: Orbis Books, 2012), 58.

David Lonsdale names this focus 'a living relationship with God', which he sees as the basis for good discernment:

> A daily living relationship with God is the precondition for good discernment. To attempt to 'do discernment' in a vacuum, as it were, by simply following a set of instructions without the foundation of [a] living relationship with God is a misunderstanding of what discernment is and an impossible task.[75]

Herbert Alphonso's treatment of 'personal vocation' develops this emphasis:

> ... the single greatest grace of my life is that I discerned my truest and deepest 'self', the unrepeatable uniqueness God has given to me in 'calling me by name'... My own personal experience and my ministry of the Spirit have taught me that the deepest transformation in any person's life takes place in the actual living out of this very 'personal vocation'.[76]

The terminology is unique to Alphonso, but others recognise the same experience, expressing it in different terminology. For example, Dermot Mansfield speaks of one's 'primordial experience':

> It is vital for any spirituality, or way of prayer, or process of spiritual accompaniment, to attend to that primordial experience, when I know that

---

[75] David Lonsdale, *Dance to the Music of the Spirit* (London: Darton, Longman & Todd, 1992), 43-4.

[76] Herbert Alphonso, *The Personal Vocation* (Rome: Centrum Ignatianum Spiritualitatis, 1990), 14. Alphonso (1930-2012) was an Indian Jesuit priest, director of the Ignatian Spirituality Centre and professor of Spiritual Theology at the Gregorian University in Rome.

I have been called into existence to be uniquely who I am and to be sustained by that look of love.[77]

I develop the significance and the value of awareness of one's 'personal vocation', the 'touchstone' of one's life, in processes of discernment in chapter 4.

Discernment in Christian decision making

Some spiritual directors consider decision making, choosing between options, to be the primary purpose of discernment. They appear to give little attention to the underlying work of establishing relationship and naming the ways of the spirits within that relationship. For example, Pierre Wolff describes discernment as 'the process of making choices that correspond as closely as possible to objective reality, that are as free as possible from our inner compulsions, and that are closely attuned to the convictions of our faith'.[78]

Discernment may well ask for some decision making, but in discussing Christian decision making (chapter 7), I argue to the place of and the need for a much broader approach to discernment prior to decision making. I argue that the ground work of noticing and being familiar with the ways of the spirits in one's life is essential. Good decision making rests on this awareness of how God's Spirit and other spirits not-of-God work in one's whole life.

---

77   Dermot Mansfield, "Spiritual Accompaniment and Discernment," *The Way* 47, no. 1&2 (2008): 159.

78   Pierre Wolff, *Discernment: The Art of Choosing Well* (Liguori, MO: Triumph Books, 1993), x.

When decision making is called for, most writers follow the teaching of Ignatius Loyola. Ignatius gives three ways or 'times' for seeking God's will or making a 'good choice' in life.[79] Though they are often treated in isolation, Michael Ivens argues that even these ways are not divorced from one's relationship with God:

> [The *Spiritual Exercises*] prepare for a Christian life lived according to a spirituality characterised precisely by concern to integrate the decisions of life into a person's relationship with God.[80]

Dyckman, Garvin and Liebert agree in their outline of the 'three levels to discernment', the most basic of which 'consists in a habitual discernment that flows from relationship with the Creative Holy One and comes to fruition in "putting on the mind of Christ". (Philippians 2:2) One learns and practises it continuously'.[81]

These authors are affirming the primary place of relationship with God in discernment.

The only disagreement amongst many commentators who follow Ignatius Loyola is the weighting to be given to any one of the three ways when making a decision. In chapter 7, I discuss the inter-connectedness of Ignatius' three ways of decision

---

79   Ignatius Loyola, *Spiritual Exercises*, ##175-8.
80   Michael Ivens, *Understanding the Spiritual Exercises: A Handbook for Retreat Directors* (Herefordshire, UK: Gracewing, 1998), 129.
81   Dyckman, Garvin, and Liebert, *Spiritual Exercises Reclaimed*, 248. These authors name the second level in reference to Ignatius' Rules for Discernment, 'focusing on inner feelings and inclinations', and third to do with making decision and actions, 'flowing from one's relationship with the Holy One.' The three senses of the term 'discernment' are seen to be interrelated and cyclic.

making and draw conclusions from my experience as a spiritual director.

God's Spirit and spirits not-of-God

Basic to any discussion of discernment of spirits is a belief that both God's Spirit and spirits not-of-God are present and active in human experience:

> Beloved, do not believe every spirit, but *test the spirits* to see whether they are from God. For many false prophets have gone out into the world. (1 John 4:1-2)

> Beware of false prophets, who come to you in sheep's clothing but inwardly are ravenous wolves. You will know them by their fruits... (Matthew 7:15-19)

God's self-giving love makes possible a life in the Spirit, attentive to the ever-present, ever-active Spirit that has been given to us. (Romans 5:5)

Spirits not-of-God work to block one's response to God's Spirit. The work of these spirits is often approached through awareness of how easily people can deceive themselves:

> I live in a world of conflicting desires, of conflicting groups, of conflicting claims. How can I know how to align myself with the one action of God? This is the point where discernment comes in... I must learn two difficult and seemingly incompatible attitudes: to trust myself and my reactions and to recognise how easily I can delude myself. Discernment requires that I believe that God's

desire will show itself in my experience, and that I yet be wary of mindless credulity toward that same experience.[82]

Indeed, as Edwards points out, 'it has been the constant teaching of the tradition that it is all too easy to fall into self-deception and to be led astray by outside influences...' He quotes developments in psychology, the sociology of knowledge and feminism, to make the point that 'we have learned that we are not neutral interpreters of reality, but inclined, often unconsciously, towards what serves our own interest and maintains our own privilege'.[83] May, in fact, believes that people rarely come to any relationship utterly freely.[84] For this reason, I study human *unfreedom* and inner vulnerability as prime ground for the temptation of spirits not-of-God, working against God's Spirit.

One learning from developments in psychology is that 'unconscious needs and drives', areas of *unfreedom,* can impel one's actions. These have been studied in depth by Luigi Rulla in his research into vocational motivation.[85] This has clear implications for the practice of discernment, which I develop below. In summary:

> Depth psychology shows that it is possible for a person to desire and to profess the ideals of Christ, while, without being aware of this, he is also driven by subconscious needs which cannot be reconciled with these ideals. Therefore the

---

82   Barry, "Towards a Theology of Discernment," 136. Barry, *Spiritual Direction and the Encounter with God,* 82. Edwards, *Breath of Life,* 158.
83   Edwards, *Breath of Life,* 158.
84   May, *Will and Spirit,* 1-7.
85   Jesuit priest, Luigi Rulla (1922-2002) was professor of psychology at the Institute of Psychology, Gregorian University, Rome from 1971. Rulla died in 2002.

individual is *inconsistent* in the sense that he is moved simultaneously by two opposed forces: one being the ideals which he consciously desires and the judgement of values which he makes, the other being the deep-lying needs by which he is subconsciously driven.[86]

The direction in which God's Spirit leads – towards life and relationship – is called an experience of *consolation,* though the experience may not always be 'consoling' in the usual sense of the word. The direction in which any spirit not-of-God leads – away from life, away from God – is called *desolation*, though again it may not always feel 'desolate'. This honours the Scriptural norm that 'you will know them by their fruits.' (Matthew 7:16) Based on experience, Buckley argues this same understanding:

> Consolation is any interior movement of sensibility – irrespective of the cause – whose direction is God... whether its presence is experientially pleasant or not... Consolation and desolation do not identify necessarily with pleasure and pain.[87]

Not all spiritual directors agree with this. For example, Toner, in his substantial study of discernment of spirits, argues, rather, that Ignatius meant 'ordinary usage' of the terms consolation and desolation: the former is pleasurable, the latter painful.[88] Timothy Gallagher follows Toner, agreeing that Ignatius employs the word 'consolation' according to 'the common understanding of the word': something happy and uplifting.[89] Joseph Tetlow

---

86 Luigi M. Rulla, "The Discernment of Spirits and Christian Anthropology," *Gregorianum* 59, no. 3 (1978): 546.
87 Buckley, "The Structure of the Rules for Discernment of Spirits," 29.
88 Toner, *Discernment of Spirits*, 286-7 and passim.
89 Timothy M. Gallagher, *The Discernment of Spirits* (New York: Crossroad, 2005), 49.

believes that Ignatius 'discovered that... sometimes consolation comes from a good spirit and sometimes from a bad spirit, and he noted the same thing about desolation'.[90]

My experience supports Buckley's position, arguing against many of the implications of the alternative understanding. I hold that consolation is the fruit of God's Spirit at work; it is never fruit of a spirit not-of-God.

William Barry is a significant contributor to the Jesuit commentaries on Ignatius and discernment.[91] Barry talks of discernment without any reference to making decisions: his interest is more about living in a discerning way. Though he quotes the Ignatian rules for discernment, in his later writing Barry situates the rules in the human experience of being 'in tune with' or 'out of tune with' God's intention and action in our world, before he quotes Ignatius' articulation of this experience into a 'rule'.[92] Later again, in his retrospective reflection, Barry emphasises that, as a spiritual director, he focused always on the directee's human experience.[93] I follow this approach.

Ernest Larkin, a Carmelite, is significant also.[94] He finds support in Carmelite sources to argue that 'discernment is not one discrete act in the spiritual life, but rather the whole spiritual endeavour. It is like contemplation, which is an abiding

---

90 Joseph A. Tetlow, *Making Choices in Christ* (Chicago, IL: Loyola Press, 2008), 96.
91 William A. Barry, *Paying Attention to God: Discernment in Prayer* (Notre Dame, IN: Ave Maria Press, 1990). William A. Barry, *Finding God in All Things* (Notre Dame, Ind: Ave Maria Press, 1991). Barry, *Spiritual Direction and the Encounter with God*.
92 Barry, *Spiritual Direction and the Encounter with God*, 77-87.
93 Barry, "What Is Spiritual Direction: A Retrospective Reflection," 31.
94 Larkin, *Silent Presence*. (Denville N.J.: Dimension Books, 1981)

condition of knowing God'.[95] Hence 'the first quality of the spiritual director who helps discern the action of the Spirit, is his own personal experience. Discernment is not learned from books'.[96] This statement is basic to my approach and to this book. In the following chapter, I discuss how, in fact, one learns from experience.

---

95   Ibid., 9.
96   Ibid., 27.

3
Learning from Experience

I keep the subject constantly before me,
and wait till the first dawnings open slowly, by little and little,
into a full and clear light.
Truth is the offspring of silence and meditation.[1]

In this chapter, I consider the meaning of an experiential approach to learning and build my methodology on that approach. This is the methodology of Practical Theology.

An experiential approach

In the tradition of spiritual direction described in chapter 2, I note that the focus of spiritual direction for centuries was on the external behaviour of those coming for spiritual direction, rather than on God's activity in the directee's experience. This was the spiritual direction that I received myself in my early years. Doubtless it tainted my own approach to spiritual direction when I was called to the ministry by my religious community almost fifty years ago – with no formation for the ministry. I listened well, I was encouraging, I helped with problem solving

---

1   Research scientist Isaac Newton (1642-1726), cited in James Gleick, *Isaac Newton* (London: Fourth Estate, 2003), 39.

and decision making, and I'm sure I gave my share of advice and admonition.

Even before I had the opportunity for formal formation as a spiritual director, I became aware that something was missing in this approach. The focus on behaviour did not bring about real change in the lives of the young people for whom I was spiritual director. I was challenged by my reading the works of Francis de Sales.

Francis recounts in his writing that he learned about the focus of spiritual direction from his experience of being a director. Francis wrote two books, *An Introduction to the Devout Life* (1609) and *Treatise on the Love of God* (1616).[2] The first was concerned with how to live a good Christian life, the spiritual practices recommended, examination of conscience, ways of prayer, and love of neighbour. The second, in contrast, focused on God's love and God's working in people's lives, a marked change in focus that Francis himself attributed to his guidance of a community of sisters, notably his spiritual direction of Jane Frances de Chantal.

Just as Francis de Sales learned from his experience, I learned from Francis that a contemplative listening to how God is working in the lives of my directees is a more helpful focus in spiritual direction than what I imagined my directees should be doing to live a good life. My understanding of this shift in focus is verified in what follows. A similar parallel shift happened later when I brought the same contemplative approach to formation and supervision of spiritual directors.

---

2   Francis de Sales, *An Introduction to the Devout Life* (Garden City, NY: Doubleday, 1972). Francis de Sales, *Treatise on the Love of God* (Rochford, IL: Tan Books, 1963).

Learning from Experience

People come to spiritual direction with their varied questions. *How can I pray with fewer distractions? How can I be sure that what is happening for me is from God? How do I decide what is best in this problem I have?* In my early practice, I would have attempted to answer such questions, rather than listen for God's invitation in the question. I learned that, instead of offering suggestions about how to pray, I experienced a very different response when I asked 'what happens when you try to pray?' Instead of discussing the pros and cons of a decision the directee wanted to make, again the experience was very different when I encouraged the person to sit with the options and notice what happens in their inner life. And when I asked about relationships, with God and with other people, I heard quite a different level of experience – and I found that my relationship with the directee moved to a different level at the same time. This is more contemplative listening, focusing on the individual's experience of God's Spirit and listening for God's invitation in that experience.

This focus and approach to spiritual direction permeates this book. My experience has taught me that it is only with such a focus that spiritual directors can notice and interpret the signs of God's Spirit and other spirits not-of-God at work in their directees. The approach contrasts with more deductive ways of learning, for example, in some branches of theology which begin with a theoretical concept or principle. It contrasts, too, with the ways of learning the tools of a trade, as an apprentice carpenter might learn the right way to perform some task or an apprentice spiritual director might learn rules for discernment. I believe that any 'rules' for this ministry are best discovered in one's own experience, for the sake of the internalisation described in chapters 9 and 10.

In the formation of other spiritual directors, all I brought to the beginnings of the formation program *Siloam* in 1979 was my own formation as a spiritual director and my vision of a contemplative experiential approach. I had no formation as a supervisor – indeed, to my knowledge, no formation program for supervisors of spiritual directors existed at that time. Working always with another experienced spiritual director, I learned from the experience of supervising others. Later, another supervisor and I were blessed with the support of an experienced psychological therapist who mentored our supervision for some years. And later still, I was personally supervised in my ministry of supervision of spiritual directors.

The vision of contemplative experiential learning was enhanced and often re-worked through the years of sharing ministry with other supervisors.

Learning from experience

In my experiential approach to ministry and formation, I take inspiration from Teresa of Avila who wrote in *The Book of Her Life* that 'as much as I desire to speak clearly about these matters of prayer, they will be really obscure for anyone who has not had experience [of prayer]'.[3] On another occasion, Teresa assured her sisters: 'I can speak of what I have experience of'.[4] I propose a similar learning from experience. I use the principles of discernment and an understanding of the effect of the unconscious in people's experience to address the 'obscurity' of which Teresa speaks.

---

3   Teresa of Avila, "The Book of Her Life," in *The Collected Works of St. Teresa of Avila*, 10.9.
4   Ibid. 8.5

Learning from Experience

I refer throughout to inner experience. Terminology of 'experience' is used for both one's experience as a spiritual director and one's inner experience of ministering. I am an experienced spiritual director, meaning that I have ministered to many people for many years. But to learn from experience, as did Teresa and Francis, I am invited to listen to my *inner* experience. What happens in my inner world as I listen and come to understand someone else's personal experience? What do I experience within, as I listen? What moves in me? This involves noticing and interpreting the inner experience in both my directee and myself.

When focusing on inner experience, I use the terminology of inner 'movements', noticing what 'moves' within. The word is used in the sense in which one might say 'I was deeply moved by what happened to me'. In this sense, a 'movement' describes something that happens to a person, not a person's choice to move from one place to another. Inner movements might include new insight, unexpected emotion, some memory or imagination, deepened desire, inclinations towards some action – movements that happen to a person, rather than are chosen. I use this terminology throughout.

I draw from the writing of Denis Edwards who argues that experience necessarily involves both encounter and interpretation of the encounter:

> Experience is best seen as encounter with some thing or person which has become available to consciousness through reflective awareness. It refers to an encounter that is interpreted within human consciousness. This second element, interpretation, has always already occurred

whenever we know that we have experienced something.[5]

Interpretation of an encounter is critical: two people with the same experience may interpret the experience quite differently. William Barry shares this understanding in his discussion of experience and the possibility of religious experience as the focus of spiritual direction. Barry's argument is that all human experience is 'multidimensional' and that all human experience has a religious dimension.[6] Along the same lines, I argue in chapter 6 that interpreting one's experience as a religious experience rests on the faith of the person who has the experience. Others may interpret similar experience quite differently.

There are different ways of interpreting experience: the cognitive way, analysing one's experience intellectually, the affective way, listening to the varying affective movements in one's experience, and what Larkin calls the 'mystical way' when one's experience is without doubt a mystical grace.[7] All three ways are called upon in what follows, though the affective way is the way most commonly used in the practice of discernment. I discuss the mystical way in chapters 4 and 5 under the heading of 'consolation without previous cause', the touchstone for interpretation of one's experience.

I recognise that one limitation of this methodology is the possible influence of unconscious needs and drives in those who set out to understand their experience and to make judgements on the basis of that understanding. This is clear in Rulla's research:

---

5   Denis Edwards, *Human Experience of God* (New York: Paulist, 1983), 7.
6   Barry, *Spiritual Direction and the Encounter with God*, 21.
7   Larkin, "What to Know About Discernment," 163.

> It is worth emphasising the point that this is particularly true when such defects have remained unconscious and have not been recognised. There will then be a tendency for such defects, limitations, or distortions to be preserved and repeated, because frequently they are in the service of unconscious needs...[8]

Indeed, I acknowledge the possibility that 'unconscious needs and drives' may well influence my own memory of my spiritual direction ministry, the primary source of material for this reflection. I know that I cannot claim accurate memory with absolute certainty: the limitations to human freedom that are the lot of all human people will necessarily affect my memory recall to some extent. Those limitations can result in what is called 'counter memory', even intentional counter memory, as it were in denial of one's true memory. On the other hand, my own formation and my experience in being supervised and in personal therapy have given me confidence to trust my memory of my ministry to people in spiritual direction. With those helps, I am more able to identify within myself the predictable dynamic when my 'unconscious needs' are demanding attention.

I am encouraged also by consistency in my memory: the experiences described were repeated often in spiritual direction sessions, and they are consistent with others' recorded experience.

Moreover the experience held in my memory and my interpretation of the experience has been validated. It has borne fruit, both for my directees and for myself as spiritual

---

[8] Rulla, "The Discernment of Spirits and Christian Anthropology," 553.

director. This is evident in the examples of spiritual direction that I describe.

Practical Theology

This way of learning from experience – reflecting on and interpreting inner experience – is the methodology of practical theology. Karl Rahner defines practical theology as:

> that theological discipline that is concerned with the Church's self-actualisation here and now – both that which is and that which ought to be. This it does by means of theological illumination of the particular situation in which the Church must realise itself in all its dimensions. Everything is its subject matter.[9]

Rahner's own spirituality and theology often uses his own experience of God as starting point. This is especially evident in his prayers.[10] Mary Steinmetz writes that 'from concrete experience of God, he attempts to understand the traditional faith of the Church. And he invites others to discover similar experiences in themselves'.[11] Rahner calls practical theology an 'independent science' and a 'fundamental one', a 'reflection oriented towards committal'.[12] Practical theology leads to concrete choices for life.

My 'particular situation' of interest is the human everyday

---

9   Karl Rahner, "Practical Theology within the Totality of Theological Disciplines," in *Theological Investigations* (New York: Seabury, 1972), IX, 101.
10 Rahner, *The Mystical Way*. Rahner, *Ignatius of Loyola Speaks*.
11 Mary Steinmetz, "Thoughts on the Experience of God in the Theology of Karl Rahner," *Lumen et Vita* 2 (2012): 10.
12 Rahner, "Practical Theology within the Totality of Theological Disciplines," in *Theological Investigations*, 103.

experience of the spirits. It is that experience that I reflect upon, seek to understand, and hope to verify through 'theological illumination' of the experience.

I stress that practical theology is a *theological* discipline. It does not simply seek after knowledge for the sake of knowledge. Rather it 'is intended to increase our knowledge and understanding of God and to enable us to live more loving and faithful lives'.[13]

The starting point in practical theology is experience, the place where the Gospel is grounded and lived out. Commentators on practical theology work from this conviction: 'human experience is presumed to be an important locus for the work of the Spirit'.[14] As Rahner emphasised, 'everything is its subject matter'.

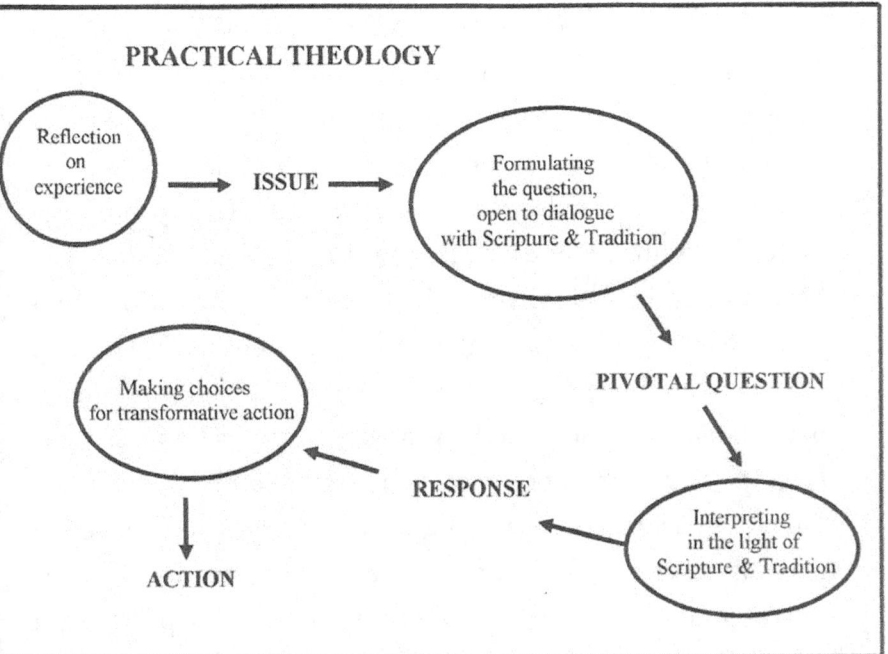

---

13   John Swinton and Harriet Mowat, *Practical Theology and Qualitative Research* (London: SCM Press, 2006), vii.
14   Ibid., 6.

Experience is then interpreted in the light of Sacred Scripture and other sources of revelation and in dialogue with others' experience.

The Methodology of Practical Theology

The diagram above is adapted from Neil Darragh, who develops his methodology along these same lines. Practical theology begins from contemporary practice, and then investigates the Christian sources in order to arrive at transformative practice.[15]

As a methodology in the formation of spiritual directors, for example, my approach to teaching discernment begins with spiritual directors' experience. I encourage the directors to notice the inner movements in themselves in their everyday experience – maybe some unexpected graced moment or some major decision they have made recently or maybe some reaction they noticed when listening to another in ministry. Facilitating such reflection on experience, I help spiritual directors to understand or interpret the movements that they have noticed in themselves. One or other may be a movement inspired by God's Spirit, another from a different spirit. This step of coming to interpret inner movements is helped by dialogue with classical teaching on the ways of the spirits (chapter 5), by listening to others' experience, and by guided reflection on the director's past experience of the spirits. In time, such reflection and interpretation of one's experience becomes habitual, as the director becomes more discerning. The last step is to seek verification of one's understanding by testing the direction in

---

15 Neil Darragh, "The Practice of Practical Theology," *Australian e Journal of Theology* 9, March (2007).

which the movements lead. Invariably, the director is led to some decision about further action. The ultimate verification comes in the fruits experienced in the person's life: 'you will know them by their fruits'. (Matthew 7:16)

This focus on the spiritual director's experience as starting point extends also to my ministry of supervision of spiritual directors. Also in a contemplative way, I listen to a spiritual director's experience in a concrete example of ministry, noticing inner movements in myself as well as in the spiritual director. Then in dialogue with the director, together we seek to interpret these movements in the light of past experience and our knowledge of the ways of the spirits. Often, the spiritual director is helped to deeper self-awareness, at times to some inner point of conversion.

In my teaching, I use the same approach in seminar work. For example, in the seminar *The Human Experience of God,* the initial topic treated is one's desire for God. I invite the participants to reflect contemplatively, prayerfully asking God to bring back into awareness examples from their own past experience when they have deeply longed for God, or when they have really wanted to pray, or when they have felt the pain of God's apparent absence. As examples come to mind, my questions are designed to help participants to fill out their experience, naming how the experience affected them at the time, what they noticed in their inner world, and where the inner movements actually led them.

This is the same diagram, applied to the experience of desire for God:

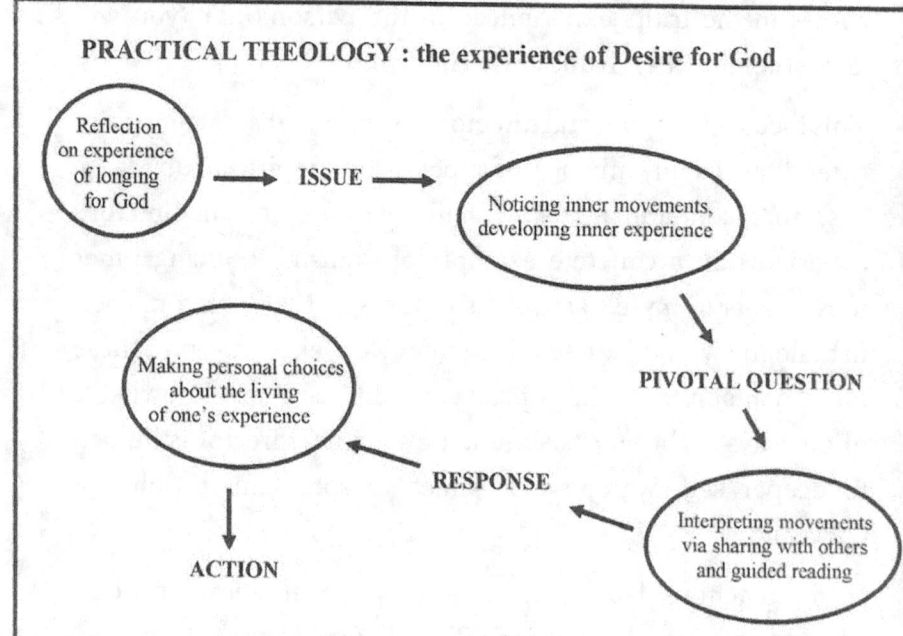

Practical Theology in seminar on 'Desire for God'

When participants are invited to share their experience with one another, invariably new light is shed on individual personal experience. Predictably, someone will say that they have just realised that the very longing for God, even though 'unsatisfied', is itself a gift of God. Someone else may develop this from a different experience and note that the way God works seems to be that the longing is forever deepened, not filled up. As others add their experience, I judge the time to introduce the teaching of the tradition in spirituality writing: for example, Gregory of Nyssa (335-395), William of St Thierry (1085-1148), Julian of Norwich (1342-1430), and John Chapman (1865-1933) all teach from their own experience that the very experience of longing for God is itself an experience of God, indeed is to know God. Desire for God is not possessive, but an openness to God in self-giving.[16]

The teaching is understood in the light of the experience itself, experience which the seminar participants have already articulated.[17] Teaching about grace, trust in God, forgiveness, true and false self, dark night, the ways of God's Spirit and other spirits, and numerous other areas of experience can be approached in this same way. I emphasise that the approach is contemplative, wanting to see and understand one's experience 'with the eyes of God'.

Darragh's outline describes my methodology accurately: one's experience as a starting point, leading to the pivotal question, and then a re-reading of Sacred Scripture and other literature from the tradition of spirituality, in turn leading to some response and to choices. Moreover, I share Darragh's hope that this approach might give birth to some 'transformative action'.

Terry Veling prefers to see the practice of practical theology more as a *craft* than a *method*, seeking understanding more than knowledge. Veling sees the approach of practical theology inviting a person to be more receptive to whatever is 'seeking to speak to us, to show itself to us, to reveal its truth to us'.[18] Veling calls this process *habitus*, 'a disposition of mind and heart from which our actions flow naturally... according to the Spirit

---

16 Sheldrake, *Befriending Our Desires*, 61.
17 This approach is affirmed by Larkin: 'Sacred writing, whether the Scriptures themselves or the writings of the saints and theologians, is the product of experience and reflection.' Ernest E. Larkin, "A Method for Reading the Spiritual Classics," *Review for Religious* 40, no. 3 (1981): 382.
18 Terry A. Veling, *Practical Theology* (Maryknoll, NY: Orbis Books, 2005).

dwelling in us'. In different language, Veling is speaking of the contemplative way to which I am committed. This way colours both my approach to spiritual direction, supervision and formation and the methodology of my present writing, focusing on experience, understanding, critical reflection and judgment.

Veling's final statement is:

> The method of practical theology is this – to become disciples, followers, listeners and doers of the Word, people of faith, people who walk the paths of God, people who seek to know and practice the purposes of God, who desire God and the ways of God.[19]

From quite a different tradition, I have been inspired also by Isaac Newton, the renowned scientist of the seventeenth century, who wrote of his approach to research work, cited at the beginning of this chapter: waiting 'till the first dawnings open slowly, by little and little, into a full and clear light...'[20] Newton, too, is speaking of the contemplative way.

The contemplative way

The contemplative way is integral to my approach to spiritual direction and the formation of spiritual directors.

John of the Cross wrote that 'contemplation is to receive'.[21] This has prompted many to see Mary, the Mother of Jesus, as the prototype of the contemplative person. Mary received the

---

19 Ibid., 241.
20 Research scientist Isaac Newton, cited in Gleick, *Isaac Newton*, 39.
21 John of the Cross, "The Living Flame of Love," in *The Collected Works of St. John of the Cross*, stanza 3.36.

Word of God literally in her womb and symbolically in every facet of her being. Mary is sometimes called the 'Womb of God'. As I wrote in *Taking God to Heart*, 'the womb is symbol of complete openness and receptivity, of expectant waiting, of total surrender, and of course, of giving flesh and birth to God's Word. The womb is pure receptivity, waiting to receive what will begin the life-process within it'.[22] Such openness and receptivity to what is given is inherent to the contemplative way.

Veling's description of practical theology as 'a disposition of mind and heart from which our actions flow... according to the Spirit... being receptive to that which is seeking... to reveal its truth to us'[23] describes the contemplative stance.

Human people are by nature contemplative beings, even though the human tendency towards independence and self-sufficiency can be a strong obstacle to 'receiving' for many people. The contemplative nature yearns to know what is real, what is true, and what is good – ultimately what is of God – in one's experience. Because discernment is concerned with what is of God, I argue that a contemplative approach is basic to the practice of discernment and to the process of becoming discerning. Indeed, the contemplative way is well established in spiritual direction literature and practice.[24]

The contemplative approach asks for an intentional focus outside of oneself. Barry calls this an experience of 'transcendence'.[25]

---

22   Brian Gallagher, *Taking God to Heart* (Strathfield, NSW: St. Pauls, 2008), 28.
23   Veling, *Practical Theology*, 16.
24   For example, Barry and Connolly, *The Practice of Spiritual Direction*, 46-64. William A. Barry, "The Contemplative Attitude in Spiritual Direction," *Review for Religious* 35, no. 6 (1976): 821.
25   William A. Barry, "The Contemplative Attitude in Spiritual Direction," *Review for Religious* 35, no. 6 (1976): 821.

Whether the object of contemplation is a beautiful flower or another person or the Word of God in prayer, the focus is entirely on the other, with no expectations or pre-conceived ideas about whatever the other will reveal of itself. Tilden Edwards describes the contemplative attitude as 'a simple, open presence to what is'.[26]

Walter Burghardt defined contemplation as 'a long loving look at the real':

> The real I look at, I do not analyse it or argue it. I do not describe or define it. I am one with it... I enter into it... The look is wonderfully unhurried, gloriously unharried... To contemplate is to be in love.[27]

In his practical suggestions to help a person cultivate a contemplative attitude, Burghardt encourages a sense of play and festivity. Most of all, he says, 'don't try to possess the object of your delight... and don't expect to profit from contemplation'.[28]

Both contemplation and discernment mean openness to surprise and newness – an attitude of interior freedom, often called 'holy indifference',[29] a basic pre-requisite in spiritual direction and discernment. Remaining indifferent means staying open to God's Spirit. Francis de Sales explains indifference: 'If I like only pure water, what does it matter to me whether it is served in a

---

26 Tilden Edwards, *Spiritual Director, Spiritual Companion: Guide to Tending the Soul* (New York: Paulist, 2001), 4.

27 Walter Burghardt, "Contemplation: A Long Loving Look at the Real" (paper presented at the National Federation of Spiritual Directors, Camarillo, CA 1975), 8-10.

28 Ibid.

29 See, for example, English, *Spiritual Freedom*, 46-50. English treats of Ignatian indifference.

goblet of gold or in one of glass, since in either case I drink only the water.'[30]

Such openness to revelation enables a person to see the object of contemplation more truly, to see as God sees. In his classic work on the prophets, Abraham Heschel called the prophet one 'who sees the world with the eyes of God', that is, one who sees the world, sees other people, and sees oneself 'with the eyes of God'. The prophet would be the true contemplative.[31]

This is the contemplative attitude, the waiting on God that grounds further discernment. Pope Francis has recommended the contemplative way for all ministry:

> ... we need to recover a contemplative spirit which can help us to realise ever anew that we have been entrusted with a treasure which makes us more human and helps us to lead a new life. There is nothing more precious which we can give to others.[32]

When spiritual directors and supervisors adopt this contemplative focus on the other person, listening, noticing, waiting, most notice movements in themselves at the same time – without actually focusing on themselves. Spiritual directors and supervisors have learned to trust these unplanned, often unexpected inner movements in themselves as indicators of the work of the spirits, as I discuss in chapter 5.

---

30 Francis de Sales, *Treatise on the Love of God*, Book 9, chapter 4.
31 Abraham J. Heschel, *The Prophets* (New York: Harper & Row, 1962), 138, 212.
32 Francis, *Evangelii Gaudium* (Strathfield NSW: St Pauls Publications, 2013), #264.

The essential attitude of waiting on God's revelation is well described by John Chapman, Benedictine Abbot. When one approaches prayer in this contemplative way, Chapman emphasises waiting on God, wanting God, but having to wait on God's gift:

> The time of prayer is spent in the act of waiting on God. It is an idiotic state and feels like the completest waste of time... The strangest phenomenon is we begin to wonder whether we mean anything at all, and if we are addressing anyone... even the word 'God' seems to mean nothing. If we feel this curious and paradoxical condition, we are on the right road.[33]

Chapman was strongly influenced by John of the Cross. John describes waiting:

> ... allow the soul to remain in rest and quietude... [We] must be content simply with a loving and peaceful attentiveness to God, and live without the concern, without the effort, and without the desire to taste or feel God.[34]

John's 'attentiveness to God' is Chapman's 'waiting on God' even when nothing seems to be happening in one's prayer. One may experience strong desire for God, which John of the Cross distinguishes from 'desire to feel God's presence'. For many, the temptation is to relieve the apparent emptiness of the prayer by looking elsewhere, rather than waiting on God. God is experienced in the waiting, though God's presence is not felt. I

---

[33] John Chapman, *Spiritual Letters* (London: Sheed & Ward, 1983), Appendix.

[34] John of the Cross, "Dark Night," in *The Collected Works of St. John of the Cross*, I,10.4.

believe that this is true of a contemplative attitude to all of life's endeavours.[35]

John of the Cross offers maybe one's first lesson in discernment: consolation is not always *felt,* and not always warm and comfortable, not always consoling, in the everyday meaning of that word. John of the Cross says later that even the experience of darkness in prayer can be a time of grace, a consolation. In chapter 4, I develop this understanding of consolation and the implied understanding of desolation: consolation is the fruit of following the Spirit of God, desolation the fruit of following some spirit not-of-God.

Within this framework and with this methodology, I research the experience of conflicting spirits (chapter 4) and how the spirits work in human experience (chapter 5). God's Spirit and spirits not-of-God are seen to attract a person differently at different stages of a person's spiritual development, but always working against one another, attracting in opposite directions. I apply these understandings to the ministry of spiritual direction (chapter 6) and to Christian decision making (chapter 7), arguing the centrality of discernment in both of these areas of a spiritual director's involvement. I conclude that to be helpful to another person, a spiritual director needs to be a discerning person.

With that conclusion, I then ask how, in fact, does one become discerning? Answering this question involves a study of human freedom and the human experience of limited freedom, impacting on the spiritual director's listening to a directee and interpreting the signs of the spirits. (chapter 8) Growth in discernment parallels growth in inner freedom. (chapter 9)

---

35 William Barry writes of a 'contemplative attitude to life' in "Spiritual Direction: the Empirical Approach," *America* April 24, 1976

4
Discernment: Consolation and Desolation

For you love all things that exist
and detest none of the things you have made...
You spare all things, for they are yours, O Lord,
you who love the living,
for your immortal Spirit is in all things.

Wisdom 11:24, 12:1

The experience of conflicting spirits

The Scriptural invitation is to 'choose life':

> I call heaven and earth to witness against you today that I have set before you life and death, blessings and curses. Choose life so that you and you descendants may live, loving the Lord your God, obeying him and holding fast to him; for that means life to you... (Deuteronomy 30:19-20)

The human experience is that this choice is not straight forward. Who has not had this experience:

> I do not understand my own actions. For I do not do what I want, but I do the very thing I hate. (Romans 7:15)

Discernment: Consolation and Desolation

Coming to terms with the mixed attractions in one's life is a constant challenge: 'I live in a world of conflicting desires, of conflicting groups, of conflicting claims. How can I know how to align myself with the one action of God? This is the point where discernment comes in'.[1]

To help an understanding of this experience, Sallie McFague contrasts the 'arrogant eye' with the 'loving eye', when commenting on Jesus' words that 'the eye is the lamp of the body' (Matthew 6:22).[2] The arrogant eye is self-serving and manipulating, exploiting others; the loving eye seeks truth and sees the uniqueness of the other.[3] I develop this below in the terminology of the two different spirits inviting response in opposing directions.

This is Anna's experience in spiritual direction[4]:

> ***Anna*** *is married woman whose children have all left school and started different careers away from home. Anna came to see me on the recommendation of a mutual friend because, she said, 'I really want to know God, but I don't know how to go about it'. When I asked about 'knowing God', Anna explained that she had heard any number of sermons and read a few books, but felt that she still didn't know God. To clarify, I asked 'What is the importance of knowing God for you?' Anna kept saying 'I just want to know*

---

1 Barry, *Spiritual Direction and the Encounter with God*, 82.

2 cf Cassian's reference to 'the sound eye and the diseased eye': John Cassian, *Conferences* (New York: Paulist Press, 1985), 54 (1:20).

3 Sallie McFague, cited in Edwards, *Ecology at the Heart of Faith*, 111.

4 As mentioned, names used in examples are pseudonyms and all examples are fictitious. No person will recognise themself in the examples, but many will identify with the experience described. The examples are written in the vernacular, in the present tense.

> God'. At one point, she added that she was looking forward to being with God somehow. My response was 'Have you said this to God? Do you talk to God about what you want and what you are looking forward to?' 'Oh no', said Anna, 'I couldn't do that'. 'How do mean, you couldn't do that, Anna?' Anna said 'It feels like it would be too risky'. The conversation continued along these lines when I asked about her feeling risk when she contemplated actually talking with God. What emerged slowly was Anna's fear 'of what God might ask of me'. The remainder of our interaction and a subsequent meeting focused on Anna's fear. She talked of not feeling safe when she tried to sit quietly and be with God and of her fear that God would ask of her more than she was ready to give. Anna was able to acknowledge the two opposing movements in her – her desire to know and be close to God and her fear that was holding her back from God. She said that she felt helpless to change.

Anna is experiencing two conflicting spirits, one inviting her to move towards God, the other holding her back from God. We realised together that her fear was the dominant spirit. But she found herself helpless in her conflict. In a subsequent meeting when Anna and I talked again about her fear, she recognised its irrationality, and prayed with the possibility that, with God's grace, she might be able to go ahead, despite her fear. I describe this in chapter 6.

Bart offers another example, typical of many similar:

> **Bart** is a local church minister who comes to the retreat centre for a few days every so often, he says 'to touch base'. On this occasion, Bart was telling me that he had

been sitting quietly, doing nothing much but relishing the view from his window, when he became aware of how blessed he was. His family, his friendships, his parish all seemed reminders of God's gift of love for him. Bart noticed that he had become quite emotional, when suddenly, he stood up and started to get active. I asked, 'what happened at that point, do you think?' 'Easy', said Bart, 'I knew I was kidding myself. It was like who do you think you are? Get on with the business of life.' As we talked further, even Bart could see that there were two quite opposite tendencies in him, one inviting gratitude to God for such blessings, the other wanting to deny the blessings.

These are examples of the two conflicting spirits.

I have noticed the same experience in my own life and my ministry. Listening to a young woman who was quite in touch with what was going on in her life and aware of God's invitation to her, I heard myself saying to myself 'this is too easy: I'm not really helping here. Do something, say something'. Again, there were two conflicting spirits, one inviting me to rejoice in this person's experience, the other urging me to 'help' when help was not needed. This latter spirit, a spirit not-of-God, is discussed in the following chapter.

Jesus' experience

Jesus knew the experience of conflicting spirits: he knew the gift of God's Spirit and he knew the spirit that tempted him away from God. Jesus' experience of consolation peaked at his baptism, clearly the turning point of his life. Jesus knew himself as beloved of God and anointed by the Spirit. (Matthew 3:16-

17) This gift of God coloured Jesus' life, his ministry, his death. Jesus' communion with God defined his identity. After such affirmation, however, Jesus then experienced temptation in the desert. The temptations of the spirit not-of-God consistently focused on Jesus' experience of being beloved. Jesus counters all the temptations of the spirit not-of-God by turning to God's Spirit, reminding the tempter of the true Word of God. (Matthew 4:1-11) Indeed, Jesus lived in the Spirit. (Luke 4:18)

Jesus' experience of conflicting spirits permeated his ministry. There are many Gospel examples of choices Jesus made during his life being true to God's Spirit: his welcome to non-Jewish people, his approach to the Pharisees, his silence before Pilate, his perseverance in suffering and 'abandonment', though even then the temptation was 'if you are the Son of God, come down from the cross'. (Matthew 27:40)

An experience in the early church

An early example of conflicting spirits is recounted in the Acts of the Apostles. The apostles were made to stand before the high priest and his council and 'the whole body of the elders of Israel' and were forbidden to preach about Jesus. When Peter and the apostles refused to obey, the council became 'enraged and wanted to kill them'. But a Pharisee in the council called Gamaliel asked to speak:

> ... keep away from these men; let them alone. Because if this plan or this undertaking is of human origin, it will fail; but if it is of God, you will not be able to overthrow them – in that case, you may even be found fighting against God. (Acts 5:38-39)

The council faced two quite opposite alternatives: one inclination was to kill the apostles, the other at Gamaliel's invitation was to leave them alone to continue their preaching. What is of God cannot be stopped and will always bear good fruit – indeed, will ultimately expose anything not-of-God. Gamaliel reminds the council of the invitation of God's Spirit.

Other examples of conflicting spirits

Examples abound in Christian literature. In the early church, St Antony of the desert knew well the struggle of conflicting spirits. Antony urged his monks 'Let us keep guard carefully, as it is written "keep your hearts with all watchfulness" (Proverbs 4:23) for we have terrible and crafty foes, the evil spirits, and against them we wrestle...'[5]

In his *Confessions*, Augustine tells of his struggle with conflicting spirits, his attraction to both the life of the Spirit and the life of 'the flesh':

> The two wills within me were in conflict and they tore my soul apart... I was quite sure that it was better for me to give myself up to your love than to surrender to my own lust. But while I wanted to follow the first course and was convinced that it was right, I was still a slave to the pleasures of the second. I had prayed to you for chastity and said 'Give me chastity and continence, but not yet'. For I was afraid that you would answer my prayer at

---

5   Athanasius, *The Life of Antony*. Antony talked of the 'demons' in ##22-43. This reference is to #36

once and cure me too soon of the diseases of lust, which I wanted satisfied, not quelled.⁶

Teresa of Avila knew similar experience:

> I was living an extremely burdensome life, because in prayer I understood more clearly my faults. On the one hand God was calling me, on the other hand I was following the world. All the things of God made me happy, those of the world held me bound. What a terrible mistake, God help me, that in wanting to be good, I withdrew from good...⁷

Teresa admitted that she didn't have the strength to move beyond what she named as some 'attachments' in her heart. These attachments were not bad in themselves, but 'were enough to spoil everything'.

In his *Autobiography*, Ignatius of Loyola told of his first experience of noticing the different, conflicting spirits in himself. Though earlier 'he was a man given over to vanities of the world, with a great and vain desire to win fame',⁸ he began to notice different movements in himself during his convalescence after surgery for wounds received in battle:

> When he was thinking about the things of the world, he took much delight in them, but afterwards, when he was tired and put them aside, he found that he was dry and discontented. But when he thought of going to Jerusalem, barefoot

---

6   Augustine, *Confessions* (Harmondsworth, UK: Penguin, 1961), VIII, 5-7, 164-9.
7   Teresa of Avila, "The Book of Her Life," in *The Collected Works of St. Teresa of Avila*, chapters 7, 9, 23.
8   Ignatius Loyola, *Autobiography*, 21.

> and eating nothing but herbs and undergoing all the other rigors he saw the saints had endured, not only was he consoled when he had these thoughts, but even after putting them aside, he remained content and happy... one day he began to marvel at the difference and to reflect on it, realising from experience that some thoughts left him sad and the others happy. Little by little, he came to recognise the difference between the spirits that agitated him, one from the demon, the other from God.[9]

Other subsequent experiences confirmed this awareness of the ways of the spirits for Ignatius.

Patrick White, Australian novelist, offers a contemporary personal example:

> During what seemed like months of rain, I was carrying a trayload of food to a wormy litter of pups at the kennels, when I slipped and fell on my back, dog dishes shooting in all directions. I lay where I had fallen, half-blinded by rain, under a pale sky, cursing through watery lips a God in whom I did not believe. I began laughing finally at my own helplessness and hopelessness, in the mud and stench from my filthy oilskin. It was a turning point. My disbelief appeared as farcical as my fall. At that moment I was truly humbled.[10]

The opposing movements in White's description – his disbelief, yet his humble acceptance of his position – work against one another and are operating at the same time in his experience.

---

9   Ibid., 24.
10 Patrick White, *Flaws in the Glass* (Melbourne: Penguin, 1983), 144.

Frequently in my ministry as a spiritual director, I hear examples of similar ambivalent experiences – wanting and not wanting, loving and hating the same reality. Alcoholics Anonymous has tackled the experience head-on for people wanting both sobriety and alcohol. Their teaching, the 'Twelve Steps', agrees perfectly with the experiences described: the necessary first step towards freedom is the acknowledgment of one's powerlessness in the conflict and one's need for a 'power greater than ourselves'.[11] The greater power, God's grace, broke through what Teresa called her 'attachment'. It was this experience that taught Teresa the value of self-awareness (the humility emphasised by earlier writers), prayer, and loving support from others.[12] Teresa learned from her experience.

Fruits of following the spirits

In all of the examples, the experience of the conflicting spirits invariably holds some emotional content – feelings of pleasure, contentment, fear, sadness. These emotions, in themselves, do not define which spirit is operating. This point will be emphasised many times in studying the experience of God's Spirit and spirits not-of-God. Feelings of dryness or struggle do not indicate God's absence, just as feelings of apparent warmth or pleasure do not necessarily indicate God's presence. John of the Cross is uncompromising on this point:

> You exalt God immensely and approach very near to him, when you consider him higher and deeper than anything you can reach... I mean, you should

---

[11] Steps 1 & 2 of Alcoholic Anonymous Twelve Step program.
[12] Teresa of Avila, "The Way of Perfection," in *The Collected Works of St. Teresa of Avila*, 4.3-4.

> never desire satisfaction in what you understand about God... Do not be like many foolish ones who in their lowly understanding of God think that when they do not understand, taste or experience him, he is far away...[13]

At the same time, in the above examples, the *direction* in which one or other attraction leads is quite clear. This is more telling: the fruits that emerge when the attraction of the spirit is followed are the best indicators of which spirit is operating. Examples of some of the fruits of following the Spirit of God are the subsequent happiness, gratitude and humility in Teresa's experience, whereas feeling bound and discontented are fruits of some spirit not-of-God. Other examples are given below.

This is how the experience of the spirits, once understood, is verified: the fruits of following one or other spirit become evident in other areas of the person's life, most obviously in relationships. God's Spirit is relational. One certain fruit of following God's Spirit is more loving relationships: people become more accepting of one another, more tolerant, more caring. Whereas spirits not-of-God, though more subtle in their tempting, ultimately lead to isolation and breakdown of relationships.

Bart's experience is an example: God's Spirit was inviting gratitude for the blessings he was experiencing. In that Spirit, Bart would have gone home with deeper appreciation of his family and his friends and his parishioners. On the other hand, had Bart turned away from that awareness, as the contrary spirit invited him, his relationships would have suffered. In my own

---

[13] John of the Cross, "Spiritual Canticle," in *The Collected Works of St. John of the Cross*, 1.12.

example, had I acted on the spirit tempting me away from God's activity in the person to whom I was listening, under the guise of being more 'helpful', I would have harmed both her relationship with God and her relationship with me. This understanding of the ways of the spirits is developed further in the next chapter.

Understanding consolation and desolation

The examples above illustrate that the felt experience of following the attraction of one or other spirit does not, of itself, indicate whether the attraction comes from God's Spirit or some spirit not-of-God. I discuss now what, in fact, does define the different spirits and the consolation and desolation that are the fruits of following different spirits. In my experience, the norm is that God's Spirit leads towards life and relationship, towards God, while spirits not-of-God lead away from life, away from God. The *direction* in which the spirit leads defines the spirit.

God's Spirit leads in a direction towards what is called *consolation*. Any spirit not-of-God leads in a direction away from God, called *desolation*. I have indicated already that the experience of consolation need not necessarily feel consoling and the experience of desolation may not always feel desolate. This is Buckley's experience and teaching:

> Consolation is any interior movement of sensibility – irrespective of the cause – whose direction is God, and whether its presence is experientially pleasant or not... Consolation and desolation do not identify necessarily with pleasure and pain.[14]

The defining element for consolation and desolation is the

---

14   Buckley, "The Structure of the Rules for Discernment of Spirits," 29.

direction in which the prompting leads. Dyckman, Garvin and Liebert agree:

> Consolation and desolation... are neither *simply* happiness and sadness, nor an 'up' or 'down' mood, though these feelings may play a role... Rather, consolation is the affective reverberation of the Holy Spirit that draws towards God, and desolation is the affective reverberation of the antispiritual that pulls in the opposite direction. Consolation and desolation are spiritual realities.[15]

My experience and my research unquestionably support this understanding, defining consolation and desolation by the direction in which the movement leads, towards or away from God. As noted in chapter 2, Toner and others maintain that Ignatius meant 'ordinary usage' of the terms consolation and desolation – the former is pleasurable, the latter painful.[16] This approach does not align with my theology of the Holy Spirit: I do not believe that the Spirit of God is limited to what is pleasurable or happy. Nor does it align with my personal experience as a spiritual director and supervisor, as illustrated in the examples that follow.

The fruits of following the different spirits, the consolation and desolation described, are well captured in Rahner's 'prayer for Pentecost':

> Grant us the understanding, validated by daily life, that by looking at and longing for you, we may experience your spirit emerging as the spirit of calm, of peace and confidence, of freedom

---

15   Dyckman, Garvin, and Liebert, *Spiritual Exercises Reclaimed*, 254.
16   Toner, *Discernment of Spirits*, 286-7, passim. See also Timothy Gallagher, *The Discernment of Spirits*, 49.

and simple clarity, while all unrest and fear, narrowness and leaden pride are recognised as at most our own spirit or the one of the deep dark... [We] ask you for the spirit of consolation and strength, of joy and confidence, of growth in faith, hope and love, of noble service and praise of your Father, for the spirit of quiet and peace. From our hearts, drive out spiritual desolation, darkness, confusion, inclination to what is low and earthy, distrust, hopelessness, lukewarmness, sadness, the sense of loneliness, ambiguity, and the strangling notions that would lead us away from you.[17]

Consolation

I now consider consolation in more detail, with the understanding that consolation is the fruit of following the attraction of God's Spirit.

In all of the examples of conflicting spirits above, God's Spirit broke through the conflict, resulting in experiences of consolation. This happened for Anna, for Bart, and for Augustine, Teresa of Avila and Ignatius Loyola, the fruitfulness of whose lives presents clear evidence of the consolation experienced. God's Spirit bears fruit in the time of consolation and in the person's whole life. Ignatius offers another example from his own life:

> The greatest consolation he received was to look at the sky and the stars, which he often did and for a long time, because as a result he felt within

---

17   Rahner, *The Mystical Way*, 69-70.

himself a very great desire to serve Our Lord. He often thought about his intention and wished to be healed completely now, so he could take the road.[18]

Ignatius' desire 'to serve Our Lord' is the fruit of the experience of consolation.

One implication of this understanding is that someone experiencing sad tears of sorrow over some past failure, for example, will still know the consolation of 'God's closeness, peace and tranquillity'.[19] Acceptance of the tears leads such a person closer to God. Even though consolation is not always consoling, it is always relational, always leading to deeper relationship with God and with other people.

There are also experiences of consolation – a deepening of faith, hope and love in a person – that have no felt emotion at all. These experiences have been termed 'hard consolation'[20] or 'painful consolation',[21] but consolation, none the less.

Still other experiences of consolation can feel quite desolate, in the ordinary sense of that word. Jesus' experience of apparent abandonment on the cross and John of the Cross' experience of 'dark night' are classic examples of this experience of consolation. The experience may feel desolate, but is actually a time of grace, 'the inflow of God', 'the loving wisdom of God',[22] drawing one closer to God.

---

18 Ignatius Loyola, *Autobiography*, 45.
19 Mark Thibodeaux, *God's Voice Within* (Chicago, IL: Loyola Press, 2010), 16, 44.
20 Sheldrake, *Befriending Our Desires*, 111.
21 Dyckman, Garvin, and Liebert, *Spiritual Exercises Reclaimed*, 255.
22 John of the Cross, "Dark Night," in *The Collected Works of St. John of the Cross*, II, 5.1.

Connie's experience is a good example:

> **Connie** *is a prayerful, committed young woman, who desires God deeply. She often talked to me about her prayer. On this occasion, when I asked about her prayer, her immediate response was 'awful – God seems far away; I just don't get any comfort in my prayer these days'. 'So what do you do' I asked. Though her prayer is 'awful', Connie went on to tell me that she still wanted God, wanted a deeper relationship with God. 'But God doesn't seem to be coming to the party?' I suggested. 'No, but I'm not going to give in', she said, 'I have no happy feeling right now, but I just sense that it's ok somehow'. 'How do you mean?' I asked. 'Well, I'm being invited to a deeper trust in God, aren't I? I know God won't abandon me.' Listening, I identified with Connie, also sensing that this is ok. I asked Connie, 'What else is happening in your life? How's work?' Quite enthusiastically, Connie talked about her friendship and her enjoyment of life, not at all aware that she was confirming for me that her prayer is truly ok.*

Connie's story typifies many in my experience. Because their inner experience feels empty and painful, many people imagine that something has gone wrong, that they are truly in a place of 'desolation', that God has abandoned them. Connie did not think that. She was attentive enough to notice the feeble sense that 'it's ok somehow'. As I listened, I knew also that 'it's ok somehow'. I recognised God's Spirit alive and active in Connie's experience. Later when we talked of the invitation to deeper trust, we saw together that it means trusting, even when there is no felt consolation. Confirmed in Connie's experience, consolation is not dependent on feeling good. Connie's consolation, even in apparent desolation, is confirmed by her ever-present desire for God, her awareness that her prayer 'is ok, somehow', and the fruits of God's presence in the rest of her life.

Dave's experience is another example of consolation:

> *Dave is a young teacher, married with a young family, active in parish life. He has come to me several times for spiritual direction. On this occasion, Dave mentioned that the parish pastoral worker had recommended the poems of St John of the Cross to the prayer group that he attends weekly. Not having heard of these poems, Dave checked on the net. He said he was attracted to one entitled* The Living Flame of Love *and had now read that a few times. 'There is something about that poem. Do you know it?' I said 'Yes, I know the poem – would you like to read it now?'*
>
> *Dave began reading*
>
> > Flame, alive, compelling
> > Yet tender beyond all telling
> > Reaching the secret centre of my soul
>
> *Dave stopped, his eyes moist, head down. After some time of silence, he said 'That really gets to me. God touches deep inside me, and yes, so tenderly'. 'What does it do to you, Dave?' Slowly, Dave put words on his emotion – 'feeling deeply loved... hard to believe'. We talked more of the gift of being loved and how he wanted to live that in his family and his parish. His biggest surprise was 'I came here intending to talk about the next verse of the poem and how that had touched me a couple of nights ago – but then this happened'.*

I experienced this as a sacred time of spiritual direction. Indeed, I had no question about Dave's experience of true consolation. As spiritual director, I too felt joy and awe in listening to him.

I have talked with Dave a number of times since: it heartens me to hear and to see Dave living truly and happily. Dave's relationships, including his relationship with God, have noticeably matured since. And he seems able to pray more quietly. 'It wouldn't matter if I never experienced that ever again', says Dave, 'I'm more than happy to give time to God.' I judge this as validation of Dave's experience.

'Spiritual consolation'

With their different understanding of Ignatius Loyola's teaching, Jules Toner[23] and Timothy Gallagher[24] are obliged to make a distinction between 'spiritual consolation' and 'non-spiritual consolation'. They say, correctly, that not all 'happy, uplifting experiences' in one's life have direct reference to one's life of faith and desire to pursue God's will.' They call these non-spiritual consolations. They give examples of the joyful appreciation of nature and some inner stirring when listening to beautiful music – experiences which do not necessarily lead one closer to God. They name these experiences 'consolation' because they feel consoling, 'non-spiritual' because they are not relevant to one's faith life.

The distinction they make flows out of their understanding of consolation as an experience that necessarily feels consoling. I argue rather that consolation is the fruit of following God's

---

23 Toner, *Discernment of Spirits*, 79, 94-121.
24 Gallagher, *The Discernment of Spirits*, 48-51.

Spirit, always leading in the direction towards God. Granted that the experiences Toner and Gallagher call 'non-spiritual consolations' are not relevant to one's life of faith, then in my understanding, these experiences are simply not consolations. They may feel consoling, but they are not strictly experiences of consolation – precisely because such experiences do not, of themselves, lead a person closer to God.

Certainly, Ignatius Loyola used the terminology of 'spiritual consolation'.[25] It was this that prompted Toner to conclude that there must exist also some 'non-spiritual' consolation. In fact, Ignatius did not use the terminology of 'non-spiritual consolation'. Indeed, his description of 'spiritual consolation' does seem to speak of a movement towards God:

> I call it consolation when an interior movement is aroused in the soul, by which it is inflamed with love of its Creator and Lord... It is likewise consolation when one sheds tears that move to the love of God, whether it be because of sorrow for sins or because of the sufferings of Christ our Lord, or for any other reason that is immediately directed to the praise and service of God. Finally I call consolation every increase in faith, hope and love, and all interior joy that invites and attracts to what is heavenly...[26]

I am convinced that, for Ignatius, the direction or the movement towards God defines consolation.

In summary, consolation is the inner experience that prompts movement towards a deeper life of faith and love of God.

---

25   Ignatius Loyola, *Spiritual Exercises*, #316.
26   Ibid.

Consolation is the fruit of the work of God's Spirit, attracting and leading in the direction towards God, deepening relationships. It may be experienced in laughter or in tears, in joy or in discomfort, depending on one's inner disposition and spiritual development, the subject matter of the next chapter. Clare of Assisi called such consolation 'enlightenment of the heart', beautifully expressing both the inner experience and the gift.[27]

Consolation without previous cause

There is a specific experience of consolation that merits further reflection. Ignatius Loyola called it a consolation 'without any previous cause', a consolation certainly from God:

> God alone can give consolation to the soul without any previous cause. It belongs solely to the Creator to come into a soul, to leave it, to act upon it, to draw it wholly to the love of his Divine Majesty. I said without previous cause, that is without any preceding perception or knowledge of any subject by which a soul might be led to such a consolation through its own acts of intellect and will.[28]

This teaching, too, came from Ignatius' personal experience. In his autobiography, Ignatius recounted his own experience on the banks of the river Cardoner:

> The road ran next to the river. As he went along occupied with his devotions, he sat down for a little while with his face toward the river which was running deep. While he was seated there, the

---

27 J. M. Begunartea, "Clare of Assisi and the Discernment of Spirits," *Greyfriars Review* 9, no. supplement (1995): 24.
28 Ignatius Loyola, *Spiritual Exercises*, #39.

eyes of his understanding began to be opened. Though he did not see any vision, he understood and knew many things and matters of faith and of learning, and this was with so great an enlightenment that everything seemed new to him... Even if he gathered up all the many helps he had had from God... he does not think they would amount to as much as he had received at that one time.[29]

In spiritual direction, I have noted numerous experiences that do appear to fit this description of consolation. This is Eve's experience:

> *Eve came for her monthly spiritual direction and said she wanted to talk about an experience she had had recently that had 'thrown her' in its intensity and its aftermath. Eve recounted sitting in a crowded bus, when suddenly she became aware that she was seeing her 'self' differently, somehow deeper, truer than the 'self I know and live in'. 'It was like "a balloon bursting"'. Struggling to find the words to express her experience, Eve said 'my true self is always there. I don't have to discover it, or improve it. I don't have to do anything'. I listened, somewhat mystified, until Eve added 'I feel free, utterly joyful, ready for whatever God wants'. I think my first response was 'My goodness, Eve, what a gift this is'. 'Yes, certainly a gift, she said, 'it was the last thing on my mind. I was more preoccupied with how slowly the bus was moving.'*

We talked afterwards about the aftermath Eve had mentioned at the beginning of her story. Indeed, the fruits of her experience

---

29 Ignatius Loyola, *Autobiography*, 39.

convinced me that her experience was of God. Eve speaks now of her inner calm and stillness and her different, 'easier' relationship with the people with whom she works. In talking about that, I was touched by the way Eve could speak of her experience without claiming anything for herself. She seems to recognise the gift she has received. This confirmed her experience for me, though initially I found Eve's experience mystifying. There seems to me to be ample evidence that this consolation is the work of God's Spirit, and that there was no previous cause.

I'm aware of numerous other examples. In Scripture, the first example is Mary's experience, hearing the words of the angel Gabriel:

> Greetings, favoured one! The Lord is with you...
> The Holy Spirit will come upon you and the power of the Most High will overshadow you...
> (Luke 1:28, 35)

Mary's response 'let it be with me according to your word' expresses her experience of God's Spirit.

John of the Cross wrote of his personal experience in similar words:

> You looked with love on me
> And deep within, your eyes imprinted grace.
> This mercy set me free...[30]

Merton describes his experience in down-town Louisville on his first visit outside of his monastery since joining the community of Trappists many years earlier:

---

30   John of the Cross, "Spiritual Canticle," in *The Collected Works of St. John of the Cross*. This translation is taken from John of the Cross, *Centered on Love: The Poems of Saint John of the Cross*, 20.

Discernment: Consolation and Desolation

> I was suddenly overwhelmed with the realisation that I loved all those people... The whole illusion of a separate holy existence is a dream... Not that I question the reality of my vocation... but the conception of 'separation from the world' that we have in the monastery too easily presents itself as a complete illusion – the illusion that by making vows we become a different species of being...[31]

For Merton, this breakthrough experience of consolation coloured the way he lived thereafter.

Etty Hillesum, another young Jewish woman, offers an example in a letter she wrote from Westerbork, a transit camp in the Netherlands, her last stop before Auschwitz:

> You have made me so rich, oh God... My life has become an uninterrupted dialogue with You, oh God, one great dialogue. Sometimes when I stand in some corner of the camp, my feet planted on Your earth, my eyes raised toward Your heaven, tears sometimes run down my face, tears of deep emotion and gratitude. At night, too, when I lie in my bed and rest in You, oh God, tears of gratitude run down my face and that is my prayer.[32]

All the examples of consolation given earlier had obvious cause – an unexpected encounter with a loved one, a passage of scripture or some poetry that touches new depths, or the beauty of creation. In contrast, consolation without a cause

---

[31] Thomas Merton, *Conjectures of a Guilty Bystander* (Garden City, NY: Doubleday, 1966), 140-1.

[32] Etty Hillesum, *Letters from Westerbork*, ed. Jan G. Gaarlandt (London: Grafton Books, 1988), 116. The letter sent to her friend Tide (Henny Tideman) was dated August 18, 1943. Etty died at Auschwitz on November 30, 1943.

suggests that the consolation comes without the thoughts and images that most often precede experiences of consolation. Harvey Egan refers to consolation without previous cause as an 'unexpected, disproportionate consolation... the paradigm of all consolations... a first principle against which all other consolations can be measured'.[33]

Buckley explains it this way:

> Very simply, this kind of experience is that a man finds himself deeply loving God without being aware of how he came to this. There could be a note of suddenness about it or surprise, but neither is particularly necessary.[34]

Buckley argues that for Ignatius, such an experience is 'self-authenticating' as a movement towards God, a *yes* which contains no experience of *no*.

Lonergan speaks of this consolation as 'being-in-love', which he likens to Otto's *mysterium fascinans et tremendum* and Tillich's 'being grasped by ultimate concern'.[35]

Egan's description of such experiences of consolation without previous cause as the 'paradigm of all consolations' finds support in other writers. For example, John English sees such an experience as 'the touchstone for all other experiences of consolation'.[36] Brian O'Leary writes of 'the foundational faith experience which reveals who we are before God...' He also

---

33 Harvey Egan, *Christian Mysticism: The Future of a Tradition* (New York: Pueblo Publishing Company, 1984), 65.
34 Buckley, "The Structure of the Rules for Discernment of Spirits," 33.
35 Bernard J. Lonergan, *Method in Theology* (New York: Herder & Herder, 1972), 106.
36 English, *Spiritual Freedom*, 220.

Discernment: Consolation and Desolation

calls this experience the 'touchstone' for evaluating any new experience.[37]

The same consolation is described by Herbert Alphonso in his concept of 'personal vocation'. I have found this particularly helpful in my ministry. Alphonso believes that the experience of one's 'fundamental consolation', one's 'God-given uniqueness', which he calls one's 'personal vocation'[38] is not only the ground of one's relationship with God, but is foundational in any process of discernment:

> the single greatest grace of my life is that I discerned my truest and deepest 'self', the unrepeatable uniqueness God has given to me in 'calling me by name'... My own personal experience and my ministry of the Spirit have taught me that the deepest transformation in any person's life takes place in the actual living out of this very 'personal vocation'.

Alphonso argues that one's personal vocation 'becomes the criterion for discernment for every decision in life, even for the daily details of decision-making'.[39] He supports his argument reflecting on Jesus' personal vocation, 'captured in but one single word "Abba"'.[40]

Based on his personal experience, Merton makes a similar claim:

> I have my own special peculiar destiny which no one else ever has had or ever will have... Because

---

37 Brian O'Leary, "Discernment and Decision Making" *Review for Religious* 51, no. 1 (1992): 60.
38 Alphonso, *The Personal Vocation*, 14.
39 Ibid., 58.
40 Ibid., 31-2.

> my own individual destiny is a meeting, an encounter with God, that God has destined for me alone... it is a gift of God to me which God has never given to anyone else and never will.[41]

Merton, Hillesum, and John of the Cross are all describing what Alphonso has called 'the fundamental consolation of his life', against which all else in life is measured.[42] Such experiences of 'fundamental consolation' give words to describe one's vocation, maybe already lived for years, but discovered or discerned only in later experience.

I note that Egan's description of consolation without previous cause as 'a first principle against which all other consolations can be measured' uses the same terminology as Alphonso's description of one's personal vocation, the fundamental consolation of one's life, 'against which all other consolations can be measured'. Both are speaking of touchstone experiences. This is relevant to an understanding of the way God's Spirit attracts interiorly free people, in the next chapter.

The importance for discernment is that noticing and interpreting the invitation of God's Spirit in one's life depends on comparison of experience with past experience. Because the experience of one's fundamental consolation is unquestionably God's gift, the affective movements that flow from the experience in oneself become a personal norm or a 'touchstone' for subsequent recognition of the activity of the Spirit of God. I find this awareness essential for discernment practice and later for good decision making.

---

41 Thomas Merton in a letter to Mark van Doren, March 30, 1948. see Robert E. Daggy, ed. *The Road to Joy: Letters of Thomas Merton to New and Old Friends* (New York: Farrer, Straus, Giroux, 1989), 22.

42 Alphonso, *The Personal Vocation*, 59.

Futrell goes so far as to say that 'unless one has already had the experience of discovering his own personal identity in Christ... he is incapable of comparing it to his experience in the choice of a specific action, and it is impossible for him to discover the word of God'.[43]

Desolation

By definition, desolation is the very opposite of consolation. Desolation is the fruit of following some spirit not-of-God, being led in a direction away from God. With practical examples, I discuss some learnings that emerge from an experience of desolation.

This is Ignatius Loyola's description of desolation:

> I call desolation what is entirely the opposite of what is described in the third rule (concerning spiritual consolation): darkness of soul, turmoil of spirit, inclination to what is low and earthly, restlessness arising from many disturbances and temptations which lead to want of faith, want of hope, want of love. The soul is wholly slothful, tepid, sad, and separated, as it were, from its Creator and Lord.[44]

Desolation is the fruit of following some spirit not-of-God, being led away from God, rather to places of disquietude and agitation, 'separated, as it were, from its Creator and Lord'. Though some people choose to turn away from God, most of the examples encountered in spiritual direction ministry are of people who are not aware that they have followed the attraction

---

43   Futrell, "Ignatian Discernment," 79.
44   Ignatius Loyola, *Spiritual Exercises*, #317.

of a spirit not-of-God, until they find themselves in a place of desolation. Only then, and usually with the help of a spiritual director, these people know that they have to look back to discover where they have misread the spirits.

Fred's experience is an example of desolation:

> **Fred** told me of the time when he was leading a seminar for a group of senior priests. He thought the seminar was going well enough till one day, an acknowledged elder of the group criticised something that Fred had said in the morning's input. Fred said that, there and then, he decided that he needed to finish the seminar and go home. He said, 'Obviously, I was not being appreciated by the group'. In fact, Fred did not act on that impulse, if only because another priest said to him that he found that morning's input very helpful.

Fred's reaction to the first feed-back comes out of a time of desolation. After the apparent criticism of his work, Fred listened to a spirit not-of-God. In the next chapter, the discussion of the ways of spirits not-of-God explains the dynamic behind Fred's reaction, which Fred was unaware of at the time. For now, his experience illustrates desolation. When Fred spoke of what might have happened had he gone home, as he was tempted, he could see readily that he would have been left miserable and the group would have been left confused. This would be the fruit of following a spirit not-of-God.

'Spiritual desolation'

In an exact parallel with the previous discussion about consolation, Toner,[45] Timothy Gallagher[46] and Tetlow[47] make a distinction between 'spiritual' and 'non-spiritual' desolation. And for similar reason: they define desolation as any experience that feels desolate. I acknowledge that there are certainly times in life when one feels desolate but, as I have described, these times are not strictly experiences of desolation or separation from God. Jesus' desolate experience on the cross, apparently 'abandoned' by God, is a perfect example: in his desire for God and his crying out to God, Jesus was actually in a place of consolation.

On the other hand, there are also experiences in life where one feels anything but desolate, but when one *is* truly in desolation, moving in a direction away from God. Buckley's oft-quoted example of 'men with their arms locked, singing bawdy songs on their way to the local whorehouse' is perfect illustration of this.[48] These men are in desolation.

Having made the distinction between spiritual and non-spiritual desolation, Toner then found it necessary to introduce the term 'anti-spiritual'. He writes that 'spiritual desolation is, strange as it may sound, an anti-spiritual experience'.[49] By this, Toner means that it is against God, for it resists any growth in faith or movement towards God. He then argues that there is 'no contradiction in terms in calling spiritual desolation an anti-spiritual experience'. I believe that they are the same reality:

---

45 Toner, *Discernment of Spirits*, 128-38.
46 Gallagher, *The Discernment of Spirits*, 61.
47 Tetlow, *Making Choices in Christ*, 89.
48 Buckley, "The Structure of the Rules for Discernment of Spirits," 29.
49 Toner, *Discernment of Spirits*, 127, 41.

both are describing what I simply call 'desolation'. If desolation is defined as the fruit of some spirit not-of-God leading in a direction away from God, the terms 'spiritual', 'non-spiritual', and 'anti-spiritual' do not arise.

Learning from desolation

God desires only consolation for God's people. If someone finds themselves in desolation, understood as a movement away from God, whether through conscious or unconscious choice, this is not a place of God. It is not of the nature of a loving God to want anyone to experience desolation. Indeed, I believe that God always works against any experience of desolation, constantly inviting a person to consolation.

This raises questions for me about the understanding of desolation in some commentators. For example, I query such statements as 'God's reasons for allowing desolation...'[50] 'God may allow a period of desolation...'[51] and 'Why doesn't God remove pain and affliction?'[52] My conviction that God always invites to consolation offers quite a different understanding from the presumption behind 'why does God allow us to experience desolation?'

God's Spirit is always present and active, even though the spirits not-of-God sometimes seem to dominate in one's experience. I believe that when someone finds themselves in a place of desolation, God's invitation to life, may be quieter, almost hidden, but is never absent. With Ignatius Loyola, I believe that it is possible to resist the temptations of spirits not-of-God 'with

---

50 Ibid., 182.
51 Edwards, *Breath of Life*, 164.
52 Manney, *What Do You Really Want?*, 83.

Discernment: Consolation and Desolation

the help of God, which always remains, though (we) may not clearly perceive it'.[53]

I find support for my understanding in Ignatius' writings. Ignatius gives three 'principal reasons why people suffer from desolation':

> The first is because we have become tepid and slothful or negligent in our exercises of piety, and so *through our own fault* spiritual consolation has been taken away from us. The second reason is because God *wishes to try us...* we are left without the generous reward of consolations and signal favours. The third is because God wishes to give us *a true knowledge and understanding of ourselves...* to know that all (consolation) is the gift and grace of God.[54]

If we find ourselves in desolation, Ignatius says, it is through our own fault. We have moved away from God, maybe unconsciously. It is not our fault in any blameworthy sense, but still we have moved away. Such an experience is not God's choice. The only sense in which God allows desolation is that God does not intervene to prevent a person's choice, but I disagree with any implication that God chooses or wants a person to experience desolation. I believe the opposite: God wants consolation and continues to invite people back, out of desolation, to consolation.

On the second reason: rather than saying that God wishes to try us, Fleming translates Ignatius as saying that it is 'a trial period allowed by God'.[55] It is important to note that Ignatius is

---

53   Ignatius Loyola, *Spiritual Exercises*, #320.
54   Ibid., #321. The emphases in the quotation are my own.
55   Ibid. in David L. Fleming, ed. *A Contemporary Reading of the Spiritual Exercises* (St. Louis, MO: The Institute of Jesuit Sources, 1976).

speaking only of this specific time of trial when one has turned away from God. Such a trial is of a person's own making. (There are other trials in life which are quite unrelated to a choice to turn away from God.) This trial becomes a test of a person's patience, perseverance and willingness to turn back to God's Spirit.

Thirdly, good can come from an experience of desolation. 'We know that all things work together for good for those who love God.' (Romans 8:28) Good comes certainly when someone acts against the spirit not-of-God that has brought about the desolation. The good one experiences is growth in self-awareness, the first step towards inner freedom, and in humility, knowing more truly that consolation is utterly gift of God.

For example, this is Gus' experience:

> *Gus talked in his spiritual direction about the struggle he was experiencing in his community. Gus is a young religious brother. He recognises that when he is under pressure, as he was recently when preparing for his exams, he tends to spend less time with the other brothers. He says he needs space for himself. But his relationships suffer. We talked about his relationships. Gus said the worst thing was that relationship with God seems to suffer, too. 'Tell me about that, Gus.' He said it was like he didn't feel 'comfortable' in his prayer time. Gus prays daily with the scripture readings of the liturgy, but the readings 'weren't speaking' to him anymore; he just 'couldn't settle' in prayer. Listening as spiritual director, my own discomfort started quite early in the conversation, when Gus talked of cutting himself off from his confreres, so I gradually*

Discernment: Consolation and Desolation

> turned the conversation back to that. 'They wouldn't understand the pressure I'm under – they don't know what it's like', he said. 'You haven't told them?' 'No, he said, 'they would think I was grand-standing, kidding myself. They don't really know me. I don't think they even like me.' I knew then that Gus was in a place of desolation, of his own making. We decided to meet the following week to see whether anything had changed. It was almost as an aside that Gus mentioned that an older brother, George, had said to him, 'How's it going, Gus?' I replied 'and that was important to you?' 'Yes', said Gus, 'he really sounded like he was interested. It was the first time that I thought to myself that I might be the one who is withdrawing'. That was the turning point for Gus.

The broken relationships with his community and with God were the clearest sign of Gus' desolation. Unconsciously and unintentionally, Gus had cut himself off, because of false thinking about his self-worth: *I don't think they even like me.* Then Gus heard the gentle voice of God's Spirit through George's genuine interest in his welfare. I had been listening for this voice, knowing from experience that God's Spirit would still be active in Gus.

Ignatius' 'reasons why we suffer from desolation' are all present in Gus' experience. His desolation was his own 'fault', a difficult 'trial' time of his own making, and he certainly benefited in his new self-awareness. Significantly, Gus experiences growth, freedom and new life only after he has heard and responded to God's Spirit. There is no life in his desolation. Such experiences verify my understanding of desolation, as described above.

One other rule from Ignatius (I think accepted by all spiritual directors) is that times of desolation are not times to make major decisions or changes in one's life:

> In time of desolation, we should never make any change, but remain firm and constant in the resolution and decision which guided us the day before the desolation... For just as in consolation, the good Spirit guides and counsels us, so in desolation the evil spirit guides and counsels.[56]

This advice, grounded in experience, is further evidence of Ignatius' understanding of consolation and desolation. He says clearly that in a time of desolation, the 'evil spirit' is guiding us: it is a time when we have moved away from God. The alternative understanding of desolation – any experience that feels desolate – is incompatible with this rule. As spiritual director, I have worked with many people in their experience of dryness in prayer when God seems to be absent, but for whom life goes on. These people are not in desolation, evidenced by the fact that their relationships and their ministry are unaffected. These people are, in fact, in a time of consolation, meaning that they are being drawn closer to God. Even in their painful experience, they have no problem with decision making, for the rule does not apply to them.

Ignatius also stresses the value of meditation, of patience, and of some penance in times of desolation, in order to work against the spirit not-of-God that has caused the desolation.[57] These are practical ways in which one consciously turns back to the Spirit of God.

---

56 Ignatius Loyola, *Spiritual Exercises*, #318.
57 Ibid., ##319, 21.

In summary, desolation is the inner experience that prompts movement away from God. The experience of desolation is not necessarily painful or desolate. Desolation is the fruit of following some spirit not-of-God, which invariably leads to broken relationships, isolation and lifelessness.

5
THE WAYS OF THE SPIRIT

Beloved, do not believe every spirit, but test the spirits
to see whether they are from God,
for many false prophets have gone out into the world.

1 John 4:1-2

With the conviction that consolation is the fruit of following God's Spirit and desolation the fruit of following a spirit not-of-God – 'by their fruits you will know them' – I now examine how, in fact, the different spirits work in human experience to lead a person into consolation or desolation. Again using examples from my own and from others' experience, this chapter studies the workings of the spirits, particularly noting how the spirits work differently for people at different stages of their spiritual development.

The attraction of the Spirit of God

The ways in which God's Spirit invites us to new awareness and the subsequent fruits, the new life, flowing from the Spirit's prompting are quite different experiences. Invariably a person notices some signs of the Spirit's invitation before choosing to follow that spirit. For example, someone may become aware of an inner excitement or a sense of wonder in themself, readily and accurately interpreting this as God's gift. This is different from the experience of the fruits that follow after the person responds to the Spirit's invitation.

This section is concerned with the initial signs of the activity of God's Spirit. Its importance in discernment is that one needs to be able to recognise these signs in order to make one's judgments about whichever spirit is active in one's immediate experience. Only after responding to whichever spirit is inviting will one notice the fruits that follow. When one follows the Spirit of God, the fruits – the consolation experienced, as defined in the previous chapter – confirms one's action.

Spiritual directors, in fact, are more interested in these initial signs of the Spirit's invitation in order to encourage a creative response. My experience suggests that the spiritual director is often in a better position to notice the signs than the person who is actually experiencing them. Someone who senses themself being challenged, even affirmed, or who notices some strong emotion within, is not always confident about the origin of these movements. The spiritual director, on the other hand, recognises the signs and knows the fundamental principle that when a person is being drawn towards God, 'the inner movements prompted by God's Spirit will be at one with this direction',[1] and when a person is being drawn away from God, the work of the spirits will be the very opposite.

As is evident in the examples that follow, God's Spirit, always drawing towards Godself, works differently for people at different stages in their spiritual development. Ignatius Loyola

---

[1] Edwards, "Discernment of the Holy Spirit," 8.

first noticed these differences, now widely accepted amongst spiritual directors.[2]

I discuss the ways of spirits not-of-God later in the chapter. The distinction between the initial signs of the spirit and the fruits that follow after one has responded is even more obvious and significant when discussing the workings of the spirits not-of-God.

For people whose basic orientation is turning away from God

There are people whose basic disposition in life neglects God. They may be people who habitually turn away from God, or people whose main interest is themselves, their comfort, pleasure, wealth or status. Ignatius Loyola referred to these people as 'those who go from one mortal sin to another'.[3] Though few people in this category actually request spiritual direction, I do have examples. From experience I recognise that the Spirit of God works in these people, using the light of reason, prompting sound judgment about their behaviour, inviting them to remorse and to right relationship with God.

This is Hal's example:

> **Hal** *is a happy-go-lucky fellow, quite successful in business, a popular and well known tennis champion, around 30 years of age. Hal has never married, but he does have a full and enjoyable social life. In fact, Hal said to me that his one serious interest in life is to have*

---

    2   Ignatius Loyola, *Spiritual Exercises*, ##313-5. and see, for example, Toner, *Discernment of Spirits*, 49ff. Edwards, "Discernment of the Holy Spirit," 21-9. Larkin, *Silent Presence*, 24-7.
    3   Ignatius Loyola, *Spiritual Exercises*, #314.

a good time, to enjoy himself. Which it seems he has been doing up until now.

Hal sought me out, on the suggestion of a friend of his, because he was feeling unhappy, even losing interest in his good time – 'something was wrong'. I asked about the change he was describing: when had he first noticed things changing? Had something happened that seemed to bring on this change? Hal was quite lifeless when he was talking to me, but I must say that I quickly sensed that whatever was going on probably needed to be going on.

It wasn't long before Hal told me that a woman friend whom he knew well and whose company he enjoyed had had a car accident a few weeks ago. It looked like she would never walk again, never dance, never play, never make love. 'I don't know why this has affected me like it has, because there are plenty of other lovely women in my life.' 'Sure', I said, 'but it has affected you, hasn't it. Is that what we need to talk about?' Silence. After some time, I asked 'What is it doing to you, Hal?' A quick response: 'I'm miserable'. We talked about feeling miserable and how unusual that feeling is for him. I had been presuming Hal was miserable because of his friend's accident, but no, eventually he said, 'it's making me ask questions that I don't want to face'.

Slowly, but maybe predictably, Hal owned that the questions were about his life-style and where his life was heading. 'Hetty's accident really makes me ask what life is all about? What do I want from life?' I tentatively suggested that the 'values' he lives by were being questioned. Hal responded quickly: 'Exactly: what are my values?'

> *I asked whether he would like to continue this conversation at another time: 'yes'. And might it be good to spend some time reflecting on your values, even before we meet: 'yes'. Hal left, still looking unhappy, but actually with more energy than he had when he arrived.*

Hal's experience is typical enough of people whose basic orientation is/has been away from God. In his case, his whole life seemed to focus on himself and his pleasure. Spirits not-of-God strive to promote that way of living. The throw-away line about all the other women in his life, suggesting that he could just as easily continue the past life-style, is the work of such a spirit not-of-God. But God's Spirit gradually invites a more reasoned approach. God's Spirit asks questions that challenge Hal's past life-style. This example of the work of the spirits for people whose basic stance had been away from God illustrates that point: the Spirit of God challenges their life-style, appeals to their conscience, and invites them to think again about the futility of their way of living. With these people, God's Spirit works through sound reasoning, not through their affectivity.

My own feelings when listening to Hal confirmed for me the presence of the spirits working in him. I was quite flat when he spoke initially about his life and the way he lived. My interest sparked only when he talked of something changing, sure sign for me of the way the spirits were working. Though his friend's accident brings sadness, I was relieved when he told me of the questions that the accident had raised in him. Recognising these movements, I judged that God was working in this young man through the questions that his experience had raised for him. Though I would not normally introduce new words myself when I minister as a spiritual director, I did suggest the word 'values' to Hal. Apparently this was helpful to Hal, but I'm aware of the risk that my introducing a new term could side-track Hal, even block the wisdom emerging for Hal.

This dynamic is confirmed by others. For example, in his earlier life, Augustine describes himself as someone whose basic orientation was away from God:

> As I grew to manhood, I was inflamed with desire for a surfeit of hell's pleasures. Foolhardy as I was, I ran wild with lust that was manifold and rank.... I was pleased with my own condition...[4]

Gradually, some shift happened for Augustine: appealing to Augustine's reason and his conscience, God continued to invite him to a desire to break from his old life-style and to turn back to God, to freedom and to authentic life. Slowly, and struggling with the pull of opposing spirits, Augustine began to 'hear' God's invitation:

> In my worldly life, all was confusion... I should have been glad to follow the right road, to follow our Saviour himself, but I could not make up my mind to venture along the narrow path.
>
> The voice of truth told me that there are some who have 'made themselves eunuchs for love of the kingdom of heaven...'[5]

While Augustine heard and wanted to follow God's call, he attests in his *Confessions* that the spirit not-of-God maintained its insistent prompting to continue as he was, encouraging

---

4 Augustine, *Confessions*, Book II, 1, 43.
5 Ibid., Book VIII, 1, 157-8.

'apparent pleasures'. (I examine this below.) Augustine's prayer 'Make me chaste, but not yet' captures the two spirits perfectly.[6]

Another example is Patrick White's story in chapter 4. White had apparently rejected God. His basic orientation was away from God. And so, in his fall with the bucket of scraps, his immediate response was to 'curse God', exactly as the spirit not-of-God prompted, supporting his rejection of God. But God's Spirit invited a more reasoned response that saw how 'farcical' was his predicament and his initial reaction. He heard and accepted that invitation of God's Spirit, feeling 'humbled' and establishing relationship with God.

Based on these examples, I conclude that for people whose basic orientation is away from God, God's Spirit works through their reasoning, not through any affectivity. In fact, the affective experience of these people is ambiguous. For example, a sense of peace does not indicate God's Spirit, but rather some spirit not-of-God, confirming their stance away from God. In fact, God's Spirit will not leave such people in peace.

Ignatius Loyola came to the same conclusion:

> In the case of those who go from one mortal sin to another, the enemy is ordinarily accustomed to propose apparent pleasures. He fills their imagination with sensual delights and gratifications, the more readily to keep them in their vices and increase the number of their sins.
>
> With such persons, the good spirit uses a method which is the reverse of the above. Making use

---

6   The passages quoted in chapter 4 describing Augustine's experience of conflicting spirits refer to the same period of his life.

of the light of reason, he will arouse the sting of conscience and fill them with remorse.[7]

This was precisely the case in the examples of Hal and Augustine, above.

For people whose basic orientation is towards God

People most commonly encountered in spiritual direction are those who basic orientation is towards God, persons who are sincere in their desire to know God, even though they still carry some *unfreedom* (or some unconscious 'attachment', in Teresa of Avila's word). The Spirit of God attracts people like this in ways that encourage their inner desire for God, it is said, 'sweetly and gently'. God's Spirit seems to work in these people in an affective way, prompting felt consolation in their desire for God, inviting to deeper intimacy with God and enhancing relationship with God:

> It is characteristic of the good Spirit to give courage and strength, consolations, tears, inspirations, and peace. This, he does by making all easy, by removing all obstacles so that the soul goes forward in doing good.[8]
>
> I call it consolation when an interior movement is aroused in the soul, by which it is inflamed with love of its Creator and Lord...[9]

This is Iain's example:

> *Iain is a young man, late 20s, unmarried, a youth worker and a carpenter by trade. Iain comes to talk*

---

7   Ignatius Loyola, *Spiritual Exercises*, #314.
8   Ibid., #315.
9   Ibid., $316.

with me every month or so because, he says, he wants to be generous with his life, wherever life is leading him.

On one occasion recently, Iain said that he had had a powerful experience, but he wasn't quite sure where to go with it. He had been preparing timber for a cabinet he had been asked to make, cleaning and sanding a piece of King Billy pine. Iain said that he always notices the grain in the timber. This time, he was looking at the grain in the timber when, quite unexpectedly, he stopped and couldn't believe the beauty of what he was looking at. Iain reckoned it held him still. He didn't dare speak or move, let alone move on, probably for some minutes, though he admits he quite lost track of time.

I asked him what was going on in himself during those quiet still minutes. 'Nothing much', he said. 'I don't think there was a thought in my head.' I responded 'Ah, you weren't thinking anything, but was there some emotion maybe? or did it bring back some memories?' 'Yes, it did', said Iain, 'it reminded me of the time that Irene, my girlfriend, took me to the Arts Centre: when we were walking around the centre viewing various paintings, I had a similar experience when I was standing in front of a Monet painting of some countryside scene. I remember how I just stood still in awe of what I was looking at.'

'In awe, eh?' I almost whispered. 'Yeah, awe, like wonder, an overwhelming kind-of feeling' said Iain. I asked 'Is it still with you? Can you still feel that feeling, as you remember these incidents?' 'Yes.' Then I suggested 'Let's just sit quietly for a few minutes and *savour the feeling. Iain, you don't need to say any more.'*

After quite some minutes, Iain said 'I'm just thanking God for such beauty and for letting me see it so clearly.' 'Oh', I said, 'you reckon it has something to do with God?' 'Yes, yes', he said, 'there's something more than human ability or creativity here, isn't there? It has to be God's work, or God's inspiration. I really am overwhelmed by such gift, I'm gobsmacked!'

Iain and I talked of the gift, noticing that he had done nothing himself to bring on the two experiences that had overwhelmed him. I was thinking of the contemplative way, though I didn't use the word, except to ask Iain 'what does it say about how you go about your work now?' He picked that up quickly: 'I would like to slow down more and notice things, really be present to where I am, who I'm with, and what I'm doing.' I replied 'maybe that answers your first question about where to go with what happened for you – seems that all you can do, all you have to do, is to slow down and be present. You might get more surprises.'

Based on the principles of discernment already discussed, Iain experienced God's Spirit on several occasions – in his experience with the timber and with the Monet painting, in his experience as he re-lived those times, and in his sharp awareness of the ongoing invitation to be more fully present. All are experiences of consolation, the signs of which Iain and I both recognised in our conversation. In Iain, the signs of the Spirit of God at work were his awe, his stillness, his gratitude in acknowledging the gift, and his awareness of the fruit of his experience. In me, I experienced something of the same wonder at God's work, great delight in what I was hearing, and an ease in being able to stay with Iain in his experience. Spirits not-of-God had no opening in Iain's experience.

Jenny offers a different example of the work of God's Spirit:

> *Jenny is a shy, withdrawn woman: she says she just doesn't relate well with people. In this, our first meeting, Jenny said she was wondering whether it would be good for her to make a retreat. When I asked where that thought had come from, Jenny told me that she gets really distracted in her prayers, even when she goes to Mass. In fact, she is trying to decide whether to give Mass away: 'I don't meet anyone at church and it's not very helpful, anyway'. She thought that the quiet place of a retreat might be less distracting for her.*
>
> *Wondering how Jenny related to God, I suggested that she delay any decisions for the moment and maybe could we talk a little about the prayers she referred to. 'How do you pray?' I asked. Jenny told me that she has an old prayer book that used to belong to her mother, full of 'quite lovely prayers', but she says she doesn't seem to be able to pray them very well these days – 'they don't give me any joy any more'.*
>
> *Responding to her lack of joy in her prayer, I asked Jenny what did she enjoy most in her life? She smiled for the first time and told me that she loved playing the piano. I showed interest in this and prompted her to talk more about her enjoyment at the keyboard. Jenny tried to down-play its significance: 'I don't know what it has to do with anything' she said to me, but gradually I heard about her gift at the piano, her joy*

> when she was playing, and her gratitude to God. At one point, Jenny even said that sometimes she felt like it wasn't really herself playing: 'something inside me carries me along'. I assured Jenny that what we were talking about was not irrelevant. I said something like 'we might just learn something important from your experience of playing the piano'.
>
> I was pleased when Jenny asked me if she could see me again sometime to continue this conversation? 'And what do you suggest I do in the meantime?' she asked. I suggested that she not worry too much about her prayer book, but I encouraged her to keep doing what she was doing, especially at the piano.
>
> As I farewelled her, Jenny noticed the piano in my lounge room. I invited her to play something for me. With obvious ability, great energy, and a wide smile, Jenny played a medley of old favourites that she seemed to put together on the spot. As we said goodbye, I was already looking forward to her next visit.

On reflection, I recall that our conversation seemed fairly lifeless initially, but that I found myself enlivened when Jenny mentioned that she 'doesn't seem to be able to pray' the prayers in her mother's prayer book. I wondered whether something of God may be at work in this change in her prayer practice, though I chose not to say that at the time. Instead, to encourage her awareness of wherever God was active in Jenny's life, I asked the question about what gives her joy. Again, I noticed new energy in myself when Jenny talked about her piano playing. I interpreted this, too, as an activity of God's Spirit. Another discernment question came when Jenny asked me for suggestions about what she could do before we met again.

Still keen to encourage her staying in touch with the invitation of God's Spirit, I suggested that she not push herself with the prayers from her mother's book.

There are other discernment issues for Jenny that we didn't discuss in this first meeting. For example, what had raised the idea of a retreat? What voice is behind the thought that she give away going to Mass? What moves in her when she plays the piano with such joy? Where are the fruits of this experience of consolation in other areas of her life?

For both Iain and Jenny, examples of people whose basic orientation is towards God, the signs of God's Spirit at work are clearly on an affective level. Their delight, enjoyment, awe, gratitude are all signs of the Spirit of God, leading to felt consolation.

I have already noted similar examples of consolation, the fruit of following God's Spirit, in the literature. The evidence Ignatius gave in his Autobiography was that he found himself 'cheerful and satisfied' when God's Spirit had touched him. Teresa of Avila noticed 'all the things of God made me happy'. These are attempts to describe the felt consolation from the Spirit of God – the 'love, joy, peace, patience...' named by Paul. (Galatians 5:22)

In these examples, different words are used to describe the fruits of the Spirit. Indeed, spiritual directors normally encourage directees to use their own language in speaking of their experience, as a further help to claiming their experience. For example:

> Experiences of inner joy and peace, moods of confidence and encouragement to faith, a sense of being in harmony with oneself and with

God, times of true creativity, and so on, are true consolation, signs of the presence of the Spirit...[10]

There is a sense of our own worth... something lifts from us, we feel lighter, liberated... we grow in compassion and sensitivity to the needs of others.[11]

For this group of people, the experience of consolation is always on an affective level. Later in the chapter, I note that spirits not-of God also produce affective responses in people whose basic orientation is towards God. And so, discernment of the Spirit of God at this point, for people whose basic orientation is towards God, is a discernment of one's feelings. One's feelings do point to whichever spirit is at work, but they need to be discerned.

As noted above, the experience of what many people call *peace*, often encountered in spiritual direction, is a classic example of the need to discern one's feelings. For a person whose basic disposition is away from God, peace does not indicate God's presence. For different reasons, this is sometimes true also for people whose basic orientation is towards God. Barry and Connolly noted earlier that 'relief at having made a decision can seem like peace'.[12] As well, spiritual directors often hear a 'peace' that is no more than an avoidance, a denial of the real experience, a pseudo peace.

Toner considers this ambiguity about the experience of a peace in some detail, especially distinguishing between a 'spiritual' and a 'non-spiritual' consolation of peace:

---

10   Lonsdale, *Dance to the Music of the Spirit*, 62.
11   Patrick O'Sullivan, *Prayer and Relationships* (Melbourne, Vic: David Lovell Publications, 2008), 111-2.
12   Barry and Connolly, *The Practice of Spiritual Direction*, 106.

> Any innocent feeling of peace or joy or satisfaction, exultation, delight or the like, especially if it comes during the time of prayer, is taken for a sign of the Holy Spirit's acting on the one who experiences it. The distinction between a spiritual and a non-spiritual consolation is ignored.[13]

My different definition of consolation and desolation argues to the same conclusion, except to say that 'non-spiritual consolation' is not consolation at all. Some experiences may feel 'peaceful', but are quite irrelevant to growth in faith and closeness to God.

From a scriptural standpoint, Dubay's description of peace confirms this understanding:

> Shalom... is not emotionally felt (though feelings may or may not accompany it). It is delicate, quiet, spiritual. It is not produced by human effort, but is given by the Holy Spirit.[14]

Thomas Green names 'peace' as the 'defining quality of consolation':

> Consolation can take many forms. It may involve strong emotion – being inflamed with love, shedding tears of love and praise – or it may be quiet and deep. The common denominator, I would say, is *peace* in the Lord – whether the soul be deeply and strongly moved... or quietly consoled... The defining quality which makes it consolation is peace.[15]

---

13 Toner, *Discernment of Spirits*, 89-94, 285.
14 Dubay, *Authenticity*, 218-9.
15 Thomas H. Green, *Weeds among the Wheat* (Notre Dame, Ind: Ave Maria Press, 1984), 97.

If this is the case, my experience suggests that the spiritual director's listening carefully to the experience behind the word 'peace' and noting the fruits of acting upon the experience is all the more important. Even more so for people who do not trust their feelings. In truth, acceptance of one's feelings opens the possibility of learning to discern what one's feelings are revealing.

If one is to trust one's feelings and interpret them accurately, one's 'fundamental consolation' in life takes on added significance. Knowing the experience of one's 'personal vocation', that 'fundamental consolation' of one's life, discussed in chapter 4, better prepares a person for the grace to hear and respond to this invitation of God's Spirit. For example, the sense of being freed and the spontaneous response of adoration that John of the Cross described when God 'looked with love' upon him became the consistent touchstone of his life. John was able to recognise the same Spirit, God's loving look and the subsequent felt freedom, even in the dark times of his later experience. In that sense, the signs of God's Spirit are quite personal and predictable, recognised from past experience.

For people who are interiorly free, not struggling with inner attachments

It was Ignatius Loyola who recognised that there is yet a third category of people (whose experience he termed 'second week', in contrast to the 'first week' experiences above) for whom the spirits work differently again. These are the people whose basic orientation is towards God, certainly, but who are experiencing, even if only temporarily, freedom from any attachment. These are people whose affectivity is more ordered. As Ignatius discovered in his own experience again, for these people, the Spirit of God continues to offer the consolation of responding to the Spirit in an affective way, but spirits not-of-God become more subtle, attracting the person 'under the appearance of good', as discussed below.

It was for these people that Ignatius named the experience of consolation 'without any previous cause', the consolation certainly from God,[16] as discussed in the previous chapter:

> God alone can give consolation to the soul without any previous cause. It belongs solely to the Creator to come into a soul, to leave it, to act upon it, to draw it wholly to the love of his Divine Majesty.[17]

This single statement, mentioned by Ignatius Loyola only once in the *Spiritual Exercises*, has prompted extensive discussion amongst Jesuit commentators.[18] Buckley and Toner both quote a little-known article of Karl Rahner (written originally in 1956): Rahner sees 'this unique and infallible experience of consolation as the core of the Spiritual Exercises'. Buckley accepts this, Toner does not.[19] Buckley and others recognise the significance of such consolation, Toner considers the experience rare.

Larkin, a Carmelite, making no mention of the disagreement amongst Jesuits, writes:

---

16 Ignatius Loyola, *Spiritual Exercises*, #330.
17 Ibid.
18 Toner, *Discernment of Spirits*, Appendix IV.
19 Buckley, "The Structure of the Rules for Discernment of Spirits," 33. Buckley accepts Rahner's argument, as does Harvey Egan, *The Spiritual Exercises and the Ignatian Mystical Horizon* (St. Louis, MO: The Institute of Jesuit Sources, 1976), passim. Toner (*Discernment of Spirits*, Appendix IV) and others quoted by Toner, argue rather that Ignatius' meaning is not entirely clear and that such consolation may be quite rare.

The consolation without previous cause is the root of all discernment through affective movements. When love breaks into our lives, we are at that moment caught up and totally open to God. There is no longer both yes and no in our response, no consolation-desolation, but pure consolation, pure yes to God.[20]

Larkin calls such consolation 'the experience of pure transcendence'. He gives examples from Teresa of Avila and John of the Cross to make the point that 'such mystical moments are by no means restricted to the extraordinary or the higher realms of mystical life'.[21] Larkin calls such experience 'falling in love', which he argues can happen to any Christian.

In the previous chapter, I noted the parallel of Egan's description of consolation without previous cause as 'a first principle against which all other consolations can be measured' and Alphonso's description of one's personal vocation, the fundamental consolation of one's life, 'against which all other consolations can be measured'. Both authors recognise that the consolation is given when one is in a place of freedom, not influenced by inner attachments, namely people in this third group of Ignatius' teaching. Because these people are living more freely, spirits not-of-God have little opportunity to tempt the person away from God. The consolation becomes a 'touchstone' for this reason: it is unquestionably gift of the spirit of God. My earlier examples of personal vocation – from John of the Cross, Thomas Merton, Etty Hillesum, and 'Eve' – are also examples of this Ignatian consolation without previous cause.

---

20 Larkin, *Silent Presence*, 35. see also Larkin, "What to Know About Discernment," 167.
21 Larkin, *Silent Presence*, 33.

In summary, the Spirit of God always works to draw people towards loving relationships – with other people and with creation – ultimately towards God. For people who are essentially committed to God's ways, the Spirit offers affective consolation, feelings of inner joy and peace. For people whose commitment is more self-focused, turning away from God, the Spirit tends rather to invite remorse by appealing to the person's reasoning.

The attraction of spirits not-of-God

In this section, I examine how spirits not-of-God attract at a person's point of vulnerability, in order to hold a person back from God.

Teresa of Avila uses the word 'attachment' as a help to understanding how the spirit not-of-God had such a strong hold on her personally. Teresa did not have the language of discernment or of today's psychological theory, but from her own experience and from her ministry to her sisters, she knew the experience of human *unfreedom*. Pseudo-fervour was high on Teresa's list of illusions:

> On the witness of St. Teresa, manifestations of religious fervour and spiritual consolations sometimes contain elements foreign to the life of the Spirit, often unconscious tendencies in which the spiritual person is seeking, without perceiving it, his own sensible satisfaction more than the love of God.[22]

---

22 Pierluigi Pertusi, "Spiritual Direction in the Major Works of St. Teresa," in *Carmelite Studies: Spiritual Direction*, ed. John Sullivan (Washington, DC: Institute of Carmelite Studies, 1981), 37.

The Ways of the Spirit

I suggest that any study of spirits not-of-God builds on an understanding of attachments, disordered affections, compulsions, *unfreedoms*. These are discussed in detail in chapter 8.

As with God's Spirit described above, so with spirits not-of-God, the signs of the spirits' attraction are quite different from the later fruits, the desolation that one experiences if one follows the direction in which the spirit not-of-God is leading.

Spirits not-of-God work against God's Spirit. The direction in which the spirits not-of-God attract is the very opposite of the direction in which God's Spirit is leading. Spirits not-of-God work to hold one back from God, to resist God's invitation, to break any true relationship with God. Discernment is always about relationship with God.

I have learned from experience that spirits not-of-God attack where they are most likely to have success: at a person's point of vulnerability. Ignatius favoured the image of a 'shrewd army commander' who studied the place he wished to conquer to find where the defences were weakest.[23] Commenting on this observation of Ignatius, Manney stresses that 'the enemy attacks everyone... but he also attacks each individual at the point of their greatest vulnerability'.[24] I find this a helpful image: in spiritual direction, I listen for indicators of this experience of vulnerability 'where the defences are weakest'.

Every person has some vulnerability: vulnerability has been called humanity's common patrimony.[25] Earlier I introduced the

---

23   Ignatius Loyola, *Spiritual Exercises*, #327.
24   Manney, *What Do You Really Want?*, 94.
25   Luigi M. Rulla, *Anthropology of the Christian Vocation* (Rome: Gregorian University Press, 1986), 14.

work of Luigi Rulla. Rulla speaks of unconscious inconsistencies in human nature, noticing how a person can be moved simultaneously by opposing forces, one's ideals and one's inner needs. He found in his research into Christian vocation that 'psychodynamic factors may influence the degree of freedom with which the individual is disposed to the action of grace'.[26]

As noted, when speaking of the human experience of freedom, Rulla uses Lonergan's term 'effective freedom',[27] as distinct from 'essential freedom', and speaks of the risk of an illusory view of one's capacity to be free. I discuss one's effective freedom more fully in chapters 8 and 9. Rulla applied his argument to discernment of spirits. As quoted earlier:

> When a person responds because the object is consciously or unconsciously perceived as something which also favours his own self-esteem, this does not necessarily favour self-transcendence and the internalisation of the ideal... For example, one may be attracted to and aspire to an imitation of the generosity of Christ, while in reality and in the last analysis, one gives in order to receive.[28]

This is an example of what Rulla calls a choice for an apparent good, flowing out of a place of *unfreedom* or unconscious inner need or attachment. Such limited freedom is an expression of human vulnerability. The ways in which spirits not-of-God tempt a person at this point of vulnerability is discussed below.

---

26 Rulla, "The Discernment of Spirits and Christian Anthropology," 541.

27 Bernard J. Lonergan, *Insight: A Study of Human Understanding* (London: Longmans, Green and Co., 1957), 619-24, 92-3.

28 Rulla, "The Discernment of Spirits and Christian Anthropology," 545.

One's vulnerable spot has its own history in one's early life experience, but it is not of one's own making or choice.[29] Psychiatrist Karen Horney explains how one becomes vulnerable. She wrote of 'the tyranny of the *should*', suggesting that the '*shoulds*' which most people seem to ingest in early years leave them vulnerable in later years. Horney gives numerous examples of how vulnerability develops:

> (The neurotic) sets to work to mould himself into a supreme being of his own making. He holds before his soul his image of perfection and unconsciously tells himself 'this is how you *should* be – and to be this idealized self is all that matters. You should be able to endure everything, to understand everything, to like everybody, to be always productive... to be the utmost of honesty, generosity, considerateness, justice, dignity, courage, unselfishness...'[30]

Horney's reference to 'the neurotic' is her way of naming what she sees as universal human experience: all people develop some vulnerability in this way.

Awareness of one's inner dictates can enable behavioural change, but the point of vulnerability remains, as illustrated in Paul's experience begging God to take away 'the thorn in his flesh'. But no, it remains as the constant reminder that 'my grace is sufficient for you'. (2 Corinthians 12:7-9) One's vulnerable spot offers the same ever-present reminder that one cannot save oneself, that one is utterly dependant on God's grace.

---

29 Brian Gallagher, *Taking God to Heart* (Strathfield, NSW: St Pauls, 2008), 35-40.

30 Karen Horney, *Neurosis and Human Growth* (New York: W W Norton & Co, 1950), 64-5.

For people whose basic orientation turns away from God

The way God's Spirit works in people whose basic disposition is away from God, people caught in some ongoing web of unfree self-serving behaviour, has been seen to be quite different from the ways of the Spirit in people whose basic disposition is towards God. So too with any spirit not-of-God: with people whose basic orientation is away from God, a spirit not-of-God has only to encourage their present behaviour in order to target their vulnerable spot. To do this, the spirit appeals to their imagination, affirming the felt pleasure that such persons experience when following the attraction of the spirit not-of-God.

Hal's experience, quoted earlier in the chapter, is typical of how a spirit not-of-God attracts people whose basic orientation is away from God: the temptation of the spirit not-of-God very obviously encouraged Hal to continue his happy-go-lucky life style.

Similarly, in Augustine's early life when his basic orientation was unquestionably away from God, the spirit not-of-God continued to encourage him in his life's orientation, deepening his 'enjoyment' of his self-indulgent behaviour. Augustine's 'I was pleased with my condition', described as running 'wild with lust',[31] illustrates the ways of spirits not-of-God. Augustine's attachment to his pleasure was his point of vulnerability. The spirit not-of-God attacked at this point.

---

31 Augustine, *Confessions*, Book II, 1, 43.

For people whose basic orientation is towards God

As discussed in relation to the work of God's Spirit, most people who come for spiritual direction are people whose basic orientation is towards God, even while they may still be struggling with inner *unfreedoms*. In other words, they are sincere people, but people whose affectivity is not yet ordered. Experience has shown that the attraction of spirits not-of-God for these people comes via false, irrational messages that they find themselves listening to in their inner life. These messages appeal to their vulnerability and sound credible.

Here are some examples:

> **Ken** is school chaplain / pastoral worker in a large regional Catholic college. He comes to me for spiritual direction, a little irregularly, but he talks about his work with the students happily and enthusiastically almost every time we meet. We had met maybe five or six times, more or less monthly. To my surprise, when Ken arrived in a hurry on this occasion, his first words were 'I've decided to quit'. I said 'hold it: what has happened?' Ken told me a lengthy story:

> The principal, Kerrie, whom Ken knows well and would have considered a friend, called Ken to her office last week to tell him that there have been complaints from some staff members about Ken's liturgies with the senior students. She said that 'others are worried that you are breaking too many Church rules and giving the students false hope for their time post-school'. Ken asked who had complained, but Kerrie said that she couldn't name the people, but she thought it would be wise for Ken to listen to what people were saying. Ken became quite agitated: he had good relationships

with the students, reckoned he got good response from these same liturgies, and was confident that he was supporting the students' religious involvement and growth – and now these unnamed people were complaining behind his back. 'Why can't they talk to me about their concerns?' he asked. Kerrie wasn't able to say any more, except that she thought she was doing Ken a favour by telling him what was going on. At that point, Ken had said 'Kerrie, I'm out of here. I can't possibly work in an environment where I'm not appreciated'.

As we reflected on this, Ken was quite adamant that this was the right and only possible decision for him. 'You can't work in a place where you are not appreciated' he repeated. I tried to slow him down and talk about his work with the students and what that meant to him. Yes, he was very happy doing what he was doing and got on really well with most of the young people he worked with. He acknowledged that it will certainly be hard having to tell the students that he is leaving, but 'what other options do I have? Even Jesus said that you have to "shake the dust from your feet", when you are not accepted.' Taking another tack, I asked what else was going on in him when he felt not appreciated. There isn't much more to say, said Ken, but he told me that he had felt the same when he left his last school – for the same reason!

As we finished our time, I suggested that he might consider not acting till we talk again next week. Ken said he would think about it!

When Ken told me of his decision, and insisted on it without pause for further reflection, I was very aware of my discomfort.

The Ways of the Spirit

I was even more disturbed when Ken mentioned that exactly the same thing had happened for him at his previous school, which suggested to me that there was some pattern in Ken's experience. Spirits not-of-God tend to attract a person always at the same point of vulnerability.

Only on his second visit a week later, we were able to talk more about what it was like for him when he was told that others were being critical and not appreciating him.

> At some point, I asked Ken 'what are you really saying when you say that you can't work in a place where you are not appreciated?' His initial response was something like 'why would you question that?' Slowly we talked more about what it meant, about what he was really saying to himself when he made that statement. Ken said it again in different ways, till he finally caught himself and paused. 'Am I being realistic? Can I honestly expect everyone to appreciate me all the time?' When I held him there, Ken himself said 'It's almost like I'm saying that I'm no good unless everyone likes me!' I sensed that this was the moment: 'Is that true, do you think?' Ken came to see that he was making major decisions on a false premise. I helped him to see also that when he makes decisions on that premise, he ends up alone and suspicious of everyone, needing to check constantly that he is not being watched or criticised.

Both the acting on false messages – *You can't work in a place where you are not appreciated* – and the resulting loss of inner freedom and relationship are evidence of a spirit not-of-God leading Ken. We talked also about Ken's vulnerability around self-esteem, the weak spot in his make-up that the spirit not-of-God was appealing to.

Sometime later, Ken and I looked back over the whole experience, listening this time for the voice of God's Spirit in Ken's experience. God's Spirit was there all the time, inviting him to a freer place where he did not depend on others' appreciation (let alone everyone's appreciation), but the voice was faint and was quite overshadowed by the strong attraction of the spirit not-of-God. Ken's experience is an example of discernment for people who want God, but still struggle with their unfreedoms.

Lee offers another example:

> *Lee came for a weekend retreat because, she said, she needed 'time out'. Lee told me that she was 'burnt out', tired, no energy, no life, flat. To my questions, she thought it was probably because she was working double time this year, studying 'full-time' at the same time as holding down her full-time job. 'Sounds crazy, I know, but I really need a Uni degree' she said. To which I think I responded something like 'well yes, Uni degrees are valuable, but what is the urgency?' 'Last year', Lee told me, 'I applied for three different jobs to upgrade a bit and was rejected every time, because I didn't have that piece of paper, a degree. That was when I decided what I had to do.' I added 'And you are burnt out in your first year! Lee, how did it affect you personally when you kept getting rejection for those job applications?' 'Well, the message was "you're no good to us without a degree". It was pretty clear: I'm no good.' This sounded to me like the crux of the matter. I said simply: 'No good, eh?' Lee then said 'If I can't get a*

job, I'm no good, am I? I'm good for nothing'. It was the absoluteness of the statement that touched me – Lee had taken her job rejections to the point where she was seeing herself as no good.

It took some time before Lee could listen carefully to the inner message she was giving herself about her personal 'goodness' and the false conclusion that her goodness depended on others offering her jobs. The pressure she had put herself under to get her degree came from a false belief about her goodness, already fragile and tentative because of past experiences in her story which I heard only later.

Teresa of Avila's experience is an example of the same dynamic. Teresa records in *The Book of Her Life* that for twenty years she wasn't able to shake off her attachment to some friendships. I imagine the inner messages Teresa was giving herself to be: 'Why break good friendships?' or 'I don't think I would be happy without such good friends' or 'I would be no good without my friends'. These messages are quite subtle and can sound credible to someone who is vulnerable because of her need for affection. Teresa acknowledged that there was nothing wrong with the friendships in themselves, except that she was not free in relation to them. The deeper messages that Teresa was giving herself are clearly false when looked at dispassionately and objectively. For example, 'I'd be no good without my friends' is not a true statement.

These examples illustrate how the spirit not-of-God targets people at their point of vulnerability. This is the way that spirits not-of-God work against God's Spirit. It is also why the inner messages, however subtle, become quite repetitive, even predictable: the tempter continues to attack at the vulnerable spot. I agree with Lonsdale's suggestion that the recurring pattern in a person's temptations points to that person's inner vulnerability.[32]

The inner messages are objectively false. But they sound credible because of their appeal to one's vulnerable spot. In my experience, these deeper inner messages are almost always related to self-esteem. If a person is vulnerable because of poor self-esteem, as in the examples above, then any message that says 'I'm no good unless...' will sound true. Such a message will even bring a kind of satisfaction, a peacefulness, for it becomes a place that the person is at home in. This is a pseudo peace, a non-relational peace.

This was the point of my earlier observation that for people whose basic disposition is towards God, the discernment required has to focus on their feelings. The feelings need discernment, because some have their source in a spirit not-of-God. And because these feelings result from false thinking, then clear thinking is needed to do that discernment.

The spirits are put to the test by checking the direction in which one or other attraction is leading – towards or away from relationship with God. When a person does, in fact, follow and act out of the invitation of the inner messages of the spirit not-of-God, then the person ends up in a place that is the very opposite of where God's Spirit is leading. This is the experience properly called 'desolation'.

This experience of desolation has been described as 'a feeling of being stuck or trapped... a pervasive sense of heaviness',[33] in Lee's experience, a 'flatness and a lack of energy'. Teresa of Avila

---

32 Lonsdale, *Dance to the Music of the Spirit*, 73.
33 O'Sullivan, *Prayer and Relationships*, 113.

wrote that when she continued to listen to the false messages and continued to believe their message, she was miserable because of her 'wretched habits'. For Teresa these were the signs that she was being led away from God, to a place of desolation.

Also evident in the experiences described is that God's Spirit is still active, though often not recognised. For Teresa of Avila, for example, the quieter, gentler voice of the Spirit of God was inviting and deepening Teresa's desire for freedom and for life. Similarly, in Ken's experience in his school chaplaincy, God's Spirit continued to offer Ken another course of action. As noted, Ken could not hear the invitation initially, since it was dominated by the louder, more strident voice of the spirit not-of-God. Indeed, this too is very common human experience. Ignatius offers the telling image of a drop of water gently penetrating a sponge for God's Spirit, and the violent, noisy water falling onto hard stone for the spirit not-of-God.[34] God is experienced in the 'sheer silence' or the 'gentle breeze'. (1 Kings 19:12)

I have witnessed this dynamic where the spirit not-of-God tempts via false reasoning many times in people who have come for spiritual direction. I believe it is frequent human experience, since most people live with some degree of *unfreedom*.[35]

At the same time, my experience as a supervisor suggests that this way in which spirits not-of-God work in people is not widely appreciated by spiritual directors. Certainly, many acknowledge Ignatius Loyola's reference to 'fallacious reasonings that disturb the soul'.[36] But the personal experience of how these false

---

34 Ignatius Loyola, *Spiritual Exercises*, #335.
35 Psychotherapy recognises this same dynamic. For example, Cognitive Behavioural Therapy (CBT) aims to unearth irrational thinking in a client's experience. Rational insight modifies the impact of poor self-esteem.
36 Ignatius Loyola, *Spiritual Exercises*, ##314-5, 29.

suggestions actually appeal to a person's vulnerability has received little attention in any writing on spiritual direction.

Ignatius suggests also that the way a spirit not-of-God uses 'fallacious reasonings' may not be the only tactic of the spirit at this point. His 'rule 2' says:

> It is characteristic of the evil spirit to harass with anxiety, to afflict with sadness, to raise obstacles backed by fallacious reasonings that disturb the soul. Thus he seeks to prevent the soul from advancing.[37]

I find that false reasoning, appealing to a person's vulnerability and self-esteem underpins all that Ignatius proposed in this 'rule'.

For people who are interiorly free, not struggling with inner attachments

As in the earlier discussion about the ways of God's Spirit, the temptation of any spirits not-of-God is different for people whose growth in inner freedom has been realised in greater self-awareness and self-acceptance, people who are not struggling with inner attachments. The temptation of the spirits not-of-God is more subtle now: the spirits not-of-God tempt these people, still with false suggestions, but 'under appearance of good'.[38] Rose Hoover uses Ignatius Loyola's imagery to describe 'the Prince of Darkness as an Angel of Light' to describe this way of the spirit not-of-God.[39]

---

37   Ibid., #315.
38   Ibid., ##10, 332.
39   Rose Hoover, "The Prince of Darkness as an Angel of Light," *Review for Religious* 47, no. 6 (1988): 858-67.

Morrie's experience is an example of conflicting spirits for interiorly free people:[40]

> Morrie is a single man, an experienced doctor who had been in charge of a ward in the hospice for almost ten years. Morrie is a committed Christian. He is a prayerful person and two or three years ago felt drawn to spend longer periods of time in prayer. He then decided to leave the hospice and take on part-time nursing for an agency, in order to be able to give more time to prayer. Later Morrie sought admission to a contemplative religious community, quite against the advice of some friends. After twelve months with the community, Morrie was advised to leave. He came to see me, feeling confused, angry with God, and 'lost'.
>
> Morrie's anger came from his feeling let down by God. He had acted in good faith, was strongly attracted to a deeper life of prayer, and had chosen what he saw as a further commitment to God. Morrie thought he was responding generously to a call from God, as he had been generous throughout his life.
>
> I encouraged Morrie to talk more about feeling 'let down'. With tears, he felt his anger and hurt again. Finally he said, 'But God isn't like that.' 'What is God like for you?' Morrie talked about his past experience of God, then realised that 'I've made a mistake somewhere?' My response was to suggest that we go back over the whole story. If there was some 'mistake', it would have to have been in his interpreting the attractions he was experiencing.

---

40   The description of this example borrows from and adapts Lonsdale's example called Jane: Lonsdale, *Dance to the Music of the Spirit*, 64.

> *Together we saw that each time Morrie made a choice for what was clearly a good thing (his prayer life), it was always at the expense of some other good (his profession, later his friends' advice). There is no question about the value of all of those involvements, but were they right for him? Morrie was able to say 'you don't choose something just because it's a good thing'.*

Morrie was tempted by a spirit not-of-God, but 'under the appearance of good'. Even as I listened to his story for the first time, I noticed my uneasiness when he cut down his time at work in order to give more time to prayer. He could admit later that there was a feeble inner voice in him lamenting that he was deciding to do less in the hospice – and again later when he was deciding to give it away altogether. In going back over the whole story, we 'heard' this voice that Morrie had not listened to earlier.

It is a delicate point of discernment: one 'voice' seems to be inviting Morrie to quit his work as a doctor in order to give more time to prayer, another seems to be saying that where he is and what he is doing is equally of value. Morrie had ignored the latter voice when he made his decisions. He recognised later that the new suggestion had somehow seemed stronger in its invitation. But, as he listened more carefully, he wondered whether the possibility of staying and caring for his patients might also be from God – and might even be more fruitful for him and for many other people. We recognised together that the 'test' would be to see where the invitation of each voice would actually lead him.

Lonsdale offers several examples of people tempted in this way. He stresses that they were 'good people, acting in good faith', but their good qualities – prayerfulness, generosity, openness, integrity – 'by some kind of perversity' led them into paths that turned out to be debilitating and destructive. These people 'were in pursuit of a greater good, but found themselves deceptively drawn to what in the end turned out to be a lesser good'.[41]

Ignatius discovered this also from his own experience: in his autobiography, he tells of his dogged determination to go to Jerusalem to visit the holy places and 'to be of help to souls'.[42] Despite several setbacks and contrary advice, Ignatius thought this was God's call. Once he arrived in Jerusalem, he came to see that his desire was not from God. Indeed, he was forbidden to stay there and threatened with excommunication if he disobeyed. This was enough evidence that he was not meant to stay in Jerusalem. Of course, he obeyed and left. Yet he must have wondered about his earlier 'certainty' that he was being called to Jerusalem. Ignatius' words were 'the bad angel disguises himself as an angel of light'.[43]

Ignatius recommends looking back to 'review the whole course of the temptation... the series of good thoughts and how they arose'.[44] In this way, he hopes that, at least in retrospect, one might recognise which of the 'goods' offered was from God's Spirit and which (the lesser good) was from some spirit not-of God. Morrie did just that.

Earlier, I noted another suggestion of Ignatius Loyola that has proved helpful in my experience: a person looking back on how

---

41 Ibid., 64-6.
42 Ignatius Loyola, *Autobiography*, 46, 49.
43 Ignatius Loyola, *Spiritual Exercises*, #332.
44 Ibid.

they have been tempted in this way does well to remember that God's Spirit is delicate, gentle, delightful, like a drop of water soaking into a sponge, whereas the action of spirits not-of-God is violent, noisy and disturbing, like water falling onto stone.[45] Lonsdale's examples suggest that one aspect of the harshness of the spirit not-of-God is its insistence: though it is offered as a 'good', the insistent demand of the invitation suggests it is not the invitation of God's Spirit. Silf uses similar terminology in her description of her experience of feeling 'driven' by the spirit not-of-God, in contrast to being 'drawn' by the Spirit of God. Ignatius captured this in his other image of a 'spoiled child... with petulant ways': 'the child is merciless in wheedling his own way'.[46]

The same point of disagreement between Toner and other Jesuit commentators, noted earlier, arises again here: Egan argues that the 'consolation' offered by the spirit not-of-God is only apparent consolation, since only God can give consolation.[47] Toner disagrees, seeing no contradiction in the possibility that a bad spirit can lead to genuine consolation. He says that the spirit not-of-God, acting as an 'angel of light' can bring the same consolation as God's Spirit.[48] Both authors claim support from Ignatius for their positions. I have consistently followed the approach of Rahner, Egan and Buckley. My personal experience and the experience of other spiritual directors confirm that a spirit not-of-God always leads away from God, even though one may feel apparent 'consolation'.

---

45   Ibid., ##333-5.
46   Fleming, *A Contemporary Reading of the Spiritual Exercises*, #325. I use Fleming's translation and image of the 'spoiled child' in preference to the traditional reference to a 'nagging wife'.
47   Egan, *The Spiritual Exercises and the Ignatian Mystical Horizon*, 61, 83.
48   Toner, *Discernment of Spirits*, 227-8. (and see footnote)

The Ways of the Spirit

The examples given in this chapter illustrate how God's Spirit and spirits not-of-God work differently in people at different stages of their spiritual development. The examples from my personal experience are consistent with Ignatius Loyola's 'rules for discernment'. Indeed, the rules for discernment are found in personal experience.

At the same time, there are many examples above of the spirits at work also in the listening spiritual director. For example, my delight when listening to Iain's experience and the spark in me when observing Jenny's enjoyment of her piano playing were seen as signs of God's Spirit. My discomfort in hearing of Ken's decision to quit his work and my uneasiness as I listened to Morrie's cutting down his ministry in the hospice were also signs of God's Spirit in me, affirming that I was hearing the spirits in their experience correctly.

I encourage the contemplative prayer exercises used in the formation program *Siloam* described in the appendix. These exercises are designed to help spiritual directors become familiar with the signs of the spirits in their own experience, noting that the consistency of the spirits covers other areas of their lives as well as their ministry of spiritual direction.

The table summarises the ways of God's Spirit and spirits not-of-God.

	God's Spirit	Spirits not-of-God
People turning away from God	appeal to reason, inviting remorse	appeal to imagination, encouraging pleasure
People committed to God	affective attraction, felt consolation, deepening desire for God	fallacious reasoning, appeal to vulnerability, giving pseudo peace
People interiorly free	affective attraction; consolation without cause	Attract under appearance of good

Having argued the ways of the spirits in human experience, I now discuss discernment in spiritual direction (chapter 6) and discernment in Christian decision making (chapter 7).

6

DISCERNMENT OF SPIRITS IN SPIRITUAL DIRECTION

Directors should reflect that they themselves are not the chief agent, guide, and mover of souls, but that the principal guide is the Holy Spirit, who is never neglectful of souls.

John of the Cross[1]

Building on the understanding of the ways of God's Spirit and spirits not-of-God – and the consolation and desolation that result from following one or other spirit – I apply these principles of discernment to the ministry of spiritual direction.

As discussed in my survey of the tradition of spiritual direction, for many centuries spiritual directors had lost sight of the focus on God's activity in the person being directed. The focus was more on external behaviour, on living a good Christian life. I learned from my experience as spiritual director and from the experience of Francis de Sales, referred to earlier, that a contemplative listening to how God is working in the lives of my directees is a more helpful approach to spiritual direction

---

1 John of the Cross, "The Living Flame of Love," in *The Collected Works of St. John of the Cross*, 3.46.

than encouraging what I imagined my directees should be doing to live a good life. This means focusing on the directee's relationship with God or their religious experience.

As spiritual directors, we listen to another's experience, seek to understand or interpret that experience in the context of the other's relationship with God, and then verify the understanding in a way that aids the directee to new choices for mission. This way of understanding is not some detached intellectual exercise of knowledge, but rather 'a more sympathetic, compassionate listening'.[2] I believe that this is of the very nature of spiritual direction. Not unlike the way wisdom has been described as 'loving knowledge' or 'knowledge through love',[3] the spiritual director's approach might be termed loving understanding. Spiritual direction takes place in an atmosphere 'of spaciousness and underlying peace, of openness and receptivity, of a kind of quiet clarity in which it is easier to allow and let be'.[4]

In such an atmosphere, the spiritual director and the directee listen together to the movements in the directee's experience and come to new understandings together. Compassionate listening builds on the relationship between director and directee. Culligan supports this attitude when he writes of John of the Cross as a spiritual director. He believes that, even while John insists on learning and experience in a spiritual director, only 'genuineness, caring and understanding create the interpersonal atmosphere between director and directee

---

2   Veling, *Practical Theology*, 10-11.
3   Edwards, *Ecology at the Heart of Faith*, 110. Edwards, *Breath of Life*, 169.
4   May, *Care of Mind, Care of Spirit*, 113.

that promotes the Spirit's guidance'.[5] I see this 'interpersonal atmosphere' essential to the ministry of spiritual direction.

I follow Barry and Connolly who insist that spiritual direction 'is concerned with helping a person directly with their relationship with God.' They define spiritual direction as 'the help given by one Christian to another which enables that person to pay attention to God's personal communication to them, to respond to this personally communicating God, to grow in intimacy with this God, and to live out the consequences of the relationship'.[6]

In fact, as already described in my own experience, the major development in the practice of spiritual direction in recent years has been shifting the focus away from 'how to be a spiritual director' or 'what does one actually do in spiritual direction', to focus rather on what God is doing in a person's life experience. A person's relationship with God develops in spiritual direction through a focus on religious experience, 'any experience of the mysterious Other whom we call God'.[7] Religious experience is gift of God's Spirit.

In their desire to focus on this gift of God, spiritual directors discover soon enough that other spirits – spirits not-of-God – are often as active as God's Spirit. These spirits work to hold people back from the gift of God. Hence my argument that discernment,

---

5   Kevin G. Culligan, "Qualities of a Good Guide: Spiritual Direction in John of the Cross' Letters," in *Carmelite Studies: John of the Cross*, ed. Steven Payne (Washington, DC: Institute of Carmelite Studies, 1992).
6   Barry and Connolly, *The Practice of Spiritual Direction*, 8. This definition is widely accepted amongst spiritual directors. Slight variations in terminology exist in some commentaries.
7   Ibid. The phrase is attributed to Karl Rahner. Writing a Foreword to Harvey Egan's *The Spiritual Exercises and the Ignatian Mystical Horizon* (St. Louis, MO: Institute of Jesuit Sources, 1976), xiii, Rahner speaks of religious experience as a 'mystical immediacy to God'.

the practice of sifting and separating these different spirits, is integral to the ministry of spiritual direction.

I believe that spiritual directors need both an understanding of religious experience and an ability to recognise religious experience in their ministry. I discuss these in turn, with examples from my own ministry as a spiritual director, and based on my earlier definition of discernment:

> ... the process by which we examine, in the light of faith and in the connaturality of love, the nature of the spiritual states we experience in ourselves and in others. The purpose of such examination is to decide as far as possible which of the movements we experience lead to the Lord and to a more perfect service of him and our brothers, and which deflect us from this goal.[8]

This treatment of religious experience will also involve some discussion of the factors that frequently affect the spiritual director's listening and interpreting the signs of God's Spirit which they notice in their directees.

Understanding religious experience

In my theology of the Holy Spirit, I note that the Spirit of God has been given to all creation from the very beginning, 'poured into our hearts through the Holy Spirit that has been given to us'. (Romans 5:5)

---

8   Malatesta, "Introduction to Discernment of Spirits," in *Discernment of Spirits*, 9. This definition, too, is widely accepted. Significant differences are found only in the commentaries which define discernment solely in terms of decision making, as discussed in my review of the tradition of spiritual direction and discernment.

Congar reflects on this Pauline teaching:

> The Spirit who is both one and transcendent is able to penetrate all things without violating or doing violence to them... The Spirit is unique and present everywhere, transcendent and inside all things, subtle and sovereign, able to respect freedom and to inspire it. The Spirit can further God's plan...[9]

Edwards writes in a similar vein:

> The Spirit of God was present in the very emergence of the human, not simply as enabling the process of evolution from within, but as surrounding and embracing early humans in self-offering love. Humans evolved into a world of grace.[10]

Accepting that all human people are embraced in love by the gift of God's Spirit, I believe that there are many experiences in our lives, usually experiences outside of our own choice and control, that are potentially experiences of God. Such experiences have a religious dimension which may not yet have been acknowledged consciously.

The phrase 'potentially experiences of God' is intended to convey that some other factor is involved before an experience can be called a religious experience. All of the examples given already have involved people of faith: my examples of consolation, Connie's trust and perseverance, Dave's joy and commitment, Iain's overwhelming awe. So, too, Edwards' examples of religious experience, the everyday realities that

---

9 Congar, *I Believe in the Holy Spirit*, II, 17.
10 Edwards, *Breath of Life*, 33, 51.

'seem to become transparent to the light of the Spirit shining through (them)... the Spirit of God transcending our limited experience'. The crucial factor in religious experience is that people 'with a religious vision of reality',[11] people with some 'religious component' in their lives,[12] people of faith, are able to interpret their experience as an experience of God. People without faith, on the other hand, will not see the same experience as a religious experience, though it may well be so. I discuss this possibility below.

Experience: encounter and interpretation

Over and above mere sense experience (when one sees, touches or smells some object outside of oneself) and intellectual experience (when one makes rational judgments about something one has read, for example), much human experience transcends anything that the senses notice or the intellect knows. People say that they 'sense' something, sometimes they 'just know' a truth. Or a person is deeply touched by the beauty of a symphony beyond any words to describe the experience. Or someone speaks of knowing deeply how loved she is. Experiences such as these are called 'pre-conceptual' experiences, described variously as 'awareness of being without limit',[13] experiences of 'mystery, transcendent yet permeating reality',[14] and experiences 'of grace'.[15] Many people interpret experiences of this nature, happening in their ordinary

---

[11] Lonergan, *Method in Theology*, 116.
[12] Barry and Connolly, *The Practice of Spiritual Direction*, 21.
[13] Edwards, *Human Experience of God*, 12-3.
[14] John Shea, *Stories of God* (Chicago, IL: Thomas More Press, 1978), 17.
[15] Janet Ruffing, *Spiritual Direction: Beyond the Beginnings* (Malwah, NJ: Paulist Press, 2000), 71-6.

everyday, as experiences of God, the transcendent God. I name such experiences 'religious experiences'.

These examples illustrate that experience involves interpretation over and above the actual encounter. This was noted in Edwards' earlier definition of experience:

> Experience is best seen as encounter with some thing or person which has become available to consciousness through reflective awareness. It refers to an encounter that is interpreted within human consciousness. This second element, interpretation, has always already occurred whenever we know that we have experienced something.[16]

For this reason, two people with the same experience may interpret their experience quite differently. Toner's example is two people gazing at the beauty of the stars on a clear night.[17] One person is touched deeply and breaks into praise of God and desire to serve God; the other is moved to a desire to study astronomy. The former, in fact, was Ignatius Loyola who described the experience in his autobiography: clearly a person of faith, Ignatius has a religious experience. The latter person has an enjoyable experience that motivates them, but it has no relevance to a life of faith, hope and charity. Toner calls the latter experience 'non-spiritual consolation', 'consolation' because it felt comforting, 'non-spiritual' because, in his understanding, it has nothing to do with relationship with God.

I argue that this latter experience need not be called consolation at all, since it does not appear to move one towards God. At the

---

16   Edwards, *Human Experience of God*, 7.
17   Toner, *Discernment of Spirits*, 116.

same time, I would have liked the opportunity to work as a spiritual director with the person who was inspired by the stars in this way. This person has been touched; something has shifted in their inner life. Help to understand the inner movement may well reveal more to the experience than is initially obvious. Potentially, might it yet be a religious experience?

Edwards discusses a similar example of two people watching the same sunrise. For both, it is an experience of overwhelming beauty, but it is a religious experience for one only. Edwards' interpretation is that only one receives the beauty as gift. 'The second has no sense of its being a personal gift.'[18] Knowing that we are receiving a gift and that 'this moment of life is not explainable by chance or by one's own efforts' is an essential characteristic of the human experience of God. James Keegan discusses a 'genuine experience of God' in a similar way. He sees the indications of religious experience are that a person becomes 'less self-absorbed', is more 'self-revealing before God' and becomes 'more involved in community'.[19] Together, these are indications of religious experience.

William James would agree with this understanding. In his classic work on religious experience, James seems to establish what he calls the 'psychology' of an experience, but leaves open a person's interpretation of the experience:

> ... the experiences remain firm facts of human nature, no matter whether we adopt a theistic, a pantheistic-idealistic, or a medical-materialistic view of their ultimate causal explanation... The theistic explanation is by divine grace, which

---

18   Edwards, *Human Experience of God*, 64.
19   James M. Keegan, "Experiencing God," *Human Development* 18, no. 4 (1997): 42-3.

creates a new nature in one, the moment the old nature is given up.[20]

'Religious' interpretation of experience

Religious experience is not defined by the content of the experience, but by the interpretation put on the experience by a person of faith, a person with 'a religious vision of reality'. For example, merely looking up at the stars is not a religious experience in itself.

Paul Schilling asks the question 'Is there such a thing as an experience of God which is not apprehended as such by the one who has it?'[21] I agree with his affirmative answer:

> There are events in which the persons who experience them admittedly find themselves confronting an extra-human dimension that they themselves do not interpret in theistic terms, but which may be legitimately so interpreted by observers who seek to understand the meaning of God in human experience.[22]

To the question of the relationship between religious experience and the faith of the person who has the experience, Schilling names three forms of the experience of God, seen as a series of concentric circles:

> The innermost circle comprises the direct, personal awareness of the divine presence consciously

---

20   William James, *The Varieties of Religious Experience* (London: Collins, 1960), 122 & footnote.
21   S. Paul Schilling, *God Incognito* (Nashville, TN: Abingdon Press, 1974), 36.
22   Ibid.

interpreted as such by the experiencer... The second circle includes the entire range of human experiences – physical, intellectual, aesthetic, ethical, social, etc. – when seen by those who have them as manifestations of the divine presence or spheres for the service of God. The outermost circle is made up of a wide variety of intimations of a more-than-human reality, which may not be identified as divine by the persons most directly concerned, but which may nevertheless actually involve the active presence of God.[23]

Examples in the innermost circle would include the experience that spiritual directors hear often enough when someone is praying with scriptural passages that they have personalised. Neville's experience is a good example:

> **Neville**, *an older, retired man, wanted to tell me about something that had happened for him on his retreat recently. He had been praying with a passage from Jeremiah: 'I have loved you with an everlasting love; I am constant in my affection for you'. Neville recounted how the words had 'hit home' – he knew God was speaking to him with those words. In response to my gentle questioning, he said that his whole long life made sense at that point – God had been with him, loving him, all the while – and still. Neville was able to talk about the inner joy and wholeness that he had experienced that day on his retreat and his prayer of gratitude ever since.*

Examples of Schilling's second circle are experiences that are not immediately associated with God, but certainly hold the

---

23   Ibid., 39.

seeds or pointers towards God's presence. Spiritual directors meet such experiences frequently. For example, Iain moved quickly from his wonderment at the timber he was preparing to recognising an experience of God's gift. Olive offers another example:

> *In her regular spiritual direction,* **Olive** *told me that she had been invited to a silent prayer vigil on behalf of people in detention. There were only ten or so people, of all ages. 'We simply stood in silence for about an hour outside the government offices, with a single banner in front of us to tell people why we were there.' I asked Olive how she found it – the silence, the prayer, the long hour? The only other person Olive knew was Ollie who had invited her, but she said it was the most powerful experience of oneness with other people that she had ever known. 'I don't think I actually said many prayers, but I felt so close with the others. I was kind-of out of myself and yet I felt wholesome in myself.' As we talked about the experience more, Olive said something like 'Is this what Jesus meant by "may they be one"?' And, on reflection, 'It's a gift, isn't it?'*

Olive herself took the step that confirmed her experience as a religious experience.

In the outermost circle are the experiences like that of the young man who was inspired to study astronomy when gazing at the stars, mentioned above. I name this man Peter. Peter is not obviously a person of faith or someone with a religious vision of reality, but, when helped to depth his experience, he may come to interpret his experience differently. I believe that Peter's experience is potentially religious in the sense that, with a different vision of life, Peter could well interpret it that way.

Here is a snippet from a subsequent (fictitious) talk with Peter:

> Director: *Astronomy, eh? This is a new move for you, isn't it?*
>
> Peter: *Ah no, I've always been captivated by the heavens.*
>
> Director: *How do you mean 'captivated'?*
>
> Peter: *Ah, I often sit outside looking up at the stars – the sheer expanse gets to me.*
>
> Director: *How does it affect you, Pete?*
>
> Peter: *I feel small in comparison, almost insignificant – and yet I'm part of it all.*
>
> Director: *Like you are caught up in something bigger than yourself?*
>
> Peter: *Yes – I think the word is that I feel 'humble' – does that make sense?*
>
> Director: *Yes, I think I know what you mean... Pete, is it inviting you to something?*
>
> Peter: *Well, to study it properly – but more than that, I want to understand, but I also want to appreciate it better, what's it all about? Where does it come from? How can I contribute in some way?*

I see this experience with Peter as an example of Schilling's outer circle: his experience does seem to suggest God's activity, though this is not recognised by Peter. There is no direct mention of the Spirit of God.

Granted that other factors, such as depth of faith, psychological makeup, social and cultural influences, necessarily affect which of Schilling's forms of religious experience a person actually experiences at any one time, all of a person's experience is of interest to a spiritual director. Indeed, God's Spirit may be active in all of a person's experience.

This is religious experience, the focus of spiritual direction. Discernment is needed from the very beginning of a time of spiritual direction if director and directee together are to understand the experience under discussion, to recognise any spirits not-of-God in the directee's experience, and to name and verify the experience.

Recognising religious experience

When listening to the experience of another person, a spiritual director waits and listens for some sign that an experience is potentially a religious experience. The spiritual director will choose to focus on that point, helping the directee to re-live the experience. Mary Ann Scofield's description of the process of spiritual direction is helpful:

> Spiritual direction at its best entirely focuses on helping the directee to become attentive to the presence, action, and movements of God in ordinary human experiences, and on noticing the directee's own responses to these movements of the Holy. Whatever content the direction conversation may hold, however many interesting twists and turns and diverse paths it takes, the director listens for one thing only... until 'Aha, this is it.'[24]

---

24 Mary Ann Scofield, "Waiting on God: Staying with Movements of God," in *Sacred Is the Call*, ed. Suzanne M Buckley (New York: Crossroad, 2005), 52. Mary Ann Scofield was a founding member of Spiritual Directors International.

What may sound simple practice, in fact, raises many questions: How does the director remain 'tuned in' through the twists and turns of the conversation? How, in fact, does the director 'recognise the presence of God'? What signs is the director listening for? What happens if the director mis-reads the signs?

I consider that the basic question is how a spiritual director recognises religious experience in their directee. Though an experience of God may not necessarily be experienced or described in 'God language' and may not necessarily be experienced as something joyful and comforting, still my experience is that a genuine experience of God, in itself, will contain evidence that this is of God. This asks for discerning listening to recognise the signs that reveal to both director and directee that the experience is indeed an experience of God.

Signs of religious experience

Invariably there are 'twists and turns', tangents and side-tracks, conscious and unconscious, in a spiritual direction conversation. This may be because the directee needs to think through (aloud) the experience they are recounting, not yet having seen the invitation inherent in the experience or the potential religious nature of the experience. It may also be that the experience contains unwelcome challenge or unacceptable feeling that they may or may not yet be aware of. Equally, it may be that some spirit not-of-God is working in the directee's experience. The spiritual director listens attentively, Scofield suggests, waiting for the 'aha' moment. I add that this listening is not a passive waiting: the director has a role to play during the twists and turns, as well, which I discuss now.

Even in the early stages when the spiritual director is helping the directee to fill out their experience, discernment is crucial. Precisely because the directee's experience is not yet clear and they are struggling to hear its import and its invitation, the directee will often, unwittingly, take a wrong turn or become entangled in personal unfree dynamics. The director's role in listening and responding to the directee at this point is both noticing any movement prompted by a spirit not-of-God and suggesting a focus or a development of some aspect of the experience that stands out for the director as the way God's Spirit is leading.

From my own experience, I repeat that the signs of the spirits at work in another person's experience appear in the listening director, as much as in the directee who is sharing their experience. Certainly, the fruits of the experience will be most obvious in the one who has the experience, thus verifying the experience, as discussed below. But the initial signs that an experience is an experience of God may be even clearer in a director who is listening in a contemplative way. Thus, when the 'aha' moment does arrive, when God's Spirit is active in the directee, the same Spirit will touch the listening director. There will be inner movements in both directee and director.

There are several instances of this in my earlier examples: as spiritual director, I noted how 'delighted' I was at Iain's story about the timber he was working with, and how I noticed 'joy' and 'awe' in myself when listening to Dave's experience with the poem of John of the Cross. These signs are quite personal and may or may not be emotional. Indeed, the signs that a director notices in themself are often more on the level of conviction. As I listen contemplatively, I seem to know intuitively when God's Spirit is active: discernment becomes 'connatural'.

Trusting their own inner movements when listening, directors' responses will flow spontaneously, keeping the conversation on track. If a directee does slip into some place of desolation, following a spirit not-of-God tempting at a vulnerable spot, once again directors listening contemplatively will notice in themselves some movement that tells them that this is happening in the directee. In such an instance, when the director notices unease or maybe some energy loss in themself, the director will draw the other's attention to that point in the conversation. My experience suggests that the director is more likely to notice this, trusting what happens to themself when listening. This happened, for example, when I noticed my discomfort at Gus' cutting himself off from his brothers in community and when Ken told me of his decision to quit his chaplaincy job.

This is a critical area of discernment for a spiritual director. If spiritual directors are to trust the movements they notice in themselves as indicators of whatever spirit is operative in the directee, they need to be able to distinguish between these movements and others, conceivably quite similar, that belong rather to some past 'agenda' of their own. A director's own agenda, for example, might include memories of their own experience, quite unrelated to the directee's sharing, or some association with another person, or often some unfree issue that the director is not aware of and has not resolved in themself. I develop this point in my later discussion of the dynamics of the relationship between director and directee and the ever-present risk that the director mis-read the signs of God's Spirit.

Other spiritual directors support this. For example, Frank Houdek emphasises the importance of the spiritual director attending to the signs in themself. Houdek notes that when

God's Spirit is active in the directee, 'it will touch the director's own God experience'.[25] Janice Edwards, too, speaks of noticing this in her experience:

> The director's inner attraction to God supplies the means to detect God's presence in a particular session. What does this attraction look like interiorly? Many directors sense a shift in their own inner reactions when the directee becomes aware of God's presence. They experience an attraction or an allurement. Their interest is heightened, even if they were previously bored. This spontaneous felt response, essential for noticing God's movement within the directee, alerts the director to God's presence, providing an opportunity to pay more attention to God's movement.[26]

I support Edwards' emphasis on the spiritual director's own relationship with God. A director's 'sensitivity to the nuances of God's presence and initiatives' is gift of God's grace.

It needs to be said, too, that there are many experiences in spiritual direction when the 'aha' moment is much more subtle than in the examples given. For example, when directing Connie (chapter 4), whose prayer seemed to offer little consolation, the moment came when Connie was able to say 'I sense it's ok somehow', with no emotion, but real conviction. As noted at the time, the spiritual director not only heard this conviction in Connie, but also noticed the movement of God's Spirit in himself.

---

25 Frank J. Houdek, *Guided by the Spirit: A Jesuit Perspective on Spiritual Direction* (Chicago, IL: Loyola Press, 1996), 124-5.
26 Janice Edwards, "Spiritual Direction: A Delicate Weaving of Religious Experience," *Studies in Formative Spirituality* VII, no. 2 (1986): 8-9.

Another example is the experience which John of the Cross calls a 'dark night'. This has been cited as an example of consolation that does not feel consoling. John of the Cross gives signs to help a spiritual director to judge that some experience is a consolation from God, even though dark. He says that there are three signs, which must co-exist, for a spiritual director to be sure that a directee's experience is genuinely of God:

- dryness and loss of satisfaction in prayer – and finding that one has nowhere else to turn to relieve the dryness
- an inability to return to former ways (maybe more meditative prayer that one prayed in the past) – and an unwillingness to do so
- a deep desire for God.[27]

The experience of John of the Cross and the experience of many spiritual directors since affirm the value of these signs when listening to someone in this situation.[28] But, even with those helps to listening, the director cannot afford to sit back and look for the signs in the directee, as it were dispassionately. In relationship with the directee, the director will notice some inner movement in themselves when the experience under discussion is of God. It may be only then that the spiritual director notices John's three indicators of God's presence.

A similar situation arises when directing someone who is grieving a dear one. An experienced spiritual director, listening

---

27   John of the Cross, "Dark Night," in *The Collected Works of St. John of the Cross*, Book I, chapter 9.

28   Matthew translates these signs as 'I cannot pray as I used to, I do not want an alternative, but I do want God.' Iain Matthew, *The Impact of God* (London: Hodder & Stoughton, 1995), 148.

contemplatively, will know the difference between real grief and self-pity, for example, again by trusting the movements experienced in themself. The director will likely notice compassion and sadness in the former when God's Spirit is active, but some unease or withdrawal in the latter when some other spirit is prompting the directee.

This listening to another's experience in prayer takes on a different dimension when the directee prays in an *apophatic* way, as in Centering prayer[29], for example. The director often hears something like 'nothing much happens in my prayer'. In this *apophatic* tradition in spirituality, God is seen as the ever-greater God, so radically different from any of God's creation that God can be known only by putting aside all images, symbols and words to describe God. It is the way of *The Cloud of Unknowing*, for example, which teaches that nothing which could possibly be imagined or comprehended in this life can be a proximate means of reaching God, for God is ever-greater than human experience.[30]

When there is little to talk about in spiritual direction, because the experience is more like an 'emptiness', then it is critical that the spiritual director listen also to what is happening in the rest of the person's life. If God's Spirit is present and active in such prayer, then the fruits will surely be seen in other areas of life, especially in relationships, personal, professional and ministerial. Once again, the spiritual director's noticing the movements in themself when listening will affirm the presence of God's Spirit in the directee's experience.

---

29 Thomas Keating, *Intimacy with God: An Introduction to Centering Prayer* (New York: Crossroad, 2009).

30 anonoymous, *The Cloud of Unknowing* (New York: Doubleday, 1973), #70.

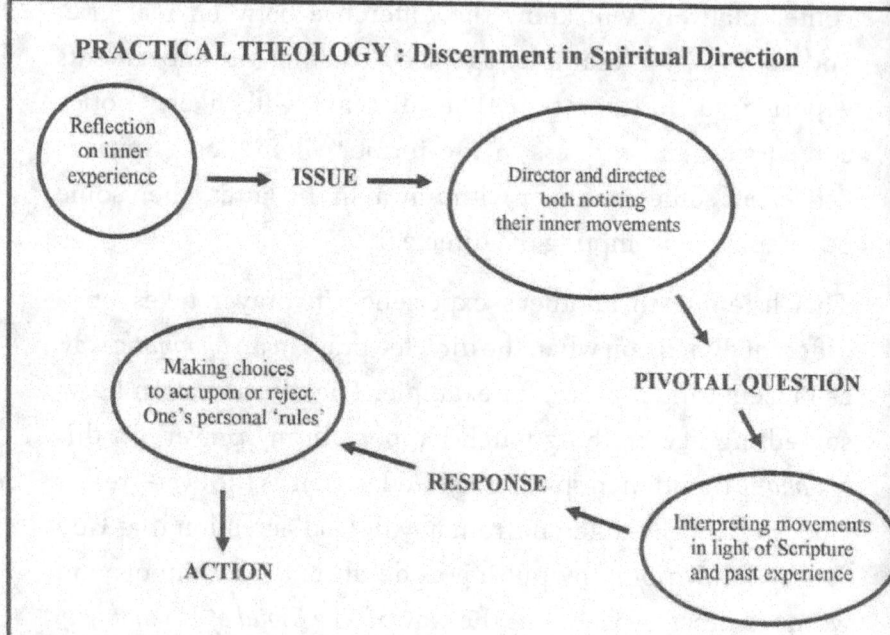

This is the way of practical theology. The diagram is the same adaptation of Darragh's diagram used earlier, applied now to discernment in spiritual direction.

The spiritual director helps the directee to be in touch with the experience being described and the inner movements prompted by the experience, notices and interprets the signs in both the directee and themself, and finally supports the directee in their decision about response and action. The example of spiritual direction with Peter earlier illustrates this. Together, Peter and his spiritual director try to understand his experience, then make some 'judgments' about it, and Peter makes his decisions on the strength of the experience.

Lonergan's way of experience, understanding, judging and deciding, perfectly parallels the spiritual director's way of helping others to notice inner movements, to understand these movements, and to act on those movements that suggest the activity of God's Spirit and reject those from spirits not-of-God.

In summary, contemplative listeners, with no hidden agenda, notice movements in themselves that they recognise from past experience as movements of God's Spirit, verified as such by later developments in the directee's experience.

Numerous commentators have listed characteristics or signs of a genuine experience of God. These include all the signs of God's Spirit named in Galatians and discussed in earlier chapters, an openness to other people and to the community of believers, and an awareness of the gift of the experience beyond human control, even beyond human comprehension.[31] Awareness of the *gift* of an experience of God stands out: this is of the very nature of religious experience. One knows in the actual experience that one could never have created the experience oneself. That very awareness will touch a person, moving them maybe to gratitude, wonder, delight, praise of God, as described earlier.

Because a directee's sharing of their experience with the spiritual director gives rise to inner movements in both the directee and the listening director, I add the spiritual director's recognition of the movement of God's Spirit in themself to the list of the signs of a genuine experience of God. An experienced spiritual director attentive to their own growth in inner freedom will recognise the movement as sign of God's presence, possibly even when the directee does not recognise the same.

Any experience of God will certainly bear fruit in the person's life. As seen in several examples, such fruit serves to validate and confirm the initial experience as gift of God. But it needs to be

---

31   For example, Edwards, *Human Experience of God*, 63-6. and Barry and Connolly, *The Practice of Spiritual Direction*, 109-17.

said that in the time of spiritual direction, neither director nor directee needs to look beyond the present experience, as though to predict the fruit or to know God's invitation in advance. The Spirit's activity and invitation is contained in whatever is already happening for the directee, in the present moment.

Signs of resistance

The signs of religious experience and the inner movements that the spiritual director and the directee notice in themselves become somewhat confused if the directee is resisting the invitation of God's Spirit. I discuss now how a spiritual director recognises resistance and best works with resistance in a directee, resistance that is almost always unconscious.

As God invites a person to deeper intimacy, invariably the human response is both desire for such intimacy, yet reluctance, even resistance. A spiritual director will be sympathetic to a directee who is resisting in some way, but the spiritual director knows that resistance cannot be left unnamed or unattended to. Indeed, the point of a directee's resistance may well be the point at which God's Spirit is inviting growth and deeper relationship:

> Resistance in prayer is not something to be condemned or pitied, but rather welcomed as an indication that the relationship with God is broadening and deepening.[32]

Anna's fear in the example discussed earlier is classic resistance. Anna dearly wanted closeness to God, but feared the implications of it, the imagined demands of such close relationship. Anna was able to name it quite quickly, but initially she was unable

---

32   Barry and Connolly, *The Practice of Spiritual Direction*, 109-17.

to move through her fear. I follow up on Anna's experience in what follows.

How does a spiritual director know if directees are resisting something in their experience that needs to be faced? I have heard directors refer to a directee who just goes round and round in circles, or who 'talks incessantly' without pause, or who 'persists in avoiding my questions', or who consistently 'forgets our previous conversation' as examples of resistance. These may well be judged as indicators of resistance, but as supervisor, I have always asked to hear more about how such behaviour affects the listening director. To that question, I have heard directors talk of becoming bored, impatient, angry, and cut off from any meaningful relationship. This is the point of discernment that supervisor and spiritual director now face.

The movements named are rather more ambiguous than those in earlier examples. Boredom in a spiritual director may come from the director's weariness or preoccupation with some personal matter, anger may come from some identification with the directee's experience, impatience may come from the spiritual director's own need to achieve and show results of their ministry, etc. The risk of a director's mis-reading the signs is discussed below. Though that discussion will introduce a note of caution, I know from experience that a spiritual director who listens contemplatively from a freer place in themself, and who has reflected upon and verified past experience will certainly learn to trust the message of any movement of boredom or sensing that they have been cut off from relationship. Resistance comes from an unconscious collusion with a spirit not-of-God, in which case some telling movement is to be expected in the listening director. At that point, the spiritual director recognises the invitation to work with the directee's resistance.

Working with resistance

In discussing how a spiritual director might work with resistance in a directee, some commentators write of the need to 'confront' resistance, an approach I do not subscribe to. Resistance is not an enemy to go to battle with. Rather, I believe that resistance needs to be recognised, named and held gently. As Ruffing says, 'do not attack' the resistance.'[33] Resistance is like a barrier between a person and what that person desires, a barrier that cannot be skirted. Once people have recognised and named their resistance, the only way forward is to move through the barrier. In spiritual direction, then, the director needs to keep the directee's focus on the resistance itself, not on the desires on the other side of the barrier.

This is how Anna's story developed in later conversations:

> *Anna was able to recognise her fear of what God might ask of her. When we talked more about the fear, deepening her experience, Anna finally named her fear that God would judge her to be not good enough for any closeness. 'And if God judged you not good enough?' 'I'd be lost, wouldn't I, doomed by God.' It was at that point that I said 'Anna, do you really believe that God would doom you like that? Is that what God is like?' Slowly, but strongly, Anna could say 'No, I do not believe that God would do that to me'. With tears, 'Why am I afraid of God?' Together, we heard the invitation to 'take a risk' to tell God how much she wanted to know God and be close to God, even though she knew she was afraid. Which Anna subsequently did.*

---

33   Ruffing, *Spiritual Direction*, 51.

Discernment of Spirits in Spiritual Direction

The discernment moment came with Anna's awareness that her fear that 'God would judge her to be not good enough' was false: to believe that would be to follow a spirit not-of-God, evidenced by the direction in which it would take her. Her conviction that 'God would not do that to me' is the work of God's Spirit.

Quinn's experience is a different example of resistance:

> **Quinn**, *a middle-aged professional man, married with family, has been coming for spiritual direction monthly for some months. He speaks easily of his everyday experiences and usually goes home with some new appreciation of God's care for himself and his family. On this occasion, Quinn told me that his father had died the previous week. I said something like 'I'm sorry to hear that, Quinn. You really haven't talked much about your father – were you close to him?' Quinn replied 'No, not really – but that's ok'. He rather quickly went on to talk about some local community meeting he had attended the day before. When we met the following month, I (innocently) asked 'How have you been since your father passed away?' Quinn: 'Ok, thanks.' We then talked of other things, though I was feeling quite unconnected with Quinn. It was several months after his father had died before I initiated the conversation with 'Quinn, I've been feeling as though I've lost you somehow. It seems we are not as open with one another these days. I think it is since your father died'. When Quinn didn't respond, I added 'Is there something there that it would be good to talk about?' 'Brian, I can't!' 'What do you mean? What stops you, Quinn?' With eyes down, Quinn said 'It's too painful – I probably need to talk, but I don't like the memories*

> – I get angry.' I assured him that I appreciated his saying that much, but I then asked 'Quinn, is it ok to get angry?' Quite strongly, Quinn said 'No, it's not ok – I shouldn't be angry with any one, let alone my father.' To that, I ventured 'I think that is what we need to talk about, Quinn...'

My early sense of being disconnected confirmed for me that Quinn was resisting something. When I eventually acted on that, we unearthed and named his resistance, namely, it is not good to be angry. That became our focus: that was the 'barrier' Quinn had to move through if he was to talk about his painful memories. His understanding of and attitude to anger were deeply ingrained, but honest talk and faithful prayer gradually gifted Quinn with a new freedom. One blessed day, he did talk about memories of his drunken father and his father's treatment of Quinn's mother. It was painful and he was quite angry, but it became the way to a healing that has brought new life to Quinn and to our relationship in spiritual direction.

The spiritual director's approach with both Anna and Quinn was to work with the resistance. And in both examples, the movements that the spiritual director noticed in himself were the clear signs of God's Spirit and the spirit that was holding the directee back from God.

Donna Markham's work with resistance to change in groups supports this approach. Markham stresses the need to 'work through' the resistance:

> Resistance, in and of itself, is neither good nor bad. It is an *unconscious* process of retarding or blocking the process of transformation. In any living organism faced with the prospect of

changing, resistance will surely be present.[34]

> The effective leader works through resistance by (i) identifying the mode of the resistant behaviour, (ii) engaging the organisation in exploring the motive behind the manifestation of resistance at this particular moment, (iii) exploring the implications that the resistant behaviour holds for the future life of the organisation if it is left unaddressed, and (iv) determining the action the organisation is willing to take to move beyond the resistance.[35]

Working through any resistance, or 'moving beyond' the resistance not only acknowledges its presence and influence, but frees the person or group to move ahead.

Spiritual directors themselves are sometimes guilty of resistance to a topic that a directee has raised. As a supervisor, I have worked with a spiritual director's resistance in his account of a spiritual direction time where he persistently side-stepped the directee's several mentions of tension in her marriage. As well, I have sensed a spiritual director's resistance in her interaction with me, the supervisor, not unlike the resistance described in Quinn's experience above. I have also met resistance to talk about areas of intimacy in cross-cultural experiences of spiritual direction and supervision, where cultural taboos are encountered. Because of the ingrained taboos, these need to be treated sensitively. Ruffing discusses similar examples in her experience, she notes, particularly in areas of intimacy and

---

34 Donna J. Markham, *Spiritlinking Leadership: Working through Resistance to Organisational Change* (New York: Paulist Press, 1999), 24.
35 Ibid., 17, 46.

erotic expression.³⁶ All of these examples are certainly issues for supervision. The same principles and the recommended way of working with resistance discussed above would apply.

Risk of mis-reading the signs

Both spiritual directors and their directees are limited human beings, fallible human beings. In this ministry, it is crucial that spiritual directors know their own fallibility and how it can affect their listening and their recognising the signs of their directees' religious experience. This is especially true of the unconscious factors that can affect a director's listening.³⁷

I find Edwards' terminology of the 'interpretative framework' helpful in understanding the risk of mis-reading or mis-interpreting the signs of the spirits when listening:

> Contemporary philosophy and theology would say that the human person brings an interpretative framework to every new experience... Our interpretative framework, with all its possibilities and biases, enters into the interpretation of experience at every stage. All experience, no matter how profound, is filtered through our finite human preconceptions and limited human knowledge.³⁸

The interpretative framework includes one's biases, one's preconceived expectations, one's past experience in similar situations, and one's inner attachments and unfreedoms.

---

36 Ruffing, *Spiritual Direction*, 112-21.
37 See, for example, Rulla, "The Discernment of Spirits and Christian Anthropology," 541.
38 Edwards, *Breath of Life*, 167.

All of these affect a spiritual director's own inner dynamics, and in turn, how the director understands or interprets the experience of their directee. The ambiguity of many of the signs that directors notice when listening to a directee – for example, 'peace', 'impatience', 'boredom' – is due to different interpretative frameworks underpinning how different directors describe their experiences.

The most frequently encountered factors contributing to a director's mis-reading or mis-interpreting the signs are the director's own inner dynamics and the dynamics of their relationship with the directee. I discuss each, in turn.

Unconscious dynamics in the spiritual director

As a supervisor, I have encountered numerous examples of a spiritual director's lack of awareness of their own inner dynamics affecting accurate listening to a directee. I recall spiritual directors who have had pre-conceived notions about their directee's experience – and that is precisely what they think they hear! This seems to happen when the director has had similar experience and presumes that the directee's experience is the same.

Moreover, a spiritual director who is not interiorly free will imagine that they are noticing signs of God's Spirit in the directee, but signs which flow from their own unconscious needs being met. Examples could be a director who has an inner need to achieve ('I think we have worked that out satisfactorily, haven't we?') or a need for order ('Let's make sure there are no loose ends!') or a need for affirmation ('Was that helpful today?') will experience apparent 'joy' or 'peace' when those needs are satisfied, an 'apparent good, not a real good'. Such a director will miss the true signs of God's working in the directee.

This is my experience as supervisor for spiritual directors who have, in fact, misread the signs of the work of God's Spirit. The director's unconscious inner needs or vulnerability have influenced their listening. Paralleling the way in which a directee is tempted at a point of vulnerability, a spiritual director may also be tempted in this way, invariably involving some emotional response. Moreover, as Rulla insists, 'the more the emotions are unconscious, the greater their effect in rendering memory and imagination selective'.[39]

This is especially so when one judges one's emotions. Considerable psychological study of the relationship between emotions and rational thinking is inconclusive, but 'it would be safe to say that, regardless of their theoretical stance, psychologists investigating these issues widely agree that emotional feeling states and cognitive processes are frequently, if not typically, highly interactive'.[40]

I find Magda Arnold's study of emotions helpful and relevant to spiritual direction. Arnold argues that:

> We are aware of the attraction that draws us to the thing or situation which we have judged suitable for us... An emotion will always occur when something is recognised as attractive or repulsive... The individual must perceive and

---

39 Rulla, *Anthropology of the Christian Vocation*, 87-88.
40 Michael J. O'Sullivan, "Trust Your Feelings, but Use Your Head: Discernment and the Psychology of Decision Making," *Studies in the Spirituality of Jesuits* 22, no. 4 (1990): 19.

judge the object in relation to himself (as suitable or unsuitable, good or bad for himself) before an emotion can arise. The emotion will follow this judgment, whether or not it (the judgment) is correct... Such evaluation is immediate, based upon a perceived similarity of this situation with situations in the past.[41]

This is illustrated in Arnold's table on the following page.[42]

Different types of emotion are explained in terms of the objects toward or away from which the tendency is directed. Arnold orders emotions according to their aim as directed toward a suitable object and away from a harmful one into 'positive' and 'negative' emotions; and according to their operation, their degree of impulsion, into 'impulse emotions' and 'contending emotions'.

---

[41] Magda B. Arnold and Gasson John A., *The Human Person: An Approach to an Integrated Theory of Personality* (New York: The Ronald Press Company, 1954), 294-5. Magda Arnold (1903-2002), noted American psychologist, was Professor of Psychology at Spring Hill College, Alabama.

[42] Ibid., 298.

Set Me Free

BASIC EMOTIONS

i. Emotions differ according to their *object* (as it is suitable or harmful to the self). Therefore we distinguish
   positive emotions (tending toward suitable objects) and
   negative emotions (tending away from harmful objects)

ii. Emotions differ according to their *operation*, the degree of impulsion. Therefore we distinguish
   impulse emotions (tending toward or away from an object when conditions are favourable and
   contending emotions (contending for or against something when conditions are unfavourable

A: Impulse emotions	Emotion toward object as such – present or absent	Object not present (tendency toward or away from)	Object present (rest in possession)
Object suitable (good)	love	wanting, desire	delight, joy
Object unsuitable (evil)	hate	aversion, dislike	sorrow, sadness

B: Contending emotions	Degree of difficulty	Object not present (tendency toward or away from)	Object present
Object suitable (*good*)	If judged attainable	hope	
	If judged unattainable	despair	
Object unsuitable (*evil*)	If to be overcome	daring	Anger
	If to be avoided	fear	

Arnold argues that an emotion is based on a spontaneous judgment about what is good and attractive, and what is not so. Arnold calls this an 'intuitive appraisal'. This judgment, in turn, is based on one's perception of the similarity of the present experience with some past experience in what is called one's 'affective memory', leading to an 'affective appraisal'.

There is a point where spiritual directors risk mis-reading the signs that their emotions suggest. The very mixed bag of one's past experience, including for example all of the early childhood experience is held in one's affective memory. This, in turn, gives rise to one's vulnerability around inner needs, as described earlier.

Arnold says of affective memory:

> Indeed, affective memory is ubiquitous, yet intensely personal, because it is the living record of the emotional life history of each person. Being always at our disposal, playing an important role in the appraisal and interpretation of everything around us, it can be called the matrix of all experience and action... But it is also the intensely personal reaction to a particular situation based on an individual's unique experiences and biases.[43]

In stressing how unfree this leaves a person, Kiely refers to past events which may have been inadequately interpreted and then largely forgotten. He argues that 'it is quite possible for an individual not to understand fully his own emotional attitudes'.[44] In other words, one risks making judgments about

---

43   Magda B. Arnold, *Feelings and Emotions: The Loyola Symposium* (New York: Academic Press, 1970), 187.
44   Bartholomew Kiely, *Psychology and Moral Theology* (Rome: Gregorian University Press, 1987), 135.

one's present experience, the judgments that give rise to one's emotional reactions, based on one's inner *unfreedoms*. In the terminology I use, such judgments offer apparent goods, not real goods. This is usually unconscious, but such judgments result in the spiritual director's mis-reading the signs of God's Spirit.

Only a 'rational appraisal' can discover the real good in one's affective memory. This is why clear thinking is needed, for example when spirits not-of-God tempt with 'fallacious reasoning' or false messages appealing to one's vulnerability. Only clear thinking can recognise the falsity.

Remembering that, most often, one's emotional or affective reactions give the signs of the active spirits in a directee's experience, it seems important to know the interaction between thinking and feeling and to recognise the judgments that have given rise to one's emotions.

Transference in the spiritual direction relationship

I consider now the dynamics of the relationship between director and directee. A frequent experience in spiritual direction, though again without awareness, is when transference happens in the relationship.[45] This happens when a directee relates to the director as if they were some other person. A key indicator is when the directee spends most of their prayer time or most of the time with the spiritual director reflecting on the relationship with the director.[46]

---

45 Barry and Connolly, *The Practice of Spiritual Direction*, 157-74. Ruffing, *Spiritual Direction*, 168.
46 Barry and Connolly, *The Practice of Spiritual Direction*, 163-4

May defines transference:

> Transference refers to specific situations in psychotherapy in which a patient unconsciously invests the therapist with qualities and attributes pertaining to the patient's mother, father, or some other person of childhood significance, and then proceeds to act *as if* the therapist really were that person.[47]

It is to be noted that transference happens in an ongoing relationship and results in a person relating to the therapist *as if* the therapist really is father or mother or authority person.[48] When transference occurs, it is usually 'one-sided (one often feels or judges that the other is simply good or simply bad), inflexible (a change in behaviour in the other will not in general produce any change in the liking or disliking), and exaggerated'.[49]

May's definition of transference applies equally to the ministry of spiritual direction, replacing the word 'patient' with 'directee' and the word 'therapist' with 'spiritual director'. If a directee is transferring onto a director qualities and attributes of their father, for example, then depending on the directee's experience and memory of the father, the director may be put on a pedestal, or may be someone that the directee imagines they have to please, or may become the target of the directee's anger. These reactions are quite inappropriate. In truth, the spiritual director does not deserve the intense admiration or the intense anger they are given. The directee is relating as they related or would

---

47 May, *Care of Mind, Care of Spirit*, 126.
48 This is quite different from 'paratoxic distortion' which is defined as predetermined ways of relating to certain people, and happens usually on first meeting. For example, someone might relate in the same way to all dark-skinned people. see May, ibid.
49 Rulla, *Anthropology of the Christian Vocation*, I, 383.

like to have related to the father. When transference happens without awareness in either spiritual director or directee, the signs the director notices and presumes to recognise are no longer accurate.

Rose's experience illustrates the inappropriateness and the intensity of transference:

> *Rose is a 40 year old religious sister who has been coming to me for spiritual direction for several months. On this occasion, Rose began by saying that she has found herself thinking about me often since our previous meeting, she would like to know me, as I now know her. 'I would like to talk about you today.' I suggested to Rose that she talk more about her feeling, even her feeling for me. She did that, even adding that she had 'talked to God about her feeling for me'. I eventually said that, while I could talk about myself, I wonder what is the best thing I could do for her right now? Did she really want me to talk about myself, or could there be something else going on in her right now? Slowly, with long silences and many tears, Rose began to touch her aloneness, her deep hurt and rejection from years back, her wanting to be loved. After a long silence, Rose said 'He's saying no'. 'He's saying no'? I repeated. 'No to our friendship.' 'How is that for you?' She said, 'I feel a kind-of loss, but it's ok'. Some weeks later, Rose experienced God's presence in her aloneness and her sadness – she told me one day that she knew no one could love her like God does.*

Rose's experience is an example of transference, but also finally of religious experience.

Interestingly, on one occasion when transference happened for Jung (though Jung did not encourage transference in his therapy), he said that he wondered if it were not, ultimately, an experience of deep longing for God.[50] This would seem accurate in Rose's experience.

Since a person's acting out of unconscious inner needs is the work of a spirit not-of-God, the director's task is to expose such a spirit, but then to point out and stay with God's Spirit in the experience shared by the directee. Effectively, the director ignores the spirit not-of-God. At the same time, it is important to say that a director does need to acknowledge the directee's transferred feelings or attitudes towards the director in some way – just as I have insisted that spirits not-of-God in someone's experience need to be named, before turning to God's Spirit. In other words, the director keeps the focus on the directee's relationship with God.

My experience suggests that transference in a situation of spiritual direction is usually mild, helped by the infrequency of monthly meetings, in contrast to the weekly meetings usual in psychological therapy. Provided the spiritual director notices and is aware of the directee's transference, this dynamic is manageable: the director simply does not take it on board.

The problem is greater when counter-transference occurs in the relationship. Counter-transference is, by definition, the situation in which the therapist/spiritual director, as it were, 'returns the favour' and relates to the patient/directee as a child. A spiritual director who accepts and acts out of the excessive praise given by the directee, or who encourages the directee's desire to please, is

---

50   Carl Jung in Joseph Campbell, ed. *The Portable Jung* (New York: Viking Press, 1971), 78.

counter-transferring. Both directee and director are acting out of unconscious inner needs and both may well feel 'peaceful' with the experience, but a pseudo peace. The noticed signs of the work of the spirits will actually be giving a false message. Supervision is essential for spiritual directors in this situation.

On rare occasions in supervision, I have also met experiences where the spiritual director is transferring, treating the directee as if they were a child, without any 'invitation' from the directee. Other psychological dynamics may be at work in such situations and again I stress the need for supervision.

Other psychological dynamics

Other psychological problems that can arise in spiritual direction, as in any helping relationship, are dependency, mutuality, and sexual attraction, all treated by May in his chapter on interpersonal dynamics. These problems can develop, he argues, because of the level of trust and intimacy that is normal in a healthy relationship of spiritual direction.[51]

Sexual feelings and sexual attraction are not uncommon in spiritual direction, but are not necessarily a matter for concern. When such feelings are *conscious*, the focus on God in spiritual direction need not be compromised in any way. My experience is that, for directees, it is usually enough for them to acknowledge their feelings with their spiritual director. If the director is experiencing sexual attraction to the directee, it is essential that the director to speak of this with their supervisor.

But a directee's *unconscious* dependence on the spiritual director or sexual attraction to the director will affect the relationship of

---

51   May, *Care of Mind, Care of Spirit*, 131-48.

spiritual direction and the typical signs of religious experience in much the same way as unacknowledged transference. However, again paralleling the ways in which a spiritual director detects transference, interiorly free directors will sense the presence of different unconscious dynamics in the directee, as they notice and trust their own reactions when listening contemplatively. Directors will then invite their directees to deeper self-awareness and openness.

Though there was no mention of sexual feelings in Rose's story, the spiritual director's desire to help Rose to self-awareness and to keep her focus on relationship with God, not with her spiritual director, describes what I consider to be the most helpful approach to this dynamic.

Once unconscious feelings are brought to awareness, feelings of this nature can usually be treated lightly and become part of the spiritual direction exchange. I fully support May's insistence on the primacy of the directee's relationship with God and the director's own discernment:

> ... that although objective analysis and psychological examination can help clarify what is going on, these should be supplements, never substitutes, for the more traditional discernments of the spiritual life and the personal prayer and meditation of the spiritual director.[52]

Quite a different and more serious scenario develops when the spiritual director also experiences unconscious sexual attraction and/or subtly responds to the directee's feelings – the parallel of the dynamic of counter transference discussed above. The situation becomes more serious again if openness becomes

---

52 Ibid., 141.

impossible. A frequent reason for this is that one or other of the director or directee is sexually inhibited or carries some sexual guilt, situations again when supervision is vital.

Just as a contemplative spiritual director senses when some unconscious dynamic is operating in their directee, a contemplative supervisor does the same for the spiritual director who presents for supervision. The supervisor will not only invite openness, but will challenge the spiritual director in concrete examples of the interaction between the director and their directee in ministry. As spiritual directors grow in awareness and inner freedom, they are better able to make choices in responding to and supporting their directees.

Finally, it can happen that some directees bring psychological problems that are beyond the scope of spiritual direction. Extreme cases where self-harm or suicide seem possible are rare and are usually quite obvious when met. More often, spiritual directors meet people who are quite unable to maintain relationship with God or with the director. I have experienced examples where the conversation focuses entirely on the person's psychological struggles. In the same way that I have described above, I've learned to trust my own reactions and inner movements to know when referral to a professional therapist is called for.

Except in the extreme cases referred to, any suggestion of referral to other professional help needs to be discussed openly with the directee. Correctly, May is careful to ensure that there is no suggestion of serious 'sickness' in the directee or incompetence in the spiritual director.[53] Formation programs for spiritual

---

53   Ibid., 191-3.

directors necessarily include an understanding of the dynamics of referral and the signs of when this practice is needed.

Verifying religious experience

Religious experience rests on a person's relationship with God. If an experience is valid, it will enhance relationship with God and with other people. The spiritual director will expect to find a person growing in compassion and acceptance of others as verification of the experience. This was pointed out in the discussion of consolation in earlier chapters: consolation bears fruit in healthy relationships and in deeper awareness of the ways of God's Spirit in a person's life. This is evident in many of my earlier examples. For this reason, a spiritual director is always attentive to the whole of a directee's life experience.

At the same time, in spiritual direction there are signs of the validity of a religious experience in the very experience. The clearest sign, mentioned above, is the directee's awareness of the gift of the experience. When this is evident, the discerning spiritual director will always notice signs in themselves, recognised because of past experience when the same signs have been verified. The spiritual director is then able to confirm the directee's experience as an experience of God.

The centrality of discernment in spiritual direction

Discernment is integral to the ministry of spiritual direction. The centrality of discernment in this ministry and in the formation of spiritual directors for the ministry became clear to me in the experience of working in formation of spiritual directors. This is true both when the director is working with a religious experience and when the focus is rather on instances of resistance or transference or other experiences flowing from places of *unfreedom*. Barry summarises my argument:

> Discernment is necessary not only because of the possible influence of the evil spirit, but also because of the multidimensionality of human experience... I experience nothing without having assimilated it to schemata or structures built up over my history.[54]

The ways in which spirits not-of-God tempt a person at points of vulnerability or *unfreedom*, support Barry's reference to the personal 'schemata or structures' that a person builds within their make-up and Edwards' reference to the 'interpretative framework' that a person uses in understanding experience. In all examples, discernment is needed to unearth the influence of spirits not-of-God holding a person back from God, and to hear the invitation of God's Spirit.

Moreover, in many examples, the invitation of God's Spirit was missed because of its subtlety and gentleness. I believe that only spiritual directors who are sensitive to their own inner movements will recognise the work of the Spirit of God in their directees' experience.

Doubtless, Barry's 'schemata' include also the healthy structures that a person has developed in their inner world as relationship with God deepened in time. This happens for both spiritual director and directee, again emphasising the place of and need for discernment in spiritual direction ministry.

---

54 Barry, *Spiritual Direction and the Encounter with God*, 29.

Spiritual direction and discernment are inseparable. As the spiritual director listens to the directee, focusing on inner experience, recognising what is of God, the director is already discerning. There is no other way.

In the chapter following, I consider the place of discernment in Christian decision making. I find discernment of spirits integral to the ministry of spiritual direction and the processes of decision making. For that reason, how a spiritual director, in fact, becomes discerning and how formation programs for spiritual directors foster the process of becoming discerning are crucial questions, treated in subsequent chapters.

7
DISCERNMENT OF SPIRITS IN CHRISTIAN DECISION MAKING

> *When religiously discerning, the ultimate question is*
> *'How will the present choice fit my relationship with God?*
> *Will it harm, preserve or promote*
> *the relationship with God that I have?'*[1]

This chapter builds on previous chapters and applies earlier learnings about the ways of the spirits to discernment of God's will or Christian decision making. The place and value of the three ways of decision making outlined in Ignatius Loyola's *Spiritual Exercises* are discussed in detail, again using practical examples. I also apply the principles I develop for decision making to communal discernment or group decision making.

God's will is understood as an expression of God's love, God's desire for each person, defined by Toner as 'God's positive, preferential, but non-necessitating will regarding a person's free choice in a concrete situation when none of the alternatives for choice is commanded or forbidden by God.[2] I use the terms 'finding God's will' and 'Christian decision making'

---

1 Edward C. Vacek, "Discernment within Mutual Love Relationship with God," *Theological Studies* 74, no. 3 (2013): 709. See also pages 683 & 692.
2 Toner, *What Is Your Will, O God*, 6.

synonymously, though my preference is for the latter because of the unhelpful associations of the terminology of 'God's will' for many people.

The principles and practice of discernment – relationship with God, the contemplative approach, openness to the Spirit, and an attitude of indifference to all alternatives – are basic prerequisites to processes of decision making. I believe that the ways suggested for discernment in decision making are of little value without the preliminary work of noticing and becoming familiar with the ways of God's Spirit and spirits not-of-God in one's whole life, as discussed in earlier chapters. For this reason, most commentators make clear distinction between discernment of spirits and discernment of God's will, insisting on a 'living relationship with God'[3] as the essential foundation of any discernment of God's will. This is consistent with my foundational statement that discernment is primarily about relationship with God, not about decision-making.

Discernment of God's will

Christian decision making, discernment of God's will, is a collaborative process, built on relationship with God. It is not mere discovery of God's will. I find this understanding in several commentators. For example, Edward Vacek develops the collaborative process within the context of a 'mutual love relationship with God' as the basis of all discernment:

> When Christians live out this relationship, the religious question is not primarily *what does God want?* or *what is good for me?* but rather *what*

---

[3] Lonsdale, *Dance to the Music of the Spirit*, 43-4.

> *should we (God and I) do?* or *what is appropriate to our mutual love relationship?* While God is the ontological originator, sustainer and inspirer of this relationship, we also have a contribution to make to its development and fulfilment.[4]

A commitment to knowing and carrying out God's desire does not exempt one from the human activity of listening to, growing awareness of, and interpreting the movements of the spirits in one's inner experience. In any situation, God may well prefer one or other of the alternatives one is facing, but God's preference, God's will, is discovered only through the human work of discernment, described above and applied below. As Toner observes, 'Divine influence supplies us with what no human efforts could possibly achieve, but it does not replace those efforts'.[5]

In much of the writing, the treatment of decision making is more on the level of practical helps, rather than the actual step of making one's decision. For example, Mark Thibodeaux lists 'typical phases' involved in any process of discernment: get quiet, gather data, dream the dreams ('tapping into deep desires'), ponder the dreams ('weighing consolations and desolations').[6] A step often overlooked is gathering the data. It seems an obvious step, but I have witnessed many decisions that had to be reversed for no other reason than that the person did not have all available facts prior to making the decision.

---

4 Vacek, "Discernment within Mutual Love Relationship with God," 699.
5 Toner, *Discerning God's Will*, 38.
6 Thibodeaux, *God's Voice Within*, 152-76.

Mary Margaret Funk offers 'five steps to making a decision'[7] from the monastic tradition:

> We ask the Holy Spirit to help, even to clarify the question we are facing.
> We make a virtual decision, a tentative answer that seems the most likely solution.
> We ask for a confirming sign, as we 'live into' the decision.
> We then make our decision, taking action, even ritualising the decision. And finally, we watch thoughts and guard our heart, especially guarding against second thoughts of doubt or recalculating risks.

Similarly, in working in discernment with women especially, Kathleen Fischer suggests several guidelines to help reflect on one's decisions:

> Listen to your deepest self.
> Affirm your own as well as others' needs.
> Trust the insights that come from your body, intuition and feelings.
> Be aware of the social and cultural forces influencing a situation.
> Interpret your affective experiences in the light of women's social conditioning.
> Try to generate alternatives when you feel trapped.
> Take account of the price of change.[8]

Liebert approaches decision making from different standpoints, finding helps through memory, imagination, awareness of one's body, feeling and reason, and nature. For example, she

---

7   Funk, *Discernment Matters*, 133-9.
8   Fischer, *Women at the Well*, 114-28.

offers practical suggestions like 'imagining how each of the alternatives could work out, one at a time' and 'if your body could talk, what would it say to you about your discernment?'[9] With these helps to decision making, Liebert outlines a seven-step process:

> Seek spiritual freedom, the inner disposition on which discernment rests.
> Discover and name the issue.
> Gather and evaluate appropriate data.
> Reflect and pray.
> Formulate a tentative decision.
> Seek confirmation.
> Assess the process.[10]

Bakke lists similar steps towards making a decision.[11] Silf, in her practical suggestions for decision making in everyday life, adds that one 'consult one's inner wisdom as much as the wisdom of external wisdom people'.[12]

Francis de Sales stresses the basic pre-requisites in Christian decision making. Francis outlined 'a short method to know God's will' in his *Treatise on the Love of God*. He insists that one must wait on God's revelation, be open to whatever God asks, and be prepared to follow God's good pleasure without question. Francis sees the temptation to doubt one's decision as the work of some spirit not-of-God.[13]

---

9   Elizabeth Liebert, *The Way of Discernment* (Louisville, Ky: Westminster John Knox Press, 2008), 56, 96, 134.

10   Ibid., 19-21.

11   Jeannette Bakke, *Holy Invitations: Discovering Spiritual Direction* (Grand Rapids, MI: Baker Books, 2000), 218.

12   Margaret Silf, *On Making Choices* (Oxford, UK: Lion Hudson, 2004). passim

13   Francis de Sales, *Treatise on the Love of God*, chapter 14.

Discernment of Spirits in Christian Decision Making

Accepting these helps to decision making, I now focus on the actual moment of making one's decision.

This is Syd's experience:

> **Syd**, *a young committed scientist, unmarried, was head-hunted and offered a new position in marine biology research, the area of his interest and expertise. The position was in a branch of CSIRO, fully government funded, recently established in Antarctica. Syd sat with the offer for a couple of days and decided that he would accept – even before he had talked with anyone else about this offer of a new job. Syd said 'it just felt right'.*
>
> *Questions came when Syd did begin to tell people. Syd's parents reacted quickly. They reckoned he was crazy: why move to a place called Sorin ('never heard of it!') in that freezing climate. 'It couldn't possibly be good for your health.' Syd's present boss could not understand why Syd would accept such a pay cut. And Syd's cricket mates felt let down: Syd is easily their best batsman and he must know the struggle the team is having even to stay in the competition.*
>
> *Syd came to talk with me, recommended by a mutual friend. He began by saying that he thought he had made a good decision till 'all these objections came up'.*

Syd's dilemma is about how best one makes such an important decision in life, indeed how does one balance one's own preference with others' reactions.

One way of decision making, often encouraged, is to compare the advantages and disadvantages of the options that one faces. Syd could do that easily. This new job offer seems to have more disadvantages than advantages. Indeed, staying in his present position appears to have the advantages – no disruption, a steady salary and certain future, a good social life and good friends. Were Syd to follow this method of making his decision, he may well decide to reject the offer of the new position.

Another way of making decisions is more affective than rational. This way works on the level of inner reactions. Syd had said that 'it just felt right', a phrase that spiritual directors frequently hear. Hearing that and sensing the significance of it, I opted to talk with Syd about this alternative way of decision making – the way, in fact, that he had used. Our conversation continued:

> 'Syd, what are you actually feeling when you say that your decision felt right?' Syd struggled to name his feeling. Words came slowly: 'it felt right... like good and true... maybe I felt at home with the possibility, at ease, comfortable... even contented. It's hard to put words on feelings, isn't it?' 'OK', I said 'so what you are saying is that feeling comfortable and content with the thought of the new job seemed right to you. I wonder what makes it right? Is it a familiar feeling for you? You must have felt this before?' Syd said 'I don't think I have put words on it quite like I have now, but yes, I do know this feeling. Even in little decisions every day, whenever I feel like this, I know I'm in the right place'. I could see that Syd was actually trusting his own past experience, fairly spontaneously recognising that this inner experience, however difficult to articulate, was actually a sign for him of the right way to go. Because it had paid off in the past. This seemed more important to Syd (and to me) than all the arguments for and against such a decision.

Discernment of Spirits in Christian Decision Making

I asked Syd about the different reactions of his friends. He reckoned that he could understand what they were saying and he would certainly want to be sensitive in his helping them to accept his decision. But 'I believe that if this is best for me, it will end up being good for others, too.' 'OK, so where are you now?' I asked. Syd said quickly 'Oh, I'm going. I'm excited about the new possibilities. I'm looking forward to contributing to some worthwhile research.'

In Syd's experience, the two ways of making his decision, the more rational and the more affective, would appear to result in different outcomes. Syd has learned from past experience to 'trust his gut', even though he finds it difficult to explain. In fact, this way of making a decision that Syd followed is quite common. It is very personal. The signs of what is right for Syd are unique to Syd. Others will say 'it's not rational'!

Interestingly, the traditional treatment of ways of decision making in Ignatius Loyola's *Spiritual Exercises* includes both of the possible approaches that Syd faced.

Ignatius Loyola, in fact, offered three ways or 'times' for seeking God's will or making a 'good choice' in life.[14] Ignatius places his teaching on decision making after a succession of meditations that he recommends to ensure that one comes to the decision making exercise quite freely.[15] Ignatius uses the term 'indifference', which he uses also in his 'First Principle and Foundation'.[16] As described earlier, 'indifference' is understood

---

14   Ignatius Loyola, *Spiritual Exercises*, ##175-8.
15   These are the meditations on 'Two Standards' (*Spiritual Exercises*, ##136-148), 'Three Classes of Men' (##149-157), and 'Three Kinds of Humility' (##165-168).
16   Ignatius Loyola, *Spiritual Exercises*, #23.

as freedom from inner attachments, not the everyday understanding of not caring or having no reaction. Ignatius sees indifference as the essential pre-requisite to any process of decision making. Francis de Sales uses the same term in this way.

Most commentators follow Ignatius' teaching on the three ways of making decisions. The only disagreement amongst some is the weighting to be given to any one of the three when making a decision. I discuss this in what follows.

Ignatius Loyola's three ways of making decisions

The first way

In the **first way** suggested by Ignatius, discovered in his own experience,[17] God 'so moves and attracts' one's will that the decision to be made cannot be doubted. Ignatius gives Paul's conversion experience on the way to Damascus and Matthew's responding to Jesus' call as examples of this way of making a decision. Roger Haight suggests that Ignatius' examples are rather too 'supernaturalistic', risking one's overlooking 'ordinary human decisions'.[18] More everyday examples might be a person's clear, unmistakable decision based on some unexpected gift of God in prayer or in a dream, when one 'knows' God's invitation with certainty. My experience affirms that people do sometimes know, without any doubt, the decision they need to make in a particular situation. Haight agrees: 'it is not rare that values, talents, situation and circumstances meet in a constellation that

---

17 Toner, *Discerning God's Will*, 109-10. Toner reflects on Ignatius Loyola's experience recounted in his *Autobiography*, #27
18 Haight, *Christian Spirituality*, 224.

Discernment of Spirits in Christian Decision Making

seems to decide an issue for a person'.[19] Indeed, Houdek claims that this is 'common' experience.[20]

This way of decision making is not strictly discernment, since the decision to be made is abundantly clear: the decision makes itself. The second and third ways of making a decision outlined below are quite different: they rest upon a person's familiarity with the ways of the spirits in one's life and the principles of discernment discussed. In spiritual direction, I experience the second and third ways more frequently than the first way.

Toner raises the question whether any decision made in this first way is an experience of consolation.[21] Toner argues that one cannot necessarily call such an experience consolation because feelings of joy and peace do not necessarily accompany it. His reasoning is valid, but his initial premise is arguable. I believe, rather, that a decision that 'makes itself' and leaves no doubt in the mind of the person is certainly a gift of God's Spirit. In which case, such a decision can be seen as an experience of consolation since it will undoubtedly lead one towards God, irrespective of whether it is accompanied by feelings of joy and peace.

Others, Egan and Manney for example, argue that the gift of such a certain decision may even be an experience of consolation without previous cause.[22] My examples above would appear to support this argument. A good decision need not be accompanied by consoling feelings, as discussed earlier for any

---

19 Ibid.
20 Houdek, *Guided by the Spirit: A Jesuit Perspective on Spiritual Direction*, 129.
21 Toner, *Discerning God's Will*, 114-8.
22 Egan, *The Spiritual Exercises and the Ignatian Mystical Horizon*, 140-1. Manney, *What Do You Really Want?*, 128.

experience of consolation. I believe that this is why Ignatius emphasised one's will, not one's affectivity, in this first way of decision making.

Ignatius' second way

Ignatius' **second way** is based on affectivity, when a decision is made 'through experience of desolations and consolations and discernment of diverse spirits'.[23] This is the most common way for making decisions. In this way, discernment of spirits and discernment of God's will come together. In practical terms, this way involves noticing and listening to the movements of affectivity in one's inner life when prayerfully considering the alternatives one is facing.

I emphasise the value of a guide or spiritual director – ideally a guide who knows one's past experience of the spirits. To appreciate which spirits are operating in their experience, people often need help to understand where their inner movements have originated and where the movements are leading.

Syd's experience above is an example of Ignatius' second way, though without mention of discernment terminology. Syd trusted the affective movement in himself when he gave time to the possibility of accepting the job offer.

Trudy and Tom offer another example in this difficult decision they were facing:

> **Trudy and Tom** talked of how difficult their marriage had been: they had been together for a little over ten years and had tried hard to communicate and share life. When they came to see me, they were both at

---

23   Ignatius Loyola, *Spiritual Exercises*, #176.

the point of weariness: 'we can't do it anymore.' And, they said, this is not the first time we have faced the possibility that we might separate. I asked about the previous times: Trudy and Tom agreed readily that every time they had raised the possibility, one or other of them had said something like 'maybe we haven't tried hard enough – let's give it one more try!' I suggested that it might help to look more carefully at what was going on in them at those times and what is different this time.

As we did that, they were able to say that even though they had been sincere every time they had decided to try harder, and even though it sounds like the 'right thing' to do, the evidence is that those earlier decisions have not been life-giving for them. The evidence is clear: not only are they both exhausted, but their relationship is broken. At home they cope by living quite separate lives. So 'what prompted those earlier decisions?' A mixed bag of 'What will people think if we separate?' 'We will lose friends, for sure.' 'It's a pretty poor show when I just can't get on with someone.' Slowly both Trudy and Tom came to see that they had based their earlier decisions on the false assumption that they are 'bad people' if their marriage comes to an end.

'Is it any different now?' I asked. 'Right now, I don't care what anybody thinks. We have to do what is right for us' said Tom. Trudy was slower in saying: 'Yes, and I think I'm seeing now that what is right for us is right before God, too.' 'What makes you say that, Trudy?' She said she was feeling relief, but also a kind-of 'hope' that she said she hadn't felt for a long time. Tom agreed. They realised that this was the most

> *honest they had ever been in facing separation. They expressed gratitude to one another and in a fairly sombre mood, shared what they acknowledged was a choice for health, happiness, 'new life'. We agreed to meet again soon and talked about some practical matters and where they might go for help with the next step. I urged them not to rush. It seemed to me that they would do well to live with this 'decision' for a little while yet.*

I admired the courage and generosity of this couple. They did not have discernment language – they did not even use God language very often – but they were open and in touch, and they wanted the truth. It was good discernment, based on their growing awareness of their affective responses to the two options they were facing, to keep trying to live together or to separate. Moreover, they came to see that they had been caught out by a spirit not-of-God earlier: their reasons for staying together and trying harder were actually false reasons and had not proved life-giving. This time, they were able to sit with the possibility of separation and notice the different affective movements in themselves, the relief and the hope. They even sensed the direction in which this invitation of God's Spirit was leading them now. I, too, felt confident for their future.

I have learned from experience that the alternatives one is facing in a decision to be made need to be considered *one at a time*, and sometimes over fairly prolonged periods. One needs to sink deeply into each alternative, to live it as though it were the decision already made, and to notice the movements associated with that alternative. All one's previous experience in discernment of consolation and desolation, then, becomes the reference point for interpreting movements associated with living the alternatives of this decision to be made: which alternative 'fits' with what one already knows of the ways of God's Spirit in one's experience and which alternative 'jars'? This proved helpful in both examples, for Syd and for Trudy and Tom.

Rahner has Ignatius express the process in this way:

> When I placed the available possibilities and their potential outcomes before me in light of the impending free choice to be made, I discovered that one option clearly fitted into the wide freedom of God and remained transparent toward him, while the other did not, even though all options could be small signs of this infinite God which, each in its own way, derived from him. While it is difficult to make clear, this is approximately how I learned to distinguish... between what held the incomprehensibility of the infinite God who wanted to be near me and what remained somewhat dark and non-transparent toward God...[24]

One remains 'transparent toward God' via the discernment of one's 'experience of consolations and desolations', in Ignatius' earlier terminology.

When the first alternative obviously sits comfortably with one's personal vocation and one's past experience of consolation from God's Spirit, it may be that in some situations the second alternative doesn't need to be considered at all. Still, even then, spiritual directors usually encourage the person discerning to give time to the other alternative as a way of confirming

---

24   Rahner, *Ignatius of Loyola Speaks*, 19.

one's decision. Indeed, one would always hope for some later confirmation of one's decision, often via the third way, yet to be described.

As mentioned earlier, the awareness of one's personal vocation has immense value in this way of making decisions: even when one has attended to the alternatives of the decision and noticed one's inner movements, one needs a norm against which to interpret the movements. Rahner, Alphonso and Futrell, cited in earlier chapters, emphasise the fundamental consolation of one's life, the 'touchstone' of one's experience as the personal norm for interpreting one's inner movements. This example illustrates the point:

> **Ursula** *is Vietnamese, having come to Australia by boat at the time when many were fleeing their country threatened by Communist take-over. Ursula says she is quite settled now, has a happy marriage and a young family. Somebody we both knew recommended that Ursula talk with me because there was 'a big decision' she was struggling to make: a friend she had met at the kinder invited Ursula to come to church with her one Sunday. Ursula told me that she was a Catholic, but she had married a non-Catholic man and had hardly been to church since that time. On the Sunday she did go with her friend, Ursula said she felt 'really free – accepted with no demands. Free to be myself.' But 'I've offended God by not going for years, haven't I? I'm not worthy to go back now.'*
>
> *I opted first to ask about her feeling free to be herself in church. I said something like 'it must have been a nice feeling when you did go that Sunday?' 'Oh yes, it reminded me of the times back in Vietnam when*

> I was a little girl. I remember feeling like that many times.' Ursula could see that 'feeling free to be herself' is a gifted place for her, a feeling she likes to savour: she said that it's when she feels 'close to God'. Ursula knew this from her past experience.
>
> When Ursula started to think that maybe she could go back to church, predictably, her 'buts' returned. 'Is it true that you have offended God, that you are not really worthy?' I asked. That led us to talk about God's goodness, forgiveness and what we mean by 'sin'. We talked about what it's like to be invited back to church. Ursula was quick enough to recognise that the 'voice' saying she is not worthy is trying to stop her from responding to God again. She made her decision there and then. I suggested that it might be worth our talking again in a few weeks, thinking to myself that several weeks of attending church will surely bring confirmation of her decision.

Reflection on past experience enables Ursula to recognise the invitation of God's Spirit: she knew the sign in herself that tells her when God's Spirit is present and active. It may be that 'feeling free to be herself' is Ursula's fundamental consolation in life: certainly whenever it is present, God is present. Ursula was vulnerable around her 'worthiness', due in part to her misunderstanding of God's goodness and human sin. This was ripe ground for the spirit not-of-God to tempt her away from the invitation of God's Spirit.

This approach to decision making is helpful even in quite mundane experiences of making decisions. I helped a friend to decide which house to purchase in exactly this way. He had been comparing his two possibilities, finding advantages and disadvantages for both, and unable to decide. Only when I encouraged him to sit with his options one at a time, he imagined himself happily settled in one of the houses, not at all concerned that the other house cost less money. Though, interestingly, when the decision was made by noticing affective movements in himself, my friend began to notice also more and more advantages of the alternative he had chosen. In this way, his decision was confirmed. In my experience, a person may well expect that the different ways of decision making will complement and confirm one another. Though personally I had no preference about the two houses, a further confirmation for me was noticing positive energy in myself after the decision had been made. I read this as a sign of God's Spirit in us both.

When decisions are made in this way, discerning one's experience of consolation and desolation, it needs to be said that there is always the possibility of delusion, of mis-reading one's inner experience. I discuss this possibility in chapter 8.

Ignatius' third way

The **third way** of making decisions is needed when a decision has not been made in either the first or the second way. Ignatius says this way is called upon only in a 'time of tranquillity', meaning that there are no affective reactions to the alternatives under consideration. A decision cannot be reached in the second way and so one has to turn to one's 'natural powers'.[25] Still presuming an attitude of openness, and still after honest prayer, one decides which is the 'more reasonable' alternative by weighing the pros and cons, the advantages and disadvantages, of the alternatives.

---

25 Ignatius Loyola, *Spiritual Exercises*, #177.

Though many commentators consider this way of making decisions to be less favoured than the second way,[26] 'of limited usefulness',[27] at best, a 'last resort',[28] some others still question whether it has been undervalued.[29] In my experience, this third way is unsatisfactory when used alone. Invariably, both alternatives under consideration will have advantages and disadvantages. When does one have enough advantages? How many more advantages than disadvantages are needed to make a decision? I am supported in this by Rahner who believes that 'reliance on pure reason is a deficient mode of discerning'.[30] Still, some commentators do present this way as the normal way of making decisions.[31]

There are good arguments for seeing this third way as a useful preliminary step, whatever way one adopts to make one's decision: Larkin[32] and Edwards[33] call this 'cognitive discernment', stressing that before any decision-making, one needs good knowledge of the scriptures, tradition, and all relevant information.

Michael O'Sullivan, too, argues the value of both cognitive and affective approaches to decision making. He believes that, while Ignatius emphasised the affective way (the consolations and

---

26 Nicholas King, "Ignatius Loyola and Decision Making," *The Way Supplement* 24, no. Spring (1975): 57.
27 Larkin, *Silent Presence*, 31, 34.
28 Stefan Kiechle, *The Art of Discernment* (Notre Dame, IN: Ave Maria Press, 2005), 41. Valles, *The Art of Choosing*, 86. Edwards, *Human Experience of God*, 109.
29 Toner, *Discerning God's Will*, 257.
30 Karl Rahner, *The Dynamic Element in the Church* (New York: Herder & Herder, 1964), 103, 08. See also Vacek, "Discernment within Mutual Love Relationship with God," 692.
31 For example, Silf, *On Making Choices*, 75.
32 Larkin, "What to Know About Discernment," 165.
33 Edwards, *Breath of Life*, 161.

desolations of the second way, above), psychological models of decision making focus more on the rational or cognitive. Because cognition and emotion are 'highly interdependent and interactive', having 'both positive and negative influences upon one another', one needs a balanced perspective. For this reason, O'Sullivan concludes with the title of his paper: 'it is all right to trust our feelings as long as we use our heads',[34] favouring some combination of the Ignatian second and third ways of making decisions.

O'Sullivan's conclusion is especially true and helpful when confronting spirits not-of-God tempting via false messages, as discussed in chapter 5. A person's strongest resource at that point is clear thinking in order to counter the false message of the spirit not-of-God. In the earlier examples, Trudy and Tom benefited from such clear thinking. As did Ursula.

One certain value of the third way of making decisions is that it offers a way of confirming decisions made in the second way: when a decision has been made via one's affective movements, as in the second way, often one then realises the many 'advantages' of the decision made, thus confirming the decision. Indeed, Egan is of the opinion that:

> the three times [three ways of making a decision] are not three distinct ways of finding God's will, but actually aspects of one core experience and election in which all three aspects are present in varying degrees of intensity.[35]

---

34   O'Sullivan, "Trust Your Feelings, but Use Your Head: Discernment and the Psychology of Decision Making," 36.
35   Egan, *The Spiritual Exercises and the Ignatian Mystical Horizon*, 152. see also Haight, *Christian Spirituality*, 225. Haight shares this view.

In summary, discernment of God's will normally involves decision making in one or other of three inter-related ways:

First way	A time when God's gift cannot be doubted	The decision 'makes itself'
Second way	A time when one finds affective movements in oneself in relation to the alternatives	Decision is made by noting the inner movements in oneself, the consolations and desolations, when contemplating the alternatives
Third way	A time of 'tranquillity' when there are no emotional reactions to the alternatives	Decision is made rationally, listing pros and cons of the alternatives and weighing against one another

This chapter highlights the essential place of discernment of spirits in Christian decision making, as the previous chapter did in the ministry of spiritual direction. Discernment of spirits is integral to the ministry of a spiritual director. With this background, I now ask 'how does one become discerning?' This is the focus of the chapters that follow.

8

BECOMING DISCERNING: THE GIFT OF FREEDOM

> *God said: Let us make humankind in our image,*
> *according to our likeness.* (Genesis 1:26)
> *Authentic freedom is an exceptional sign*
> *of the divine image in all people*[1].
> *Where the Spirit of the Lord is, there is freedom.*
> (2 Corinthians 3:17)

Based on my experience, I believe that the theory and practice of discernment of spirits is integral to the ministry of spiritual direction. I now examine how a person becomes discerning, arguing that the process of becoming discerning is a process of growth in inner freedom. I begin the argument in this chapter with a practical theology of human freedom, God's gift of freedom and the human experience of limited freedom, unique to each person. In the following chapter, I develop an experiential approach to growth in inner freedom. Growth in inner freedom is the way to become discerning.

---

1   Vatican II, "Gaudium et Spes (Constitution on the Church in the Modern World)," in *The Documents of Vatican II*, #17.

The gift of freedom

In the gift of the Spirit, God's self-giving love endows all creation with life and sustains all creation in its evolving life. Edwards builds on Rahner's theology of creation:

> God chooses to give God's self in love to what is not divine, and so creation comes to be... the central insight of Christian revelation is that God gives God's self to us in the Word made flesh and in the Spirit poured out. This self-giving can be understood as defining every aspect of God's action in creation, redemption, and final fulfilment.[2]

God's loving self-bestowal, in creation, incarnation and redemption, the life of grace and final fulfilment, is seen to be the one divine act. In the moment of creation, the indwelling life-giving Spirit of God enlivens and frees all of God's people, making self-transcendence possible. This is the gift of God's grace: all people are created free.

Essential Freedom

Christian philosophers, psychologists, anthropologists and theologians all agree that to be human is to be free. Inner freedom is the core of a person's identity.

For example, philosopher Max Muller argues that we can never be deprived of our freedom because it is part of our 'equipment' as human beings.[3]

---

2 Edwards, *How God Acts*, 39-40.
3 Max Muller, "Freedom: Philosophical," in *Encyclopedia of Theology: The Concise Sacramentum Mundi*, ed. Karl Rahner (New York: Crossroad, 1975), 535.

Psychiatrist and anthropologist, Luigi Rulla, introduced earlier, makes the same point:

> Freedom is not only a property of our actions, an adjective – it is the *being* of every man. The human species is not simply gifted with freedom as other species are gifted, for example, with fins and with wings; I *am* my freedom.[4]

Ignatian scholar, Roger Haight, commenting on the anthropology underpinning Ignatius Loyola's *Spiritual Exercises,* summarises:

> ...the primary meaning of freedom equates it with the human person itself: a person *is* freedom.[5]

Theologian, Karl Rahner, agrees fully:

> Freedom, precisely speaking, is not the possibility of always being able to do something else, the possibility of infinite revision, but the capacity to do something uniquely final, something which is finally valid precisely because it is done in freedom. Freedom is the capacity for the eternal.[6]

A person *is* freedom. To be human is to be free. Even though the human experience of this inner freedom is limited – some say 'flawed' – my experience suggests that one's essential inner freedom is never lost. Indeed, one glimpses one's essential freedom from time to time. Even in difficult times, one often senses the possibility of acting quite freely.

---

4 Rulla, *Anthropology of the Christian Vocation*, 238. Rulla quotes and affirms this comment on the *Pastoral Constitution on the Church in the Modern World* of Vatican II, but does not acknowledge the origin of the comment.
5 Haight, *Christian Spirituality*, 87, 103.
6 Karl Rahner, "Theology of Freedom," in *Theological Investigations* (New York: Seabury, 1969), VI, 186.

Becoming discerning: the Gift of Freedom

Walter offers this example:

> **Walter** is regular in his spiritual direction. He began without preliminaries: 'Do you remember my telling you about my friend Wes, the fellow who lost his wife tragically, and then lost his job within a couple of months?' I said that yes, I remember, and I remember that you are trying to support Wes as best you can. 'Well, we went to the races last week; I had a good day and won almost $200 – I gave it to Wes. He pocketed the notes, showed no emotion, and didn't even thank me. I was so caught by surprise that I didn't say anything at the time. But since, I've been quite angry – I'm thinking that I need to confront him in some way. What do you reckon?' I said 'Wal, let's talk first about how this affected you'. Walter was quick to say that he felt taken for granted – 'he obviously doesn't appreciate what I do for him. I don't think I should let him get away with that – that would be too much to ask.' I asked 'how do you mean, too much – what makes it too much?' 'Well, Wes is $200 better off and I'm left with nothing – no gratitude, no acknowledgement.' 'And that is important to you?' 'Yes' he said with emphasis, and then stopped himself. Slowly Walter said, 'Do you mean that I could live without being acknowledged and rewarded?' 'Ah, you will have to discover that for yourself, Walter. Would you like to sit quietly with the question, right now?' We did that – for a longer time than I expected – till Walter smiled at me and said, 'I really want to stay with this – something's happening – I feel kind-of lighter.' More than happy to wait, I suggested that we talk about it again next time we meet.

Walter would not have imagined that his support for his friend was motivated by anything other than his desire to help someone who was in need. Yet, his feeling 'lighter' seemed to me to be clear sign of a freer place in Walter when he does not act out of his own unconscious need for affirmation. This is not to deny Walter's genuine conscious care for Wes, but to say that at the same time, his helping his friend is motivated also by some degree of self-interest. The possibility of not acting out of that motivation is real and close: Walter glimpses this and responds. In technical terminology, Walter learns self-transcendence.

Listening to Walter, I recalled Rahner's question in chapter 1: 'have we ever been good to someone who did not show the slightest sign of gratitude or comprehension and when also we were not rewarded by the feeling of having been selfless or decent?' Even granting the possibility that a person might answer this question affirmatively from an unfree place – hence the need for discernment – I see all of Rahner's questions as relevant to self-transcendence:

> Have we ever kept quiet, even though we wanted to defend ourselves when we had been unfairly treated? Have we ever forgiven someone even though we got no thanks and our silent forgiveness was taken for granted?... Have we ever decided on some course of action purely by the innermost judgement of our conscience, deep down where we can no longer tell or explain it to anyone, where one is quite alone?...[7]

Of these questions, the invitation to forgiveness is an experience frequently met in spiritual direction: 'have we ever forgiven

---

7   Rahner, "Reflections on the Experience of Grace," in *Theological Investigations*, III, 89.

someone even though we got no thanks and our silent forgiveness was taken for granted?' When someone has been deeply hurt, often even by a close friend with no intention of hurting and no awareness of having done so, the prospect of forgiveness with no likelihood of recognition can seem daunting. As in Walter's experience, the other person seems to be let off too lightly! Forgiveness is a complex process: the one who forgives experiences a kind of emptiness which, understandably, many people resist. But, in fact, it is a place of freedom, of self-transcendence.

With God's grace, forgiveness becomes possible. With God's grace, Walter finds himself ready and very able to give without counting the cost, without having to be thanked. In this new experience of inner freedom, Walter touches his true identity.

Rahner believes that to answer his questions in the affirmative is to experience God's 'pure Spirit', an experience of grace, the gift of freedom. The possibility of such experiences supports my argument that one's inner freedom is never lost, indeed is always within one's reach. As May says, 'we must always claim the freedom we have been given. To do otherwise would devalue our humanity'.[8] Based on the experience of years in a concentration camp, Victor Frankl claims his freedom in this statement: 'within the limits, however restrictive they may be, man can move freely... The conditions do not determine me, but I determine whether I yield to them or brave them'.[9]

In summary, to be human is to be free. One may lose sight of God's gift of one's essential freedom, for reasons discussed below, but this inner freedom is never lost.

---

8   May, *Care of Mind, Care of Spirit*, 63.
9   Victor Frankl, *Psychotherapy and Existentialism* (New York: Simon & Shuster, 1967), 60.

Freedom as personal identity

What happened for Walter is ordinary enough everyday experience. Life is made up of such choices. The choices that a person makes every day are also choices about who a person wishes to become in life:

> Man is simply not there, he does not simply grow: he has 'to be', he is a task absolutely imposed on himself or what he will be. There is no way in which he can evade this decision.[10]

Freedom by its very nature is the history of a person's coming to be themself, making choices that define who they become. This is a choice for one's 'true self'. As Rulla argues, 'this is not just freedom as self-determination, but is freedom as *self-affirmation*':

> It may be said that Christian freedom is not just a psychic capacity of making a choice of any kind, but is the possibility of realising oneself... this is not just freedom as self-determination, but is freedom as *self-affirmation*, fulfilling the capacity for theocentric self-transcendence which man has received from God.[11]

Such self-affirmation or self-realisation is the fruit of self-transcendence. Going beyond one's self, focusing on the other person is the way to authenticity. Walter's experience can be understood in this framework: his choice to transcend himself and his 'needs' was a choice for his true self, his authentic self. Such choices made by Walter and many other people, are the exercise of and the fruit of God's gift of freedom.

---

10 Muller, "Freedom: Philosophical," in *Encyclopedia of Theology: The Concise Sacramentum Mundi*, 535.
11 Rulla, *Anthropology of the Christian Vocation*, 265.

Becoming discerning: the Gift of Freedom

Moreover, a person's free choices, as affirmations of one's true self, also affirm the love of God in oneself. A person is essentially free, because loved. God's love 'has been poured into our hearts by the Holy Spirit', setting us free. Indeed, when God gifts an individual person, God is gifting all people. For this reason, as discussed earlier, a key sign of the activity of God's Spirit is that it builds communion. (1 Corinthians 12:7) This was named as an essential fruit of the work of God's Spirit: one gifted by God becomes more loving, more open and accepting of others. My mantra throughout is that God's Spirit is relational.

In his exegesis of Paul's writings, Jerome Murphy-O'Connor argues to the communal character of human freedom:

> ... such freedom is not something they possess as individuals, but something in which they share as members of a wider whole... The power of the Spirit which produces freedom is the creativity of love displayed by other members of the community.[12]

The very title of Murphy-O'Connor's book on the pastoral anthropology of St Paul, *Becoming Human Together*, captures this. He believes that the gift of freedom is given and is experienced only in communion with others.[13] One implication of this is that, as one becomes more free, one's awareness of belonging to the community and one's relationships with others will deepen, as evident in experience. Murphy-O'Connor quotes Galatians 5:13 to support his claim that the true use of freedom, in fact its ultimate constituent, is to be 'thorough love servants

---

12   Jerome Murphy-O'Connor, *Becoming Human Together: The Pastoral Anthropology of St. Paul* (Wilmington, DL: Michael Glazier Inc, 1982), 161.
13   Ibid.

of one another'.¹⁴ The importance of this focus on relationships for discernment will be emphasised in the following chapter.

Muller's exposition of the concept of freedom concludes that in the exercise of one's freedom one manifests God's image (*imago Dei*). This is freedom's gift.¹⁵ It is also the theological understanding of the human person, as exemplified in the Vatican Council document *Gaudium et Spes*. As cited at the beginning of the chapter, the Council reiterated that 'we are created in the image of God' and then related this to the exercise of human freedom:

> Authentic freedom is an exceptional sign of the divine image in all people... For God willed that men and women should be left free to make their own decisions so that they might of their own accord seek their Creator and freely attain their full and blessed perfection...¹⁶

One's free choices do indeed affirm one's true self and one's relationships. But these same choices are also gift of God's grace. With this understanding, Rulla and Lonergan both see human freedom is an expression of God's freedom:

> ... the true and ultimate meaning of man is God himself: God is the only being capable of bringing man to the full realisation of himself.¹⁷
>
> We are the fruit of God's self-transcendence, the expression and manifestation of God's

---

14   Ibid., 167.
15   Muller, "Freedom: Philosophical," in *Encyclopedia of Theology: The Concise Sacramentum Mundi*, 534.
16   Vatican II, "Gaudium et Spes (Constitution on the Church in the Modern World)," in *The Documents of Vatican II*, #17.
17   Rulla, *Anthropology of the Christian Vocation*, 148.

benevolence and beneficence, God's glory... as the excellence of the son is the glory of his father, so too, the excellence of humankind is the glory of God.[18]

Freedom, then, is not solely freedom *from* something, some attachment within, but equally freedom *for* goodness, for creativity, for life. Any choice other than truth or goodness betrays God's gift and abuses one's freedom. Freedom does not mean that one can do anything one wishes, good or evil. Congar argues that 'freedom is not a licence dependant on whim – which is an illusory freedom or a caricature of freedom'. A free person 'determines himself from within himself: that is the very definition of freedom'.[19]

Congar quotes Augustine:

> According to Augustine, the Christian into whom the Holy Spirit has poured the love of God will spontaneously observe a law which can be summed up in love: 'He is not subject to the law, but he is not without a law...' The content of the law is the norm for his action, but he is not subjected to the restraints of the law because he has interiorised the law.[20]

The quotation from Rulla earlier in the chapter supports this understanding:

> Christian freedom is not just a psychic capacity of making a choice of any kind, but is the possibility of realising oneself, by choosing that which

---

18   Lonergan, *Method in Theology*, 116.
19   Congar, *I Believe in the Holy Spirit*, II, 125.
20   Ibid.

gives meaning and realisation to one's own life, that is, by choosing the meanings given in the transcendent values of Christ.[21]

Freedom is not licence: it is a sharing in God's life and God's freedom.

Essential freedom and effective freedom

When someone chooses, consciously or unconsciously, to move away from God, to ignore the call of God's Spirit, as described in chapter 5, that person is not *freely* choosing to deny God, but is still bound by some inner attachment. Merton says an evil choice 'destroys freedom', meaning that one's *unfreedom* is compounded by such a choice.[22]

The limitation of one's freedom is called one's *effective* freedom. Kiely explains the limitations of one's freedom that flow from crucial experiences of early childhood.[23] In childhood when capacity to reflect on one's experience is poorly developed, the child is left especially vulnerable to the first experiences of separation or punishment or pain. Affective memory and inner *unfreedoms* all stem from this time of growth.

The human reality is that one is free and unfree at the same time, essentially free, but effectively unfree. With God's grace, one can still grow more fully into freedom, which I discuss in the chapter to follow.

The limitations on one's freedom mean that a totally free choice is rare. The human experience is that one has 'glimpses' of one's

---

21 Rulla, *Anthropology of the Christian Vocation*, 265.
22 Thomas Merton, *Seeds of Contemplation* (Wheathampstead, Hertfordshire: Anthony Clarke Books, 1961), 155.
23 Kiely, *Psychology and Moral Theology*, 242-3.

essential freedom, and with grace, one does actually act freely at times, as Walter realised. But one's limited, effective freedom tends to dominate in most people's experience. Choices made with limited freedom tend to be the rule, not the exception. The critical point is that they are *unfree* choices because of the unconscious factors limiting one's freedom.

This being the case, the term 'free will', as commonly used, is frequently misunderstood. Most people understand that they are free to make their own choices: a choice to go to a movie or to walk on the beach, a choice to complain or to welcome an unexpected visitor, a choice to abuse or to forgive someone who has been hurtful. In truth, how many of those choices are *free* choices? In these daily decisions that confront every person, discernment is called upon because of one's limited freedom. One's places of *unfreedom* influence one's choices. Because these places of *unfreedom* are unconscious, many choices give the appearance of being free, but they are choices for apparent goods, not real goods. My discussion of how one becomes free in the following chapter will speak to this point.

One's essential freedom is the freedom, deep within, with which all people are gifted and towards which all people aspire. When spiritual directors are listening to another's experience, directors are invited to listen from that place of inner freedom.

The human experience of limited freedom

While all people have been gifted with freedom, it is a freedom rarely fully experienced:

> I do not understand my own actions. For I do not do what I want, but I do the very thing I hate... I do

> not do the good I want, but the evil I do not want is what I do. (Romans 7:15)

Freedom becomes something of an ideal, as though removed from one's experience and glimpsed only occasionally. The quotation above from the Vatican Council document *Gaudium et Spes* continued: 'human freedom has been weakened by sin'.[24] Rahner refers to 'the powers of enslavement formed by sin, death and radical selfishness which prevents man from loving God and his neighbour'.[25] These are expressions of the human experience of limited inner freedom. My term, *unfreedom,* introduced in an earlier chapter, captures this human experience. I stress that this experience is not pathological in any sense. It is normal everyday human experience.

Traditional teaching in spirituality acknowledges the experience of limited freedom, often describing the experience in terms of the self-created image of the person that one imagines oneself to be, or the person one thinks one should be. Such a self is self-created, not God-created. It has no basis in reality, no matter how virtuous it may appear or how much time and energy has gone into cultivating it. Keating calls it 'a homemade self that does not conform to reality'.[26] It represents a pseudo freedom that shows itself in emotional habits of behaviour. May argues that one's self-image has a strong influence on one's freedom:

> The image we have of ourselves – one component of 'identity' – deeply affects how we meet the world and the attitudes with which we encounter

---

24 Vatican II, "Gaudium et Spes (Constitution on the Church in the Modern World)," in *The Documents of Vatican II,* #17.
25 Karl Rahner, *Meditations on Freedom and the Spirit* (London: Burns & Oates, 1977), 37.
26 Keating, *The Human Condition,* 14.

images of God. One's image of oneself is no more real than one's image of God. We are at core endlessly mysterious, and our self-images are simply expedient symbols of who we really are. This is true also for our images of God.[27]

In other words, when one approaches God by putting on one's 'best' self-image, one encounters only the unreal God of one's own imagination. Growth in freedom will mean bringing these false images into awareness in order to transcend them.

The term *attachments* is commonly used to describe those areas of one's inner life that are unfree. The usual psychological terminology for 'attachments' is 'addictions':

> Working against (our freedom) is the powerful force of addiction. Psychologically, addiction uses up desire... Spiritually, addiction is a deep-seated form of idolatry. The objects of our addictions become our false gods... To define it directly, addiction is a state of compulsion, obsession or preoccupation that enslaves a person's will and desire.[28]

In different translations, John of the Cross uses several terms for attachments – 'appetites', 'imperfections', 'sensory affections' – when referring to one's lack of freedom:

> ... insofar as a person is purged of his sensory affections and appetites, he obtains liberty of spirit in which he acquires the twelve fruits of the Holy Ghost. He is wondrously liberated from the

---

27 May, *Care of Mind, Care of Spirit*, 66.
28 May, *Addiction and Grace*, 13-4.

hands of his enemies, the world, the flesh and the devil.[29]

Most commentaries on John of the Cross prefer the term 'attachments'.[30] Independently of John of the Cross, Ignatius Loyola refers to 'inordinate attachments',[31] again stressing the lack of inner freedom.

Teresa of Avila used the term 'attachment' explicitly when describing her struggle with conflicting spirits:

> What a terrible mistake, God help me, that in wanting to be good, I withdrew from good... my soul didn't have the strength to reach such perfection alone – on account of some attachments that, though in themselves not bad, were enough to spoil everything.[32]

Teresa names her attachment to 'some friendships' that she imagined she could not live without. She recognised that there was nothing wrong with the friendships, except that she was 'attached' to them. More accurately, her attachment was to some inner dynamic. One's external behaviour is more likely a manifestation of some inner *unfreedom* or attachment.

Augustine was attached to his promiscuous life-style, though again the inner attachment was deeper, presumably to some felt need for pleasure through sexualised nurturance.

---

29 John of the Cross, "Dark Night," in *The Collected Works of St. John of the Cross*, I.13.11. see also "The Ascent of Mount Carmel" I.3.4

30 For example, Gerald G. May, *The Dark Night of the Soul* (San Francisco, CA: HarperSanFrancisco, 2004), passim.

31 Ignatius Loyola, *Spiritual Exercises*, #172.

32 Teresa of Avila, "The Book of Her Life," in *The Collected Works of St. Teresa of Avila*, chapter 23.

Becoming discerning: the Gift of Freedom

Examples in earlier chapters were Gus' withdrawing from his community because 'they don't know me, I don't think they even like me' (chapter 4) and Ken's impulsive decision to quit his job because he wasn't 'being appreciated' by everyone on the staff (chapter 5). Both were unfree around their need for acceptance. Though they were quite unaware of it, they were attached to this need in themselves; this had become their false self image.

I emphasise that the experience is of an inner attachment. Attachments are experiences of *unfreedom* or limited freedom in one's inner life. These attachments or *unfreedoms* in one's inner life become places of vulnerability where spirits not-of-God are more prone to attack, as described in chapter 5.

My examples illustrate that letting go of one's false self-image, transcending one's inner attachments, is not something one can do alone. Often enough, one does not even advert to the existence of the false image. Only cooperation with the grace of God, as discussed in the following chapter, makes growth in inner freedom possible.

This way of understanding human freedom, one's essential freedom and one's limited freedom, raises two questions that need clarification before I discuss how, in fact, one becomes more free and more discerning. Initially, I will outline my understanding of the unconscious and the role of the unconscious in one's experience of limited freedom. Then, following Rulla, I will discuss the anthropology on which I base my approach.

The role of the unconscious

The existence of the unconscious is widely accepted since Sigmund Freud's discovery early last century. Freud developed the concept of unconscious motivation to explain feelings or behaviour which seemed unexplainable by conscious reasons or motives. By definition, the unconscious is inaccessible and cannot be summoned to consciousness by mere force of will.

Freud distinguished between the 'conscious' where a person is immediately aware at any given time, the 'preconscious' from which memories can come readily into awareness (for example, in meditation, in counselling, even in concentrated effort to remember) and the 'unconscious', the largest and most inaccessible area that is deeply embedded below consciousness.[33] May cautions against seeing these as entities or places within the brain: rather, they are 'qualities of mental function'.[34] I use the term 'unconscious' to include everything not in one's conscious awareness.

Many of the dynamics of human relationships – defences, resistances, transferences – are understandable only in terms of the unconscious. For example, there is no other way to explain Anna's resistance, her fear that she would not be acceptable to God (chapters 4 and 6), Ken's unconscious need for appreciation (chapters 4 and 5), and Rose's transference stemming from her unconscious need for love (chapter 6). All of these are examples of unconscious dynamics beyond the person's awareness.

Similarly, there is no other way to explain the everyday examples of someone over-reacting emotionally to an innocent comment

---

33 See Rulla, *Anthropology of the Christian Vocation*, 79-89. May, *Care of Mind, Care of Spirit*, 52-4.
34 May, *Care of Mind, Care of Spirit*, 53.

from another person, or of someone whose same behaviour keeps repeating itself, as in Ken's out-of-proportion reaction to criticism and his tendency to repeat his earlier decision to leave his job.

Looking again at Quinn's experience after his father died (chapter 6), it became obvious – to the spiritual director, but apparently not to Quinn himself – that Quinn was resisting any talk of his father. The 'something else' in Quinn's experience was his unconscious belief that he should not be angry with anyone, an example of the should dictates described in chapter 5. In fact, this turned out to be pre-conscious, close enough to conscious awareness for him to name it quite quickly, once the question had been raised by the spiritual director.

Behavioural inconsistencies arise when there is disharmony between the different levels of personality. This happens, for example, when one's ideals are in conflict with one's needs, the former conscious, the latter unconscious. For some people, these needs are so deeply embedded in the unconscious that they are accessible only via dreams or through free association and slips of the tongue, according to Freud. Post-Freud, psychological therapy also uses creative music and art and numerous psychological tests to tap into the unconscious.

In my discussion of the risks that a spiritual director might misread the signs of the spirits, unconscious emotions were seen to exert major influence, because of their effect on the director's freedom in listening. A spiritual director may not be conscious of their feeling at any one time, not conscious of the processes that gave rise to the feeling, and not conscious of the feeling's connection with past experience. Rulla argued this way:

> The more the emotions are unconscious, the greater their effect in rendering memory and imagination selective. This selectivity limits or preconditions our knowing, deciding, and acting on (our) values... Some will be distorted, others will receive privileged attention, others again will be overlooked.[35]

One's past experiences and their associated repressed emotions make up the bulk of what Arnold calls 'affective memory'.[36] Though some small part of one's affective memory may be conscious, it is because of one's unconscious affective memory that emotional reactions of the past are re-lived. What, in fact, is a past experience of joy or grief or anger is made present in a new situation, distorting its truth. This is a normal and frequent human experience. In my earlier examples, Morrie's anger and hurt (chapter 5) and Rose's emotional attraction to the spiritual director (chapter 6) are examples of this dynamic.

When a spiritual director themself reacts emotionally to a directee's sharing, because of some unconscious memory, the director's emotions are no longer indications of whichever spirit is at work:

> The paralysing effect on freedom may be particularly great in the case of subconscious motivations. (One's) needs and constraints... owe their being to a history of fulfilments and frustrations. But it is a history buried in the unconscious...'[37]

---

35   Rulla, *Anthropology of the Christian Vocation*, 87-8.
36   Arnold, *Feelings and Emotions: The Loyola Symposium*, 187.
37   Luigi M. Rulla, *Depth Psychology and Vocation* (Rome: Gregorian University Press, 1983), 169. Rulla quotes M. F. Kaplan, *Freud and Modern Philosophy* (New York: Meridian, 1957), 219

Unless the spiritual director is aware of the 'constraints' on their freedom – that is, the memories and emotions that are unconscious – their listening will be distorted. There were clear examples of this earlier: a director's feeling bored while listening may well be due to their own weariness, as much as whatever the directee is saying; a director's impatience may well be due to some inner need for achievement or need to be helpful not being met, as much as the directee resisting the Spirit.

If Rose's spiritual director had some unconscious emotional or sexual attraction to Rose, his response to her asking that the conversation focus on the director would have been quite different. Indeed, the response would have come from an unfree place in the director – and been unhelpful. Had Gus' spiritual director (chapter 4) not trusted his own discomfort at Gus' cutting himself off from his brothers, but instead been drawn in an unfree way to Gus' reference to his difficult prayer times, again the response would have been unhelpful. This is developed also in my discussion of the ministry of supervision in chapter 10.

Unconscious needs

Various schools of psychology explain differently the human experience of limited freedom, the unconscious motivations underpinning such experience, and the effect of one's limited freedom on one's way of relating to others. For example, Carl Jung built his work around the concept of the 'shadow', 'the dark side of one's being'[38] or 'the thing a person has no wish

---

38   C. G. Jung, *Memories, Dreams and Reflections* (London: Pantheon Books, 1963), 262.

to be'.³⁹ Others have developed the experience of one's 'false self' or one's self-created self, in contrast to one's 'true self', an approach favoured by Thomas Merton and Thomas Keating:

> The only true joy on earth is to escape from the prison of our own false self, and enter by love into union with the Life who dwells and sings within the essence of every creature and in the core of our own souls.⁴⁰

This self is false because its existence is based on its defending illusions. The core illusion is that the false self imagines itself to be autonomous, the centre of its own meaning, effectively holding a person back from acceptance of God's love.⁴¹ Keating's foundational premise is that 'the contemplative journey is an exercise of letting go of the false self, a humbling process because it is the only self we know'.⁴² This 'letting go' I call 'self-transcendence'.

I find that Luigi Rulla's theory of *Theocentric Self-transcendence*⁴³ speaks directly to my experience, personally and as a spiritual director. Rulla's distinction between one's 'essential freedom' and one's 'effective freedom' gives me a helpful framework in my listening to and interpreting the movements of the spirits in spiritual direction. Rulla borrowed these terms from Lonergan.⁴⁴ He names the two anthropological realities within

---

39   Wilkie Au and Noreen Cannon Au, *Urgings of the Heart: A Spirituality of Integration* (New York: Paulist Press, 1995), 24-42.

40   Thomas Merton, *New Seeds of Contemplation* (New York: New Dimensions, 1962), 17.

41   Thelma Hall, *Too Deep for Words: Rediscovering Lectio Divina* (New York: Paulist Press, 1988), 50.

42   Keating, *The Human Condition*, 19.

43   Rulla, *Depth Psychology and Vocation*. Rulla, *Anthropology of the Christian Vocation*.

44   Lonergan, *Insight*, 619-24, 92-3.

Becoming discerning: the Gift of Freedom

human nature: the possibility of theocentric self-transcendence – the essential freedom with which all humans are gifted – and the various limitations inherent in the human person that tend to obstruct one's freedom to live self-transcendence – one's effective freedom.

The findings of Rulla's research in Christian vocation are consistent with my understanding of the work of spirits not-of-God, tempting a person at a point of vulnerability. (chapter 5) Central to his conclusions is that 'psychodynamic factors may influence the degree of freedom with which the individual is disposed to the action of grace'.[45] The psychodynamic factors are understood to be one's inner 'needs', defined as 'tendencies to act in certain ways'.[46] This is critical in the ministry of spiritual direction and discernment: a person's vulnerability to the temptation of spirits not-of-God flows from this place of limited freedom. When one is attracted to some object or activity because it appears, consciously or unconsciously, to favour one's self-esteem, for example, then self-transcendence is highly unlikely. Rulla's conclusion rings true to my experience in spiritual direction:

> Depth psychology shows that it is possible for a person to desire and to profess the ideals of Christ, while, without being aware of this, he is also driven by subconscious needs which cannot be reconciled with these ideals. Therefore the individual is *inconsistent* in the sense that he is moved simultaneously by two opposed forces: one being the ideals which he consciously desires

---

[45] Rulla, "The Discernment of Spirits and Christian Anthropology," 541.
[46] Rulla, *Anthropology of the Christian Vocation*, 133 & Appendix B.

and the judgement of values which he makes, the other being the deep-lying needs by which he is subconsciously driven.[47]

This psychodynamic theory refers to the unique constellation of one's inner 'needs', resulting usually from early childhood experience. 'Needs' are described as 'innate tendencies... to act in certain ways'.[48] Coping in a less-than-perfect world means that children, understandably, repress the effect on themselves of their early experiences, especially their hurts. This can happen in experiences of mistreatment or abuse, deprivation or even over-gratification. The repression shows itself in later life in unfree patterns of behaviour. For example, someone deprived of affection in early childhood may well experience dependence on other's care and protection in later life, constantly seeking affection in subtle ways. Rulla calls this a need for succorance. This happens especially when the need is unrecognised or unconscious. Or again, someone who was treated harshly as a child, who was asked to obey without question, may well experience a need for submission or possibly a need for abasement in later life, always nervous of authority figures.[49] All people experience these inner needs, needs which in themselves are quite amoral.

Rulla quotes from Murray a list of twenty-two needs that have become evident in human psychological make-up: for example, the need for autonomy, for succorance (to be helped or cared for), for order, for dominance, for achievement, the need for

---

47 Rulla, "The Discernment of Spirits and Christian Anthropology," 546.
48 Rulla, *Anthropology of the Christian Vocation*, 133 & appendix B.
49 Gallagher, *Taking God to Heart*, chapter 3.

submission, etc.⁵⁰ While the constellation of needs is present in all people, different need-strengths and need-patterns emerge, depending on childhood experience. Some needs are more demanding than others, some are in more conscious awareness than others, some are quite unconscious, resulting in blocks to personal freedom.

Not all needs are necessarily negative in their impact. Rulla points out that there may be unconscious needs in a person that actually support the person's commitment to their values.⁵¹ Examples might be an unconscious build-up of healthy aggression or ambition that results from some early childhood experiences, but that now stand a person in good stead.

Ideals represent an attraction to something intrinsically good in itself, whereas needs represent an attraction to something that seems 'good for me'. For both people whose needs conflict with their values and people whose needs seem to support their values, the needs are unconscious and people are not aware of the influence of the inner needs on their behaviour. One's needs show themselves in inner attachments, which leave one unfree.

May argues similarly in his discussion of the human experience of willingness and wilfulness.⁵² Noting an element of *unfreedom* in all human relationships, May argues that all ministerial relationships involve some degree of self-interest, unconsciously and innocently, and some conscious or unconscious preconceptions about what is best for the other person. This applies no less to the ministry of spiritual direction.

---

50 H. A. Murray, *Exploration in Personality* (New York: Oxford University Press, 1938), 152-226. Rulla, *Anthropology of the Christian Vocation*, Appendix B.
51 Rulla, *Depth Psychology and Vocation*, 83.
52 May, *Will and Spirit*, 1-7.

I have stressed already that no one is ever totally devoid of freedom: everyone is free to struggle with whatever limited freedom they possess. May refers to such freedom as 'the bare edge of freedom, insured and preserved inside us by God'.[53] Walter's experience earlier illustrates this ever-present freedom within. But the question remains: how can one become aware of one's *unfreedoms* and how can one become more free in one's relationships? This is the subject matter of the next chapter.

A realistic anthropology

Before moving to the question of how one becomes more free, I clarify the anthropology on which my treatment of growth in inner freedom is based. The same anthropology underpins my approach to formation of spiritual directors.

Rulla insists that any program involving formation for mission must be based on an adequate inter-disciplinary anthropology. Otherwise, the risk is oversimplistic categorising of a person. He points out that there are irreconcilable differences between the anthropologies which underlie psychoanalytic humanistic psychology and an anthropology which is intrinsically Christian. Rulla, in fact, names several psychodynamic theories which are 'inadequate as a general view of vocation and of Christian living, in which we are called to go beyond ourselves, not primarily to a self-realisation centred upon ourselves'.[54]

For example, Freudian anthropology taught that one's personality, one's psychic life, is set in place and is subservient to the power of the unconscious. One cannot change. In which

---

53   May, *Addiction and Grace*, 18.
54   Rulla, *Anthropology of the Christian Vocation*, 18-9.

case, personal freedom and personal responsibility for one's actions are of little consequence. In this way of understanding the human person, personal needs are (unconsciously) repressed, but in fact these needs control one's behaviour. Only sheer will power prevents a life of instinctual gratification of one's inner needs. This is a rather pessimistic anthropology: such pessimism negates the freedom of the children of God and limits any possibility of growth in freedom.

At the other extreme, the humanistic psychology of Carl Rogers[55] believes that human growth is guaranteed to blossom in the right conditions. Rogers and others emphasise 'positive self-regard', self-realisation and self-fulfilment. In this understanding of the human person, consciousness dominates: one's psychic life is identical with one's conscious life, leaving few limitations to a person's freedom. The good is what one wants. Though the human capacity for creativity and intimacy is emphasised, there is no recognition of the limited nature of human freedom, in which case there is little possibility of any real formation. Self-fulfilment can lead to self-centredness, individualism and what is effectively pseudo growth.

Self-realisation and self-fulfilment are laudable enough goals in the pursuit of a worthwhile existence as a human being, but a Christian anthropology insists that they are not ends in themselves, meaning that they are not goals that a Christian person works to achieve for oneself. Rather, they are fruit of one's call to freedom for self-transcendence in love. To place self-fulfilment as a primary motive for embracing a life committed

---

55   Carl Rogers, *On Becoming a Person: A Therapist's View of Psychology* (London: Constable, 1961).

to Gospel values, in fact, would be a contradiction of the Gospel value of self-transcendence.

The Christian anthropology that Rulla himself develops he calls 'realistic'.[56] This anthropology accepts the truth that 'to be human is to be free', even though the human experience of freedom is limited because of pervasive influences, conscious and unconscious. To be 'realistic' is to be able to acknowledge one's biases, one's *unfreedoms*.[57] But self-transcendence leads to greater inner freedom and the integration of one's needs with freely chosen values. An essential characteristic of Christian anthropology is self-transcendence, not self-fulfilment: 'those who lose their life for my sake will find it'. (Matthew 10:39) I use the terminology of self-transcendence, rather than the oft-misunderstood terms 'self-denial' and 'self-sacrifice'.

Rahner presumes this same anthropology in his theology, seeing the human person as ultimately oriented towards transcendence:

> Orientation towards ultimate Mystery is a foundational characteristic of being human... to be human is to be open to the possibility of God's self-communication... the communication of God's own self.[58]

This realistic anthropology honours both God's gift of freedom and the human experience of limited freedom. Moreover, it recognises the possibility of growth in inner freedom through self-transcendence.

---

56   Rulla, *Anthropology of the Christian Vocation*, 22-5.
57   Lonergan speaks of 'critical realism', transcending 'long-ingrained habits'. See Lonergan, *Method in Theology*, 239-40.
58   Steinmetz, "Thoughts on the Experience of God in the Theology of Karl Rahner," 2.

Becoming discerning: the Gift of Freedom

Rulla sums up this way of looking at the human person by saying that 'ultimately the call to follow Christ is the necessary development and unfolding of what man has always been, a free person determined by his very nature to live with Christ'.[59] Indeed, Jesus' total surrender to God was the source of his deep freedom and deep love:

> Freedom is the presupposition of love and is fulfilled in love. One who is free can love, can lose himself for the good of the other, as Christ has done for us. The greater the freedom of a person, the more complete can be his/her donation, his/her slavery of love.[60]

Growth in inner freedom through self-transcendence, which is to say growth in humanity, is possible because of Jesus' utter fidelity to his humanity.

To understand one's true humanity, the starting point is the person of Jesus, not one's own limited experience of humanity. Because Jesus lived his humanity freely and fully, in complete authenticity, it is in relationship with Jesus that one discovers how one is invited to live an authentic life, born of freedom.

Sebastian Moore paraphrases Paul's hymn in Philippians 2:6-8 to capture Jesus' living his humanity faithfully and freely:

> Jesus, being in the form of God (as all humans are) did not translate this into being for himself (as all humans do), but on the contrary took our humanness on in an extraordinary way, its true way, a way of total self-dispossession, of freedom from ego, in which (upsetting all our

---

59 Rulla, *Depth Psychology and Vocation*, 48.
60 Rulla, *Anthropology of the Christian Vocation*, 247.

ideas of what befits divinity) he made manifest the ultimate mystery that itself is poor, for-all, has no possessions, makes rank meaningless... which fact became fully manifest in Jesus raised from the dead and receiving the name beyond all names.[61]

Jesus' 'emptying himself' was his choice to live his humanity fully and truly. This is humanity's 'true way', free of inner attachments, transcending inner 'needs', letting go of any self-focus or self-promotion. This is the way that Jesus lived, graced by God.

Murphy-O'Connor uses the same realistic anthropology when he insists that living humanly and freely is possible for all humans, precisely because one human being, Jesus, lived his humanity faithfully and fully.[62] Jesus Christ is the model of authentic humanity. Human people risk judging what it means to be human on their own limited experience of humanity, rather than on Jesus' experience.

Murphy-O'Connor gives the analogy of one human person walking on the moon, another conquering Mount Everest and another running a mile in less than four minutes. These achievements were thought to be humanly impossible, till Neil Armstrong walked on the moon, Edmund Hillary and Tensing reached the summit of Everest, and Roger Bannister ran the four-minute mile. Since, many people have achieved the same feats. In one person's break-through, humanity now knows the possibility. Murphy-O'Connor concludes that because Jesus lived his humanity truly and fully, then it is possible for all humanity:

---

61   Sebastian Moore, *Jesus, the Liberator of Desire* (New York: Crossroad, 1989), 42.
62   Murphy-O'Connor, *Becoming Human Together*, 45ff.

> Because (Jesus) lived under the same historical conditions of time and space as we do, the mode of existence displayed by Jesus Christ remains a perpetual challenge to an attainable standard.[63]

Just as Jesus' oneness with God was the source of his freedom, so too the source of all people's freedom is oneness with God. Focusing on oneness with God and on Jesus' living his life and his humanity fully and freely grounds my discussion of ways to help human growth in freedom in the next chapter.

The starting point is that God created all people free. God desires freedom for all and always works towards freedom for God's people. All people aspire to this freedom and know that, with grace, it is within reach, because of Jesus. The theological axiom from Thomas Aquinas, 'grace perfects nature', sometimes translated as 'grace builds on nature',[64] is the reminder that God's grace makes growth in freedom possible, whatever stage of human and spiritual development one has reached and however free or unfree one is in one's life. The gift of God's grace is inner freedom, the fullness of humanity.

Cooperation with this grace of God can be quite demanding. Gerald May believes it 'may be the greatest struggle any human being can face, and it may call forth the greatest courage and dedication... It is, after all, the pure, naked aspiration of the human soul toward freedom and, through freedom, to love'.[65] May summarises that 'the joy and beauty of freedom and love must be bought with pain'.[66] Growth in inner freedom, freedom from one's unconscious attachments or needs, is painful

---

63 Ibid., 56.
64 Thomas Aquinas, *Summa Theologica*, vol. VI: Nature and Grace.
65 May, *Addiction and Grace*, 19.
66 Ibid., 117.

because even when one is aware of one's inner needs, the needs still crave to be met.

Based on a realistic Christian anthropology, this chapter argues that, even though one's effective freedom is limited, one's essential freedom is never lost. Growth in freedom is always possible.

> Do not be conformed to this world, but be transformed by the renewing of your minds, so that you may discern what is the will of God, what is good and acceptable and perfect. (Romans 12:2)

In the following chapter, I discuss how growth in inner freedom comes about, with God's grace. I argue that, as a person becomes free, they becomes discerning.

Becoming discerning

The process of becoming discerning rests on growth in inner freedom. Yet, the possibility of and the dynamics of this growth in inner freedom have been given little attention by commentators on spiritual direction and discernment. Some do grant the possibility. Some even take for granted that growth in inner freedom will happen in spiritual direction:

> In its purest form, spiritual direction is a journey towards more freely and deeply choosing to surrender to God.[67]

> Spiritual direction is a singularly appropriate ministry to help us to overcome our fears and egocentrism.[68]

---

67 May, *Care of Mind, Care of Spirit*, 63.
68 Barry, *Spiritual Direction and the Encounter with God*, 5.

> The whole purpose of spiritual direction is to penetrate beneath the surface of a man's life, to get behind the facade of conventional gestures and attitudes which he presents to the world, and to bring out his inner spiritual freedom, his inmost truth, which is what we call the likeness of Christ in his soul.[69]

At the same time, a spiritual director does well to keep in mind how this movement towards inner freedom happens. Such awareness can suggest a particular focus for a person's prayer and for the spiritual direction time. The authors quoted do not discuss this aspect of spiritual direction. It is the subject matter of the following chapters.

It needs to be said also that in many instances, more than spiritual direction is needed to encourage the growth presumed in the above quotations. There are particular approaches in both spirituality and psychological therapy that help to promote growth in inner freedom. For example, at times when some form of psychological therapy is more likely to be needed than spiritual direction, therapists have developed techniques to help others touch unconscious memories and emotions. A therapist may encourage and expose transference when this occurs in the therapy, or work with music and art therapy, etc. With the person's active cooperation, God's grace works through these processes to expose what I have called one's 'false self-image'. I consider these and other possible approaches in what follows.

---

69 Merton, *Spiritual Direction and Meditation*, 8.

9
BECOMING DISCERNING: GROWTH IN INNER FREEDOM

> *Jesus, being in the form of God (as all humans are)*
> *did not translate this into being for himself (as all humans do), but*
> *on the contrary took our humanness on in an extraordinary way, its true way;*
> *a way of total self-dispossession, of freedom from ego,*
> *in which (upsetting all our ideas of what befits divinity)*
> *he made manifest the ultimate mystery*
> *that itself is poor, for-all, has no possessions, makes rank meaningless...*
> *which fact became fully manifest in Jesus raised from the dead*
> *and receiving the name beyond all names.*[1]

The previous chapter explored the basic Christian vocation to inner freedom:

> For you were called to freedom, brothers and sisters – only do not use your freedom as an opportunity for self-indulgence. (Galatians 5:13)

> Where the Spirit of the Lord is, there is freedom. (2 Corinthians 3:17)

---

[1] Moore, *Jesus, the Liberator of Desire*, 42. This is Moore's paraphrase of Philippians 2:6-8

Becoming discerning: Growth in inner freedom

In this chapter, I consider how a person becomes discerning, based on a spirituality and psychology of growth in inner freedom. In particular, I study this growth in the experience and the teachings of John of the Cross and Ignatius Loyola. I draw the implications of these ways of becoming discerning for formation programs for spiritual directors.

Growth in inner freedom

A focus on relationships

Just as human *unfreedom* shows itself most obviously in relationships, growth in inner freedom comes about also in relationships, relationships with one another and relationship with God. Initially, I discuss the experience of how human relationships normally develop. Then I argue to a parallel experience in the development of the human relationship with God.

I agree with May that all human relationships suffer from some degree of self-interest or *unfreedom*.[2] As discussed in the previous chapter, the human experience of limited freedom, one's *unfreedom*, can be understood in terms of one's unconscious inner needs. When one's inner needs are brought into conscious awareness, the possibility of transcending one's needs becomes real. One learning from experience is that awareness in itself does not ensure growth in freedom. Only the sometimes painful choice to transcend one's needs and embrace one's Gospel values ensures freedom. This choice is gift of God's grace. The learning that mere awareness of one's inner dynamics does not

---

2   May, *Will and Spirit*, 1-7.

bring about change in a person is basic to growth and formation in discernment.

There is a psychological base for the development of human relationships, but with psychiatrist Gerald May, I believe that such development is essentially spiritual:

> With all its technological advances, neuroscience is yet to produce a cure for addiction. Nor has medical science been able to replace the essential spiritual nature of recovery from addiction.[3]

May illustrates his point by noting that the spirituality of the 'Twelve Step' program of Alcoholics Anonymous so obviously portrays 'the transition from personal effort to spiritual receptivity that it might well have been written by Teresa [of Avila] or John [of the Cross].'[4]

I refer back to earlier examples: Fred's experience (chapter 4) was seen as an example of desolation when he was tempted to finish his seminar after someone in the group had criticised his work. Similarly, Ken's experience (chapter 5) in deciding to quit his school chaplaincy was discussed as an example of how spirits not-of-God tempt at one's vulnerable spot, in Ken's case, his need to be appreciated by everyone on staff. At the time, neither Fred nor Ken even considered the possibility that he could continue his ministry even though some people had been critical of his work. To continue to relate to people who have been critical would be painful for them, because both Fred and Ken are attached in some way to the comfort of their inner needs being met. But, at least now in retrospect, one can acknowledge that possibility. And how wonderfully freeing it

---

3   May, *The Dark Night of the Soul*, 160.
4   Ibid.

would have been for these men to transcend their inner needs in this way. Their way of relating to the group or staff would change noticeably. My experience in similar situations suggests that they would become more compassionate and more caring of others.

There are similar opportunities for self-transcendence for many people almost every day, particularly in one-to-one relationships: for example, in the challenge to remain faithful in a strained relationship. In the previous chapter, Walter's experience illustrated not only the possibility of transcending his *unfreedom,* but also the real possibility of acting from a truly free motivation. As well, other examples of the possibility are suggested by Rahner's question: 'have we ever been good to someone who did not show the slightest sign of gratitude or comprehension and when also we were not rewarded by the feeling of having been selfless or decent?'

This transcendence is well described by Rulla:

> Self-transcendence, besides being a gift, is also the final result of a personal conquest, which can be reached only gradually by a long personal journey of active cooperation with divine grace.[5]

Rulla speaks of both the possibility of self-transcendence, with grace, and what he calls the struggle to live self-transcendence, because of unconscious areas of *unfreedom.* Other commentators use different terminology to describe the same human experience.

Sebastian Moore writes of 'dying to ego' or 'dying to one's present ego-consciousness' to describe this movement towards

---

5   Rulla, *Anthropology of the Christian Vocation,* 145.

inner freedom. Moore describes how one's sinfulness tries to prevent one's dying to ego, keeping one in places of *unfreedom*, in the same way that spirits not-of-God work in a person, as I describe earlier. Moore highlights Jesus' different experience: 'the fully liberated human being, Jesus, is one in whom the death to ego proceeds with more vigour, undeterred by sin'.[6] Moore argues to his understanding of Jesus' experience by paraphrasing Philippians, quoted at the head of the chapter. Jesus is the 'liberator of desire', the title of Moore's book.

Carmelite Constance Fitzgerald calls the experience the 'transformation of desire':

> (This transformation is) the movement from a desire or love that is possessive, entangled, complex, selfish and unfree to a desire that is fulfilled with union with Jesus Christ and others... desire is not suppressed or destroyed, but gradually transferred, purified, transformed, set on fire... we are challenged to make the passage from loving, serving, 'being with', because of the pleasure and joy it gives us, to loving and serving regardless of the cost.[7]

The passage from being with another for the sake of the pleasure it gives to loving for the other's sake, I call self-transcendence. I identify this movement in the examples above.

---

6   Moore, *Jesus, the Liberator of Desire*, 37.
7   Constance Fitzgerald, "Impasse and Dark Night," in *Living with Apocalypse*, ed. Tilden H Edwards (San Francisco, CA: Harper & Row, 1984), 97-8. Constance Fitzgerald is an American Carmelite Sister.

Fitzgerald wrote a development of her understanding some years later.[8] Again based on John of the Cross, she discussed the transformation or the purification of memory. She says that 'the difficulty is that memories can lead us to either healing and empathy or hostility and destruction'. Arguing that the human experience is frequently some attachment to one's memories (as 'props'), Fitzgerald says that memory needs to be 'deconstructed' or purified as a further way to inner freedom:

> I strive to be faithful to and in solidarity with those who continue to remember indescribable violation and at the same time I am receptive to the transforming power of hope that deconstructs memory and to the fathomless Mystery coming to us from the future.[9]

With John of the Cross, Fitzgerald sees this growth in inner freedom applying to both one's painful memories and one's more positive memories, the consolations of one's life. She argues that the purification comes about in contemplative prayer: a person is 'dispossessed'. This is the prayer John describes as 'dark night', which I discuss below.

Gustave Thibon describes the same experience as 'the purifying of love', which he argues is normal and necessary in all relationships. He writes specifically of what he sees as common experience for married couples.[10] Thibon believes that love can be quite unrealistic in its early stages. Invariably there comes a time when 'the lover seems to have plumbed the depths of the

---

8 Constance Fitzgerald, *From Impasse to Prophetic Hope: Crisis of Memory*, vol. 64, *Catholic Theological Society of America* (2009).
9 ibid., 27 & 31.
10 Gustave Thibon, *Love and Marriage* (London: Burns & Oates, 1962). Thibon (1903-2001) was a French philosopher who published extensive works on human experience.

beloved', when one begins to doubt the other, even criticise the other. In reality, it is merely 'his own depths he has plumbed, the depths of his self-enclosed ego'.

> ... the slow discovery of the reality of the loved one destroys little by little the inner idol of the loved one, the idol that was none other than the idealised projection of the self, the image of what the lover himself lacked.[11]

I have met this in my own experience as a spiritual director: I recall a married man telling me that 'she (his wife) is not the woman I married anymore'. When this happens in a relationship, it can be a time of disillusionment, even crisis, indeed a time when some marriages break down. In fact, the idiosyncrasies that this husband was beginning to notice in his wife had always been there. The true change was that he was now seeing his wife more truly, not as someone he imagined or wanted her to be. In Thibon's words:

> Love is then at the crossroads. The flesh and the ego can no longer find sustenance in the loved one. There must be an intervention of the soul in all its depth and purity; otherwise love dies...[12]

This is the moment when love is 'purified'. If this man continues to love in spite of the disillusionment, he learns to love the other, his wife, for herself. Thibon describes the experience as 'a new joy, the solemn joy of self-surrender, silent and imperishable'.

Thibon is describing, rather more graphically than in the experience of most relationships, the purification of love that he says is normal experience. At the same time, it needs to be said

---

11 Ibid., 104ff.
12 Ibid.

that some relationships do collapse, as couples grow apart. The experience of Trudy and Tom discerning their future (chapter 7) is an example of this.

From a different standpoint, Rosemary Haughton describes the same experience. She writes in the context of conversion, offering the example of a person who is converted through an encounter with someone of quite different background and values:

> ...it is at this moment (of conversion)... that he is reconciled to *himself*, to this newly stripped and worthless and unlovely self, for it is in realising the complete worthlessness of all that he had thought worthwhile, in the rejection of all this as loathsome and futile, that he discovers his real value.[13]

Haughton's experience parallels my defining conversion as transcending one's needs, indeed transcending one's very self. Bernard Lonergan expresses this conversion in terms of unrestricted and unconditional love: one's being becomes 'being-in-love'.[14]

This is the self-transcendence that I have described in my examples. It permeates the writing of all of the authors quoted. William Johnston, writing on Christian prayer, summarises: 'nothing is more important in the Christian life than self-transcendence'.[15]

---

13   Rosemary Haughton, *The Transformation of Man: A Study of Conversion and Community* (Springfield, IL: Templegate Publishers, 1980), 97.
14   Lonergan, *Method in Theology*, 105.
15   William Johnston, *Being in Love: The Practice of Christian Prayer* (London: Harper Collins, 1988), 132.

I believe that such self-transcendence is the way to become more free in relationships, free to see, to love another truly without self-interest, even unconscious self-interest. For the psychologist, this is normal human development; for a person of faith, it is gift of God's grace. In turn, I argue that such growth in inner freedom is the way to become more discerning.

Different approaches to growth in freedom

Ted Dunn, a clinical psychologist, has written about 'some of the ways to work toward greater interior freedom.'[16] These are Dunn's ways:

- ease the defences that constrict your truth and conceal self-knowledge
- return to your touchstone faith experiences – those moments and places in your life where you best meet God
- play with possibilities, think outside the box, and suspend your judgment
- explore your own resistance in order to gain insight and become freer from it
- visualise what liberation would look like beyond the struggle, to be radically free

Dunn's suggestions are helpful on a practical level, but he does not address actual growth in inner freedom. How does a person actually grow in inner freedom?

Funk uses the term 'afflictions' to describe the experience of *unfreedom,* quoting Benedict and Cassian. She lists

---

16 Ted Dunn, "Interior Freedom: A Reflective Guide and Exercise," *Human Development* 33, no. 2 (2012): 3-10.

consciousness of food, sex, things, anger, dejection, *acedia* (weariness of soul), vainglory, and pride as the classic 'afflictive thoughts'.[17] Discernment for Funk is the process of sorting out these thoughts in order to 'root out' or 'refrain from' what is afflictive. Though she encourages the practice of lectio divina as a prayer support in one's effort to root out affliction, Funk does not speak of how a person grows in inner freedom.

'To form a discerning mind', Mark McIntosh, too, quotes from several early writers to emphasise the need to 'become aware of the pre-conceptions and urgencies' in one's thinking (Origen), the need to be open to 'the Divine more' (Cassian), to be 'attuned to God' in contemplation (Evagrius) and 'conversion to God's love' (Catherine of Siena). The human need is clear, but again there is no discussion of the process of growing in inner freedom.[18]

Liebert emphasises the need to approach any discernment with an indifferent heart, free from 'addictions, compulsions and inordinate desires', and recommends conscious prayer for the gift of inner freedom.[19] Liebert urges regular prayer with the Awareness Examen on a personal and communal level to help growth in awareness of God's activity. She notes, as I have discussed earlier, that 'discernment becomes a way of life' as one becomes more 'fine-tuned' to God's ways through this practice.[20]

When Lonsdale treats one's 'needs and desires', he concludes that the invitation is to grow in awareness: if one knows one's inner needs, their 'power is reduced' and they are less likely to

---

17 Funk, *Discernment Matters*, 13.
18 McIntosh, *Discernment and Truth*, 83-90.
19 Liebert, *The Way of Discernment*, 33-4.
20 Ibid., 35.

affect one's behaviour.[21] This is true in my experience: awareness of one's vulnerability does seem to reduce its power for one is then free to make choices. But one remains vulnerable to the temptations of spirits not-of-God. The inner needs in one's make-up still exist. Confirmed in experience, one remains vulnerable, even as one grows in inner freedom. One knows the need for God's grace, even still, as the apostle Paul discovered in his experience. (2 Corinthians 12:7-9)

I turn now to John of the Cross and Ignatius Loyola, trusting Rahner's words that 'we must put our trust in another freedom, not a threatening one, but a saving one'.[22]

John of the Cross

Based on sound psychology and spiritual experience, John of the Cross speaks with some authority on God's ways of inviting growth in inner freedom.

John of the Cross teaches that the normal development of any relationship is a process of 'purification' (in some translations, 'purgation') of one's desire and one's love for another person.[23] John called the experience of being purified a 'dark night', when one is quite helpless to change what is happening, indeed when one barely understands what is happening. In Spanish, John uses the word *oscura*, translated as 'dark'. The English word 'obscure' suggests also that the experience of a dark night is beyond one's understanding. Moreover, it is a place of waiting where one does not know the outcome. Au calls it 'liminal

---

21 Lonsdale, *Dance to the Music of the Spirit*, 83-84.
22 Rahner, *Meditations on Freedom and the Spirit*, 18.
23 John of the Cross, "Dark Night," in *The Collected Works of St. John of the Cross*, I.8.1-2.

space: the gap created by the dissolution of the old and the yet-to-emerge new'.²⁴

John's soul-friend, Teresa of Avila, knew this waiting experience well. Teresa described her need for purification quite graphically when she spoke of how unfree or 'bound' she experienced herself, and how utterly unable she was to do anything about it. In such an experience, step two of Alcoholics Anonymous' Twelve Step program, referred to above, is the conviction that 'a power greater than ourselves' is needed if we are to be freed from our attachment. Teresa's expression for the same realisation was that she hadn't seen 'how little benefit it is if we do not place our trust in God'.²⁵ She says her only prayer was 'begging' God, needing God, but having to wait on God. This was her time of 'purification' or 'transformation of her desire', her growth in inner freedom.

That John of the Cross is speaking of his own experience is evident when he writes of this experience in his poem *The Living Flame of Love*:

> Flame, alive, compelling / yet tender past all telling / reaching the secret centre of my soul / since now, evasion's over / finish your work, my Lover / break the last thread, wound me and make me whole.

> Burn that is for my healing / wound of delight past feeling / ah, gentle hand whose touch is a caress / foretaste of heaven conveying / and every debt repaying / slaying, you give me life for death's distress.

---

24   Au and Au, *The Discerning Heart*, 208.
25   Teresa of Avila, "The Book of Her Life," in *The Collected Works of St. Teresa of Avila*, chapters 8, 9, 23.

> O lamps of fire, bright-burning / with splendid brilliance, turning / deep caverns of my soul to pools of light / Once shadowed, dim, unknowing / now their strange, new-found glowing / gives warmth and radiance for my Love's delight.
>
> Ah, gentle and so loving / you wake within me, proving / that you are there secret and alone / your fragrant breathing stills me / your grace, your glory fills me / so tenderly your love becomes my own.[26]

John is describing both the purification via the 'flame' and the freedom, the wholeness, the 'tender' love.

Fitzgerald adds that 'in the very experience of darkness and joylessness, in the suffering and withdrawal of accustomed pleasure, transformation is taking place'.[27] The transformation or purification taking place is that one is being freed of inner attachments, a purification that Keating calls 'divine therapy'.[28] John's teaching is that the experience of dark night is a time of growth, personally and relationally. Later, in his poem *The Dark Night*, John calls it 'sheer grace'.[29]

When speaking of 'beginners', John of the Cross says:

> God introduces them into the dark night... There, through pure dryness and interior darkness, God weans them from the breasts of their gratifications

---

26   John of the Cross, *Centered on Love: The Poems of Saint John of the Cross*, 22-3.
27   Fitzgerald, "Impasse and Dark Night," in *Living with Apocalypse*, 97.
28   Thomas Keating, *Open Mind, Open Heart* (New York: Continuum, 1999), 93. Keating, *The Human Condition*, 33.
29   John of the Cross, *Centered on Love: The Poems of Saint John of the Cross*, 12.

and delights... by means of the purgation of this night.[30]

Moreover, John says, the experience comes upon a person with little warning:

> It is at the time they are going about their spiritual exercises with delight and satisfaction, when in their opinion the sun of divine favour is shining most brightly on them, that God darkens all this light and closes the door of the sweet spiritual water they were tasting as often and as long as they desired...[31]

> At this time, God does not communicate himself through the senses as He did before, by means of discursive analysis and synthesis of ideas, but begins to communicate himself through pure Spirit by an act of simple contemplation...[32]

John of the Cross' particular interest in describing the experience of dark night is the transition from meditation to contemplation. What John calls 'meditation' is the discursive prayer where a person exerts more effort in prayer and has more control of their prayer. In contrast, 'contemplation' is characterised more by being present and open to God. I have encountered this experience of transition many times in spiritual direction. For example, with Xavier:

> *Xavier* came for spiritual direction because he was worried that he must have offended God in some way. When I asked where that concern had come

---

[30] John of the Cross, "Dark Night," in *The Collected Works of St. John of the Cross*, I.7.5.
[31] Ibid., I.8.3.
[32] Ibid., I.9.8.

from, Xavier said 'all my spiritual life seems to have dissolved – I've lost interest in the journal writing I used to enjoy of an evening, I don't seem to be able to settle to reading my spiritual books, and honestly I just can't pray anymore'. 'How do you mean, you can't pray? What happens when you try to pray?' Xavier told me that he was in the habit of spending time with Gospel stories, often the daily reading from Mass, he would reflect on Jesus' words and the way he healed and cared for people, almost always finding some message for himself or some application to his own life. 'That doesn't seem to happen anymore.' 'So what do you do now?' I asked. 'Well, for a while I tried to work out what had gone wrong – and couldn't, so now I just sit there quietly, wanting God, hoping something will happen.' On a first visit, I chose to say no more than words of encouragement to Xavier to keep 'sitting there, wanting God'.

Xavier's experience has all the elements of a dark night: it is obscure, he cannot understand the change in his prayer and, as often happens, he thinks something is wrong and tends to blame himself. Xavier is left dry and empty, with nowhere else to turn, but he still wants God. John of the Cross emphasises that the ever-present desire for God is the surest sign that God is active in the person's experience, that nothing has 'gone wrong'. Xavier is being set free – even from attachments he didn't know he had. As in the earlier examples of human relationships, his relationship with God is being purified, freed, clearly by God's grace.

Becoming discerning: Growth in inner freedom

In my ministry of spiritual direction, I hear directees speak of an unexpected distaste for more meditative or mental prayer. People report that there is no pleasure in their prayer, no feeling, no devotion. John of the Cross describes this experience as 'such dryness that they not only fail to receive satisfaction and pleasure from their spiritual exercises and works, as they formerly did, but also they find these exercises distasteful and bitter'.[33] Often I hear a concern in people that this is their own fault. But just as often, I hear some sense of being invited to stay still and trust God in the darkness. Though the experience is described as darkness or emptiness – 'nothing much happens in prayer' – I am convinced that this is far from the reality. Indeed, Merton adds an important postscript:

> The absence of activity... is only apparent. Below the surface, the mind and will are drawn into the orbit of an activity that is deep and intense and supernatural, and which overflows into our whole being and brings forth incalculable fruits.[34]

My experience as spiritual director with many people in similar situations confirms this view.

Though Merton, too, wrote primarily about contemplative prayer, I believe that the dark night experience described by John of the Cross and Merton can and does happen in all relationships in a person's life. John says that this is a normal developmental process, which may well be expected to happen for all people in some way. May argues:

> Regardless of when and how it happens, the dark night of the soul is the transition from bondage

---

33 Ibid., I.8.3.
34 Merton, *Seeds of Contemplation*, 188.

> to freedom in prayer and in every other aspect of life... we find an ever increasing freedom to *be* who we really are in an identity that is continually emerging and never defined.³⁵

Moreover, John points out that the purification of the dark night doesn't happen once and for all: it is an ongoing process. And though it may be dark and joyless, sometimes quite painful, he says that it is the way desire is purified and freed. It is a time of consolation. John of the Cross says that 'the delicateness of delight felt in this contact is inexpressible'.

> I would desire not to speak of it so as to avoid giving the impression that it is no more than what I describe. There is no way to catch in words the sublime things of God which happen in these souls. The appropriate language for the person receiving these favours is that he understand them, experience them within himself, enjoy them, and be silent.³⁶

I see Yvonne's experience as precisely what John of the Cross is describing, a process of purification towards growth in inner freedom:

> When **Yvonne** came to me for retreat, she told me that she usually prays a kind of centering prayer. Yvonne prayed with the mantra 'My Lord and my God' to the rhythm of her breathing. I suggested that she continue that on retreat – maybe she could pray like that a few times a day. 'OK', she said, 'but I'm not much good at it – and nothing much seems to happen.' 'Well, let's trust

---

35 May, *The Dark Night of the Soul*, 132-3.
36 John of the Cross, "The Living Flame of Love," in *The Collected Works of St. John of the Cross*, 2.21. This is from John's commentary on the poem.

that God will still find ways to bless you this week' I responded.

Sure enough, when we talked each morning, 'nothing much' had happened for Yvonne, except to say that she was content to be praying as she was, enjoying a daily walk on the beach and listening to music of an evening. About day four, Yvonne told me that she had listened to Mahler's Resurrection Symphony the previous evening. Though she knew the music well, last night was a whole new experience. 'When the chorus reached the words "what you have longed for is yours", I was so overwhelmed with love, I wasn't sure whether I was crying or laughing. I have never experienced so many tears, happy tears!'

After considerable silence, as Yvonne still wiped the odd tear, I asked her what is uppermost in her heart now. Her response surprised me: 'I feel small... and inadequate... it is such a gift, no way can I lay claim to that.' Acknowledging that, I encouraged Yvonne to continue with her centering prayer.

The follow-up on the next morning turned out to be further gift. Yvonne said that she had gone back to prayer as usual, even while very aware of her inadequacy. Later she found herself re-living a time when she had been poorly treated by her boss at work. 'What I see differently now is that I had been laying claim on his acknowledging me – as if I have to be acknowledged. He was certainly ungrateful, but I don't have to be acknowledged by all and sundry, do I?' I replied 'It sounds like you are in a freer place?' 'Yes, that's the word, said Yvonne – 'I do feel free. I know that this tendency to look for acknowledgment is a

> *weak spot for me and it may kick back at me, but I can see it clearly now. I'm sure I can manage it. And I certainly want to keep up that prayer time.'*

For Yvonne, God's grace of new freedom was fruit of her faithful prayer. Even though it seems that little was happening in her prayer, as Merton says, 'the absence of activity is only apparent.' Afterwards, Yvonne became aware of the shift that had in fact happened for her.

John of the Cross goes on to say that the experience of purification in the dark night is a sharing in Jesus' own experience, modelled on and shared with Jesus:

> A man makes progress only through imitation of Christ, who is the way, the truth, and the life… Because I have said that Christ is the way and that this way is a death to our natural selves in the sensory and spiritual parts of the soul. I would like to demonstrate how this death is patterned on Christ's…[37]

John's picture of the darkness that Jesus knew in his life and death emphasises that no one is alone in the experience of 'dark night'. John could well have quoted Hebrews:

> Because he himself was tested by what he suffered, he is able to help those who are being tested. (Hebrews 2:18)

> Although he was a Son, he learned obedience through what he suffered; and having been made perfect, he became the source of eternal salvation for all who obey him. (Hebrews 5:8-9)

---

37   John of the Cross, "The Ascent of Mount Carmel," in *The Collected Works of St. John of the Cross*, II.7.8-9.

Jesus continues to live his dying and rising in human lives still.

Keating, following John of the Cross, claims that the process of purification is best helped by the regular practice of Centering Prayer. One grows in inner freedom through such contemplative prayer, as did Yvonne. Using his terminology of 'divine therapy', Keating calls this a therapy for 'the tyranny of the false self'.[38] Keating argues:

> What matters is fidelity to the daily practice of a contemplative form of prayer such as Centering Prayer. This gradually exposes us to the unconscious at a rate that we can handle and places us under the guidance of the Holy Spirit... The contemplative journey, because it involves the purification of the unconscious, is not a magic carpet to bliss. It is an exercise of letting go of the false self...[39]

Keating calls this 'the divine project': 'Only God could have thought it up'.[40] False images, hidden agendas, inner attachments, *unfreedoms,* any unconscious tendencies to control or manipulate God's work will all be revealed in such faithful prayer. Keating says that the alternative to such growth in inner freedom is that one hears only what one wants to hear – anathema to a spiritual director.

I believe that all contemplative prayer promotes the same process of purification. Thelma Hall, for example, makes a similar claim when discussing *lectio divina*.[41] In contemplation,

---

38 Keating, *The Human Condition*, 33.
39 Ibid., 20.
40 Ibid., 42.
41 Hall, *Too Deep for Words*, 29-31.

when one is honestly open to God's work, anything not-of-God will be exposed.

Green is quite mistaken in his belief that the dark night is an experience of desolation.[42] This is the very opposite of the teaching of John of the Cross. Toner also describes John's dark night as an experience of desolation, consistent with his definition of desolation as anything that feels painful, but in an appendix, he discusses in detail the contrast between John of the Cross' experience of 'dark night' and Ignatian 'desolation'.[43] The teaching of John of the Cross, the understanding of consolation and desolation presented here, and the experience of spiritual directors all affirm the grace of an experience of 'dark night'. It is indeed a time of consolation.

Because it is an experience of grace, it bears good fruit. My experience of the fruits of a dark night experience is that, as one is purified, one comes to know others more truly, as they are in themselves, not judged by one's own likes and dislikes. And one comes to know God more truly, not as one may have imagined God. In other words, one moves from loving or being with others because of any satisfaction or affirmation received, rather to loving and ministering to others for *their* sake. One becomes more truly loving, as described earlier in Fitzgerald's phrase 'the transformation of desire'. I have named this consistently as the fruit of the work of God's Spirit.

Iain Matthew names three fruits of the experience of dark night: it is a journey into truth, it develops a deep sensitivity to other people's pain, and it 'releases' a person for love:

---

42 Green, *Weeds among the Wheat*, 126 (footnote).
43 Toner, *Discernment of Spirits*. Appedix II

Becoming discerning: Growth in inner freedom

> (Night) means no longer being slave of a too-demanding self-image, knowing, not because we have been told it or read it or tried to convince ourselves of it, but because we *know* it, knowing that of ourselves we are nothing. That is freedom...
>
> Night softens the 'brittleness' towards others, which comes from being full of ourselves. When we know ourselves as we are, we can be mellow, 'gentle' John says, towards God, towards ourselves, and towards others...
>
> Night brings a knowledge of our truth which eases us off our self-importance and releases us for total love.[44]

May instances Teresa of Avila in making the point that 'often the liberation results in a remarkable release of creative activity in the world'. The same conclusion emerged in my discussion of the psychological approach to developing relationships. These are the fruits that flow from and confirm God's work.

In summary, John of the Cross' experience and teaching on the experience of 'dark night' stresses the gift of God's grace. Though the experience comes about beyond one's conscious control, even without one's awareness, one is being freed from attachments and compulsions and enabled to live and love more freely. In ministry, one is able to listen to another in a contemplative way, without ulterior motive. May's summary is true to my experience:

> (The dark night) is the secret way in which God not only liberates us from our attachments and idolatries, but also brings us to the realisation of

---

44 Matthew, *The Impact of God*, 63-4.

our true nature. The night is the means by which we find our heart's desire, our freedom for love.[45]

I develop below how such growth in inner freedom is the first step in any process of becoming discerning.

Ignatius Loyola

Ignatius Loyola is equally concerned with growth in freedom. Though there are different understandings of Ignatius' intent in writing the *Spiritual Exercises*, Rulla argues that the varying opinions come together in 'promoting an interior disposition of liberty in decision or election, which makes possible an ever closer imitation of Christ'.[46]

Indeed, some Ignatian commentators interpret the *Spiritual Exercises* precisely as 'a way to freedom'.[47] English and Haight are typical examples:

> *Spiritual Exercises* sharpen our awareness of this love (the love of God poured into our hearts by the Holy Spirit) and of the Spirit's presence making us free... Freedom is one of the fundamental graces of the Spiritual Exercises.[48]
>
> All the elements of the *Exercises* are marshalled toward breaking the attachment to things that constrict human freedom, allowing reflection on values and feeling for ideals to attract freedom... and finally taking hold of the self in a decision

---

45 May, *The Dark Night of the Soul*, 67.
46 Rulla, "The Discernment of Spirits and Christian Anthropology," 537.
47 Maureen Aggeler, "Women's Metaphors for Freedom," *The Way Supplement* 70, no. Summer (1992): 20.
48 English, *Spiritual Freedom*, 30-3.

that changes, reorients or rededicates a person's trajectory.[49]

Ignatius has in common with John of the Cross a focus on the experience of Jesus Christ, in communion with God. John's insistence on imitation of Christ is paralleled by Ignatius' desire for a felt knowledge of Christ Jesus through contemplation of Jesus in Gospel scenes.

In my ministry as a spiritual director, even in ongoing spiritual direction (not necessarily when directing the Ignatian *Spiritual Exercises*), I have often encouraged the prayer called 'contemplation of Jesus' which Ignatius recommended in the second and third weeks of his *Spiritual Exercises*. I believe that this Ignatian prayer bears fruit in growth in inner freedom.

For example, this is Zoe's experience:

> *Zoe has made several directed retreats with me. She is committed – Zoe works in diocesan youth ministry – and has deeply experienced God's love in her life. She began this retreat telling me that she had been thinking lately that she needed to be more like Jesus if she is to continue in her ministry. I suggested that the best way for that to happen might be to spend more time with Jesus and to get to know Jesus better. Yes, she would like to do that. On the second day, I suggested to Zoe that all she needed to do was simply be with Jesus (not worrying about implications for ministry), listen to him, watch him, notice how he reacts to people and to situations – what I call 'contemplating Jesus'. Sometimes you will find yourself moved or affected in some way, maybe reacting to something Jesus says,*

---

[49] Haight, *Christian Spirituality*, 49-50.

maybe attracted to something. Zoe picked up on this prayer beautifully. On different occasions, she told me how she had been drawn to Jesus' ease with people he didn't actually know, frightened by Jesus' words to the rich young man, even shocked by Jesus' silence before false accusations. Zoe had consistently taken her reactions back to Jesus and found herself talking with Jesus often. Quite near the end of her week's retreat, Zoe told me that, like Jesus, she knew she didn't have to be so worried about how she came across to people, what people thought of her, even what I thought of her! We talked about what that might be like for her, back home and back in ministry. Zoe reckoned that it was possible as long as she stayed with Jesus.

Without mention of inner attachments, Zoe has experienced a new growth in freedom through contemplation of Jesus. As described above by John of the Cross, Zoe has been invited into Jesus' own freedom. She would be the first to admit that she could not have come to this by herself, just as she recognised that she could not sustain her new awareness by herself.

This is the Ignatian way to growth in inner freedom. As a person contemplates Jesus in his life and ministry, wanting 'to know you more clearly, love you more dearly, and follow you more nearly',[50] God's Spirit leads the person gradually, almost imperceptibly, into more intimate relationship with Jesus. Growth in inner freedom, letting go of even unconscious attachments, happens as the relationship with Jesus deepens and is 'purified'.

---

50   A prayer based on Ignatius Loyola's prelude beginning the second week, *Spiritual Exercises*, #104

In his study of the Ignatian *Spiritual Exercises*, English describes such experience:

> As he works his way through (the exercises), he may gradually dispose himself to gain freedom... The basic thrust of indifference and detachment... is not so much leaving all things, as finding a person, the person of Jesus Christ. It means being so dominated by love for Christ that he is free of all else.[51]

Merton's earlier comment when referring to John of the Cross' teaching that 'the absence of activity is only apparent'[52] is relevant here. In fact, as in Zoe's experience, God's activity gifting the person with growth in inner freedom, beyond any human activity, is quite powerful – and shows itself in the subsequent fruits in Zoe's life.

As further confirmation of Ignatius' intent, Haight highlights other significant meditations that Ignatius placed into the weeks of focusing on relationship with Jesus. Haight argues that the meditations on 'Two Standards',[53] 'Three Classes of Men',[54] and 'Three Kinds of Humility',[55] are designed to challenge a person's freedom and invite to deeper commitment to the way of Jesus. Haight comments that these meditations emphasise commitment to following Jesus and conclude with 'a loving attachment to and identification with him'.[56]

---

51 English, *Spiritual Freedom*, 46-8.
52 Merton, *Seeds of Contemplation*, 183.
53 Ignatius Loyola, *Spiritual Exercises*, ##136-47. Haight, *Christian Spirituality*, 170. Haight renames this meditation 'Two Types of Life'.
54 Ignatius Loyola, *Spiritual Exercises*, ##149-57. Haight, *Christian Spirituality*, 191. This meditation is renamed 'Three Types of People'.
55 Ignatius Loyola, *Spiritual Exercises*, ##165-8. Haight, *Christian Spirituality*, 211. This meditation is renamed 'Three Ways of Commitment'.
56 Haight, *Christian Spirituality*, 212.

It is after these meditations that Ignatius introduces his meditation on 'Making a Choice of a Way of Life'[57] and his teaching on decision making, described in my chapter 7. For only then does he see a person free to make such decisions.

Having seen how one becomes free, in what follows, I discuss how one lives in a discerning way, once free. I then consider the implications for formation of spiritual directors. Several norms for an approach to formation emerge in order to ensure that formation programs promote growth in inner freedom and the living of a discerning way of life.

Being self-reflective: a discerning way of life

Growth in inner freedom bears fruit in a person's deeper self-awareness and easy familiarity with the ways of God's Spirit and spirits not-of-God in oneself. One lives a discerning way of life when this awareness is so integrated that honest loving response to God's invitation in one's everyday life becomes second nature. Indeed, 'Ignatius was interested in building, not a *process* of discernment, but rather a *person* of discernment.'[58] Such a person lives the fruits of the Spirit (Galatians 5:25): they are more loving, kind, patient, by nature.

When God asked Solomon 'what should I give you?' (1 Kings 3:5), Solomon asked for 'an understanding mind'. The Scriptural passage says that God was pleased that Solomon did not ask for something for himself, like power or riches, but had asked for the ability to discern between good and evil. God seems to be saying that the gift Solomon asked for and that God gave to

---

57 Ignatius Loyola, *Spiritual Exercises*, #169.
58 Thibodeaux, *God's Voice Within*, 151.

Becoming discerning: Growth in inner freedom

Solomon, a wise and discerning mind,[59] was not a gift *for himself*. Like all of God's gifts, the gift of wise discernment, given to an individual, is given so that others too will benefit. I have seen this in my ministry. Discerning people seem to be able to hold lightly the gifts God has given to them. Indeed, they have grown in inner freedom.

John of the Cross does not have any formal teaching on discernment, though his principles are clear in a response he wrote to a community of sisters who had asked his advice about one of their members who was claiming special religious experience. John wrote of the 'five defects which reveal that hers is not a good spirit':

> First, it seems that she has within her spirit a great attachment to possessing things... Second, she is too secure in her spirit and has little fear of being inwardly mistaken... Third, it seems she has the desire to persuade others that her experiences are good... Fourth, the effects of humility do not appear in her attitude... Fifth, the style and language she uses doesn't seem to come from the spirit she claims...[60]

In contrast, the indicators of a life lived 'in the spirit' that John of the Cross expects are detachment, openness, unpretentiousness, humility, and simplicity. John is speaking of the inner freedom that comes from the Spirit of God. Indeed, John's classic work, *The Dark Night*, which I discussed above,[61] is precisely on this point.

---

59 The Jerusalem Bible's translation is 'a heart wise and shrewd'.
60 John of the Cross, "Censure and Opinion," in *The Collected Works of St. John of the Cross*, 683-4. This is thought to have been written in the year 1588.
61 John of the Cross, "Dark Night," in *The Collected Works of St. John of the Cross*.

Persons who live in a discerning way are free people, people free to love. Such people are in tune with the Spirit, they 'respond to what is good and true connaturally, congruently, by second nature. They resonate with what is of God, because they are of God'.[62] Their freedom or detachment shows itself in the way they relate to other people, to their ministry and to the struggles and joys of life. They appear to be more human, more deeply joyful and balanced, more 'likely to engender trust', just as they themselves trust the ever-present grace of God.[63]

Hans Urs von Balthasar describes a person of discernment as 'the Christian man of prayer (who) has reached a certain finality of disengagement from himself and his expectations of experience... After all, the Holy Spirit wants nothing else than to form Christ in us'. (Galatians 4:19)[64] Similarly, Frank Houdek calls such a free person a person 'of spirit'.[65]

This inter-connection between growth in freedom and becoming discerning is argued by numerous commentators. For example, Bakke speaks of 'an underlying way of life, a *habit* (of discernment).'[66] In the same vein, Larkin writes:

> Integration follows from self-knowledge and self-acceptance. Integration is wholeness, each part in its place and all parts seen in the context of the whole. It is healing. It occurs because I know myself, my whole self which reaches all the way into God... It is self-possession, consolation,

---

62 Larkin, *Silent Presence*, 29-30.
63 Barry and Connolly, *The Practice of Spiritual Direction*, 123-4.
64 Hans Urs Von Balthasar, "Reflections on the Discernment of Spirits," *Communio* 7 (1980): 206.
65 Houdek, *Guided by the Spirit: A Jesuit Perspective on Spiritual Direction*, 124.
66 Bakke, *Holy Invitations: Discovering Spiritual Direction*, 217.

Becoming discerning: Growth in inner freedom

openness, freedom, detachment, indifference, a trusting spirit, and all the other fruits of the good Spirit. The integration we speak of is the work of grace.[67]

Dubay's succinct conclusion is that 'Only the spiritually mature, the fully purified and converted are able to discern fully'.[68]

These commentators support my argument that one becomes discerning as one grows in inner freedom. Just as growth in inner freedom is gift of God's grace, fruit of attentive waiting on God in contemplative prayer, so too is discernment. A key word in the description of a discerning person is 'integration'. The discerning person, the discerning spiritual director, has integrated learnings and growth in freedom to the point where their relationships and responses to another are spontaneous and free. My initial definition of discernment called this integration 'connaturality':

> Discernment is defined as 'the process by which we examine, in the light of faith and in the connaturality of love, the nature of the spiritual states we experience in ourselves and in others'.[69]

Edwards refers to a person's 'instinctive affinity (connaturality) for the things that are of God'.[70] In other words, discernment becomes second nature.

I emphasise that the process of becoming discerning and living a discerning way of life is a gift of God's grace. Cooperation

---

67 Larkin, *Silent Presence*, 46, 60.
68 Dubay, *Authenticity*, 60.
69 Malatesta, "Introduction to Discernment of Spirits," in *Discernment of Spirits*, 9.
70 Edwards, *Human Experience of God*, 107.

with grace asks a commitment to growing in awareness of one's unfreedoms or inner attachments and to changing one's habitual behaviour flowing from the places of unfreedom. It is in this context of living one's freedom that John of the Cross urged 'denial' of one's 'inordinate appetites',[71] and Ignatius Loyola encouraged acting against (*agere contra*) one's 'inordinate attachments'.[72] Andre Louf argues that this is the proper understanding of 'fasting' in the Christian tradition: fasting from one's addiction.[73] Only gradually, as one builds new habits of behaviour, discernment become connatural.

Fidelity to a contemplative way of prayer, openness to God, and deep desire to become free make possible a discerning way of life and ministry.

Implications for the formation of spiritual directors

The key question for formation programs for spiritual directors is not so much how to teach discernment, but how to create a learning environment which encourages and enables growth in inner freedom and the process of becoming a discerning person.

If discernment is integral to the ministry of spiritual direction and if one becomes discerning as one grows in inner freedom, as outlined above, then several implications for the formation of discerning spiritual directors follow. For a formation program to foster growth in discernment in the program's participants, I argue that the program needs to be contemplative, relational

---

71 John of the Cross, "The Ascent of Mount Carmel," in *The Collected Works of St. John of the Cross*, 19.2 & 11.1. Matthew, *The Impact of God*, chapter 7.
72 Ignatius Loyola, *Spiritual Exercises*, ##16 & 157.
73 Andre Louf, *Teach Us to Pray* (London: Darton, Longman & Todd, 1974), 82-6.

(person-focused), experiential and transformative, norms which flow from the argument of the previous chapters.

I develop these principles for formation in the following chapter and I apply them to formation programs for spiritual directors. I use examples from the *Siloam* program of formation to illustrate how the principles take concrete shape in a formation program.

10

FORMATION OF SPIRITUAL DIRECTORS

In its purest form, spiritual direction is a journey towards more freely and deeply choosing to surrender to God.[1]

With few exceptions, those who ministered as spiritual directors for others prior to 1970s relied on their own experience of God's presence in their lives, maybe some spiritual reading, and their inner wisdom. Directees generally trusted the wisdom figures in their lives. Formal formation programs for spiritual directors were rare.

Even though adequate programs for formation of spiritual directors existed in Australia and overseas, the conference of Leaders of Religious Institutes in Australia was concerned that many of their sisters and brothers were being guided by incompetent, unprepared spiritual directors. In mid-1990s, the Religious Leaders asked a chosen group to investigate ways of accrediting spiritual directors in Australia. This small group, of which I was a member, grew into the Australian Ecumenical Council for Spiritual Direction (AECSD) in the year 2000. After

---

1 May, *Care of Mind, Care of Spirit*, 63.

Formation of Spiritual Directors

years of reflection and consultation, the Council determined that the only way to ensure that spiritual directors were equipped for the task was to set standards for their formation and ethical norms for their practice. The first document of these standards was launched in 2005.[2] It was revised and renamed Guidelines in 2008[3] and a further revision entitled *Contemplatively Forming Tomorrow's Spiritual Directors* was published in 2015.[4] The accreditation of a spiritual director to minister comes from their graduation from a recognised program of formation.

The Australian Ecumenical Council for Spiritual Direction lists four key formative elements to ensure effective formation of spiritual directors:

- Applicants need to be suitably assessed
- Content and process of formation need to be comprehensive and integrated
- Ongoing processes of assessment need to be in place
- Members of the formation team need to be well qualified and competent

These elements are developed in the later document, with a strong emphasis on a contemplative ethos and practice. There is no discussion of discernment in these documents.

To my knowledge, there is no literature on the experience of creating a formation program for spiritual directors and

---

2 AECSD, *Standards for the Formation of Spiritual Directors* (Melbourne, Vic: 2005).

3 AECSD, *Guidelines for the Formation of Spiritual Directors* (Melbourne, Vic.: 2008).

4 AECSD, *Contemplatively Forming Tomorrow's Spiritual Directors* (Melbourne, Vic.: 2015).

minimal literature on the principles that might give shape to such a formation program. One exception is my own writing on the occasion of twenty-five years of the *Siloam* formation program. I detail the content of the program, its approach to formation, and the integration of personal formation, ministry as a spiritual director, and discernment of spirits.[5]

Two significant books deserve mention because they were written by spiritual directors while conducting a formation program. Both were written some years after the beginnings of the formation program, *Siloam*, but emphasise the same principles of formation.

Barry and Connolly's *The Practice of Spiritual Direction* lists the centrality of religious experience, focusing on the relationship with God, fostering a contemplative attitude, noticing inner reactions, and evaluating religious experience as principles on which their program was founded.[6] Their treatment of discernment is concerned solely with norms to 'evaluate religious experience'. They do not discuss the work of spirits not-of-God.

The other book is *Sacred is the Call*, edited by Suzanne Buckley, with several chapters written by spiritual directors and supervisors involved in formation programs, principally at Mercy Centre in Burlingame, CA.[7] Again, the book is not concerned with the creation of the program, but the articles offer suggestions around essential aspects of a formation

---

5   Brian Gallagher, "Twenty-Five Years of Siloam," *Presence* 12, no. 4 (2006). See also Heart of Life Centre, *Application to AECSD for Siloam's Recognition as a Formation Program* (Melbourne: Heart of Life, 2007).
6   Barry and Connolly, *The Practice of Spiritual Direction*.
7   Suzanne M. (ed.) Buckley, ed. *Sacred Is the Call* (New York: Crossroad, 2005).

program. These include contemplative listening, sensitivity to inner movements to hear God's voice, working with resistance, integrating psychology and spirituality, the place of and focus of supervision, etc. There is no mention of discernment of spirits.

A 2014 issue of the periodical *The Way* included several articles by spiritual directors who were involved in formation (often called 'training') of spiritual directors. Michael Smith writes of training in an academic environment,[8] Robert Marsh is concerned with teaching spiritual direction,[9] Ruth Holgate describes her experience in training spiritual directors by observation of and feed-back on their practice,[10] and Paul Nicholson argues for apprenticeships for spiritual directors.[11] Again, discernment of spirits is not discussed in any of these articles.

Holgate acknowledges that her way of 'training' spiritual directors 'is not without its critics, who see spiritual direction more as a charism than a skill that can be taught'. I am one of her critics. I speak of formation of spiritual directors, not training spiritual directors. The terminology of 'training' spiritual directors suggests that one can learn how to be a spiritual director. I believe strongly that spiritual direction cannot be taught as a skill. My approach is rather that one becomes a spiritual director as one grows in inner freedom and ability to discern the spirits.

---

8   Michael Smith, "Forming Spiritual Directors through an Academic Course," *The Way* 53, no. 4 (2014): 45-55.

9   Robert R. Marsh, "Teaching Spiritual Direction as If God Were Real," *The Way* 53, no. 4 (2014): 57-67.

10   Ruth Holgate, "Training Spiritual Directors," *The Way* 53, no. 4 (2014): 68-78.

11   Paul Nicholson, "Forming Spiritual Directors: Training Programme or Apprenticeship?," *The Way* 53, no. 4 (2014): 79-87.

In my experience of formation of spiritual directors, the key question for formation programs is not so much how to teach discernment, but how to create a learning environment which encourages and enables growth in inner freedom and the process of becoming a discerning person.

I believe that formation is a personal, dynamic, developmental reality. Its aim and its outcome are not pre-determined, not static, not measurable. For formation is essentially about personal growth, conversion, *trans*formation.

The Australian Ecumenical Council for Spiritual Direction gives some guidelines to help programs of formation. In their most recent document, the Council recommends that any program 'be structured as a transformative, developmental process'.[12] This is detailed in their earlier document on guidelines for formation:

> Integral to the personal growth component are the nourishment of a prayerful and contemplative approach to life, self-awareness and sensitivity to the movements of the Spirit. Personal experience and growth is the most important source of knowledge for the person training to be engaged in the ministry of spiritual direction...
>
> The process of spiritual direction requires appropriate relationships between directors and their directees. Therefore emphasis on the development of personal self-awareness and relational openness of the student is an essential requirement in formation.[13]

---

12   AECSD, "Contemplatively Forming Tomorrow's Spiritual Directors," #6. see also John Auer et al., "Contemplatively Forming Tomorrow's Spiritual Directors," *Presence* 22, no. 4 (2016): 50-6.

13   AECSD, "Standards for the Formation of Spiritual Directors," 2 (d).

These recommendations fully support my approach to formation. Formation to become a discerning spiritual director requires the *internalisation* of Gospel values, a process quite different from learning the values or complying with the values. Fidelity to a contemplative way of prayer, openness to God, and deep desire to become free make possible a discerning way of life and ministry.

In the previous chapter, I name several implications for formation of discerning spiritual directors: if a formation program wishes to foster growth in freedom and discernment in its participants, the program needs to be contemplative, relational (person-focused), experiential and transformative. I develop these norms for formation in what follows.

The contemplative way

The contemplative approach to spiritual direction, to supervision, and to growth in inner freedom permeates my ministry and my writing. The contemplative way focuses on God's work in a person's experience, noticing and interpreting the signs of the spirits. As described earlier, John of the Cross insisted that God's Spirit is the true director in spiritual direction. John considers the greatest mistake for a spiritual director is to tamper with God's work. Gerald May and Leonard Doohan both refer to John's image of roughening God's painting:

> From their writings, it is clear that Teresa and John felt the most prevalent error of spiritual directors was trying to do too much, meddling with the precious work of God in a soul. When this happens, John says, it is like a beautiful and exquisite

painting being roughened and discoloured by a 'crude hand' that knows nothing of art.[14]

The focus of spiritual direction then becomes the way God is at work in individual directees.

The contemplative approach is recommended not only in the practice of spiritual direction, but also in supervision and formation of spiritual directors. The earlier discussion of personal vocation emphasises the uniqueness of each person before God. Each spiritual director is unique before God, a uniqueness that is revealed only gradually in the supervisor's contemplative working with the spiritual director.

As emphasised throughout, in the contemplative approach, focusing on what God has done/is doing in the life experience of the other person, spiritual directors begin to notice movements in themselves, even while fully attentive to the other person. Their response in spiritual direction flows from this contemplative way of listening, not from any judgment about what the director thinks the other person needs, let alone any pre-conceived ideas in relation to the other person. This applies equally to the ministry of supervision.[15]

The relational, person-centered way

Growth in relationships is a key fruit of the Spirit of God. Relationships are never static. All of the spiritual directors'

---

14   May, *The Dark Night of the Soul*, 169. Leonard Doohan, "John of the Cross and Spiritual Direction," *Presence* 22, no. 1 (2016): 38. See John's own commentary in John of the Cross, "The Living Flame of Love," in *The Collected Works of St. John of the Cross*, 3.42.

15   See, for example, Paul F. Castley, "Supervision: A Contemplative Approach," *Presence* 5, no. 2 (1999): 25-30. and Janet Ruffing, "An Integrated Model of Supervision in Training Spiritual Directors," *Presence* 9, no. 1 (2003): 24-30.

relationships will be relevant to their formation: relationships with those to whom they minister, with their peers in the formation program, with their supervisors, and with God. All of these relationships will be influenced by unconscious inner needs, the *unfreedoms* that a person carries, all will be subject to the normal development of a relationship described by John of the Cross, and all will contribute to a person's growth during their formation. Moreover, all can be reflected upon contemplatively.

As one or other relationship is challenged in the formation process, its gradual 'purification' (John of the Cross' word) will affect all other relationships. The supervisor's task is to encourage integration of the many different ways in which the person being supervised is invited to growth.

Moreover, a person's call to be a spiritual director is discerned within the context of relationship with God. The ministry of spiritual direction is a charism, to which one is called. I am fully in agreement with May:

> I don't (even) think that you can 'train' spiritual directors. Certainly education, supervision and ongoing accountability are very important and can certainly enrich a director's ministry, but no amount of training will make a good director out of someone who is not called and gifted.[16]

In his introduction to the new edition of his work *Soul Friend*, Kenneth Leech goes further:

> I stand by my suggestion that the role of 'training' is extremely limited, and that this ministry is

---

16   May, *Care of Mind, Care of Spirit*, 215.

essentially a by-product of a life of prayer and growth in holiness.[17]

Recognising the charism of spiritual direction, David Fleming argues the importance of discerning a spiritual director's call:

> Spiritual direction is rooted in God's call first and our response to God's call... Persons also receive confirmation of this gift in a normal human way by means of other people with whom they live and work identifying it and calling for its use. Commonly, people who have some intimations of a God-given discerning ability find that others seek them out and want to share their life situation...'[18]

Both the person's prayer experience and the experience of being asked by others to be their spiritual director suggest a healthy relational life. The guidelines of the Australian Ecumenical Council for Spiritual Direction recognise the charism of the ministry of spiritual direction and recommend that, prior to acceptance into a formation program, the program seeks evidence of a person's call to be a spiritual director.[19] To my knowledge, most formation programs follow this recommendation.

Over and above their personal supervision, participants in a formation program are encouraged to see a personal spiritual director regularly during the program. Individual and group supervision focus on each person's relationships with those to whom they minister, with peers and with supervisors, but only

---

17 Kenneth Leech, *Soul Friend* (London: Darton, Longmann & Todd, 1994), xvii.

18 David L. Fleming, "Spiritual Direction: Charism and Ministry," in *The Christian Ministry of Spiritual Direction*, ed. David L Fleming (St. Louis: Institute of Jesuit Sources, 1988), 4-5.

19 AECSD, "Guidelines for the Formation of Spiritual Directors," 1.1.

spiritual direction focuses directly on relationship with God. A person's relationship with God is also purified and developed in the formation process.

The experiential way

All available guidelines for the formation of spiritual directors include the need for some basic theoretical knowledge of theology and psychology. I add the importance of a thorough knowledge of the ways of God's Spirit and spirits not-of-God in human experience. Moreover, I believe that such knowledge is of value only when it is grounded in experience. An experiential approach to teaching and learning, as distinct from academic learning, promotes personal transformation. This approach applies even to the so-called 'rules for discernment'. I believe that knowledge of how the spirits work in one's personal life, that is one's personal rules for discernment, is best gained from experience. The contemplative prayer exercises used in *Siloam*, described in an appendix, are designed to help such learning. Rules for discernment are not to be imposed on others, but provide a background for spiritual directors as they listen to the unique experience of the person to whom they are ministering.

The importance of the director's own experience is supported by John of the Cross:

> Although the foundation for guiding a soul to spirit is knowledge and discretion, the director will not succeed in leading the soul onward to it, when God bestows it, nor will he even understand it, if he has no experience of what true and pure spirit is.[20]

---

20   John of the Cross, "The Living Flame of Love," in *The Collected Works of St. John of the Cross*, 3.30-1.

For the same reason, I argue against an over-emphasis on skills-based formation, as though one can be taught how to be a spiritual director. Formation is not primarily about 'training'.[21] Lucy Abbott Tucker, an experienced formator of spiritual directors, advises:

> ...while I could teach someone skills that are helpful to the direction relationship, I could not make a spiritual director. It is a bit like teaching someone to dance: I can teach the steps but the rhythm needs to come from within... Training centres need to be keenly aware of the limitations of training and skills development.[22]

Rosemary Haughton's distinction between transformation and approaches to formation based on the 'law' supports this approach. Haughton argues that formation based on law, meaning formation based on behaviour according to set norms and rules, amounts to 'death by asphyxiation'.[23] I call this a 'behaviourist' model of formation.

As noted, focusing on skills or behaviour in formation inevitably encourages compliance, not internalisation, not personal growth. The definitions of these terms are:

> *Compliance* can be said to occur when an individual accepts influence because he hopes to achieve a favourable reaction from another person or group. He adopts the induced behaviour not

---

21   The Apostolic Exhortation on the formation of priests defines pastoral formation as 'more than acquiring pastoral techniques': John Paul II, *Pastores Dabo Vobis* (Homebush, NSW: St. Pauls Publications, 1992), #58. This is equally true for all ministry formation.
22   Lucy Abbott Tucker, "Professionalization: Spiritual Directors at the Edge," *The Way* 91, no. Spring (1998): 42-43.
23   Haughton, *The Transformation of Man*, 35.

because he believes in its content, but because he expects to gain specific rewards or approval and avoid specific punishments.

Identification can be said to occur when an individual accepts influence because he wants to establish or maintain a satisfying, self-defining relationship to another person or group... He adopts the induced behaviour because it is associated with the desired relationship...

Internalisation can be said to occur when an individual accepts influence because the content of the induced behaviour, the ideas and actions of which it is composed, is intrinsically rewarding. He adopts the induced behaviour because it is congruent with his value system... Behaviour adopted in this fashion tends to be integrated with the individual's existing values.[24]

Focusing on skills or behaviour – what to do, what not to do, how to respond, how not to respond – inevitably encourages compliance, not internalisation, not personal growth. In a particular way, when a person's unconscious needs dominate behaviour, the person's value system is effectively overlooked. In such a case, compliance happens because the person is acting out of need or *unfreedom*. In contrast, internalisation becomes possible with growth in inner freedom. Becoming a spiritual director is a very different process from learning about spiritual direction. Becoming discerning is a very different process from learning about discernment.

---

[24] Herbert C. Kelman, "Compliance, Identification and Internalisation: Three Processes of Attitude Change," in *Readings in Attitude Theory and Measurement*, ed. Martin Fishbein (New York: John Wiley and Sons, 1967), 470.

My insistence that formation begins with the spiritual director's personal experience flows from this understanding. Lonergan's insight in his *Method in Theology* gives the framework for developing personal experience. He writes of:

> ... our *a priori* structured drive that promotes us from experiencing to the effort to understand, from understanding to the effort to judge truly, from judging to the effort to choose rightly...[25]

Lonergan argues that this is the essential way of human knowing. His theory, called *Operations of Conscious Intentionality*, offers a way of knowing that may be summarised in the operations of experiencing, understanding, critically reflecting and judging, and making choices for action (the four ways in which human consciousness functions). This theory and methodology is applicable to any area of ministry and any area of research. Focusing on, becoming more aware of, and finally growing in understanding of one's experience makes change possible.

To summarise: in this approach to the ministry of spiritual direction and the ministry of formation of spiritual directors the focus is always on the individual's experience. The spiritual director or supervisor is encouraged to listen contemplatively to the invitation of God's Spirit in the person's prayer, ministry and life experience. Self-awareness and growth in inner freedom come about in this approach to formation.

The transformative way

I believe that formation is about transformation. If participants in a formation program are to become effective, discerning spiritual directors, growth in self-awareness and inner

---

25   Lonergan, *Method in Theology*, 103.

freedom is essential. Such growth requires inner conversion or transformation in order to rise above one's limited freedom for the sake of self-transcendent love. Though a formation program sets out to supervise participants' ministry as spiritual directors, the focus of the supervision invariably turns to the individual director's inner life. Self-transcendence is based on one's *being*, not one's doing.[26] Transformation is God's work, once again calling for the contemplative approach that I have advocated throughout.

I emphasise that only affective insight brings change. Intellectual insight, of itself, does not. Affective insight will mean coming to terms with one's affective memory which includes all of one's past experience. In chapter 6, Arnold points out that one's affective memory is the key to one's vulnerability around inner needs and attachments:

> Indeed, affective memory is ubiquitous, yet intensely personal, because it is the living record of the emotional life history of each person... it can be called the matrix of all experience and action... But it is also the intensely personal reaction to a particular situation based on an individual's unique experiences and biases.[27]

I believe that a formation program needs to offer a level of supervision that understands this dynamic and enables participants to face their vulnerabilities, transcend their inner needs and attachments, and be transformed to personal freedom. The new freedom will bear fruit in more effective ministry as a spiritual director. The psychological model of a transition from *unfreedom* to freedom and the theological model of transition

---

26 Rulla, *Anthropology of the Christian Vocation*, 272.
27 Arnold, *Feelings and Emotions: The Loyola Symposium*, 187.

from death to life describe the same human experience. This process of transformation underpins formation for discernment.

In my experience, many formation programs appear to give little attention to the place of growth in inner freedom in their spiritual directors. I'm convinced that, when spiritual directors are listening to another's experience, directors are invited to listen from that place of inner freedom. I believe that spiritual directors must know in their own life, maybe with more urgency than anyone else, that everything usually called 'mine' – my call, my ministry, my listening, my own personal experience of whatever the other is talking about – is of little worth. All are totally, utterly dependent on God's mercy and love.

Merton named this realisation an experience of 'dread': indeed, he found it so dreadful that he called it 'the hell of mercy'. It is the 'hell' of being purified of all self-sufficiency and inner attachment, and yet the 'mercy' that convinces one that only God is God.[28] This is to know true freedom.

Formation programs

I discuss now how these norms for formation programs – that the program be contemplative, relational, experiential and transformative – take shape in practice. I use the experience of the *Siloam* program to draw out implications for formation and supervision of spiritual directors.[29] This program of formation at the Heart of Life Centre in Melbourne began in 1979 when no other formation program for spiritual directors existed in

---

28   Thomas Merton, *Contemplative Prayer* (New York: Herder & Herder, 1969), 137.

29   This is the program of formation that I know best. References to the program apply to the years of my involvement. As a formation program for spiritual directors, *Siloam* continues to evolve in different ways.

Australia. In 2018, *Siloam* boasts over three hundred graduates, working throughout Australia and overseas, in more recent years in the young churches of Asia and the Pacific.

In 2007, *Siloam* was recognised by the Australian Ecumenical Council for Spiritual Direction (AECSD) as meeting its standards for formation of spiritual directors in Australia. In 2013, the program was accredited as a Graduate Diploma in Spiritual Direction by the University of Divinity.

Siloam is essentially a *formation* program, inviting participants into a process of becoming discerning spiritual directors, rather than mere learning about spiritual direction or learning how to be a spiritual director. The environment of the program is contemplative and experiential, encouraging participants to personal growth in inner freedom and discernment. Through personal formation, spiritual directors are freed to listen contemplatively and notice the movements of the spirits in their directees. In other words, individuals' personal formation in *Siloam* bears fruit in their ministry.

The name *Siloam* is taken from John's Gospel (9:7): the blind man was healed of his blindness by Jesus after he washed in the waters of the pool of Siloam. The healed blind man recognises Jesus as one sent by God: John says that the word *Siloam* means 'sent'. Jesus himself is the living water, the healing water. The very title of the formation program speaks of its vision: participants would become competent spiritual directors, and, more importantly, they would become people who see with new eyes, God's eyes, having tasted the rich symbolism of the healing waters of *Siloam*. Only then would they, too, be sent to minister as spiritual directors.

A competent spiritual director needs to be someone committed to their own prayer, someone who is desirous of and open to growth in self-awareness and inner freedom, someone who knows God's ways with humanity, someone who listens carefully and contemplatively to another, without imposing their own experience or own agenda.

Siloam's approach to spiritual direction and to supervision demands a high level of integration and inner freedom in the spiritual director and the supervisor: no strings attached, no hidden agendas, no self-interest, and no prejudice. A basic conviction in *Siloam* is that formation needs to be personal transformation to enable spiritual directors to grow in inner freedom and discernment.

A second basic conviction is that spiritual direction is primarily God's work. The focus of spiritual direction is relationship with God. In prayer, in spiritual direction and in supervision, the spiritual director is encouraged to bring the same contemplative attentiveness and focus on God's working.

These two convictions permeate *Siloam*'s approach to formation. The convictions deepened in my experience of ministering to spiritual directors in that program. They are expressed in the contemplative, relational, experiential and transformative norms for formation, described above. In turn, these norms apply to every aspect of a formation program:

- admission to a formation program
- beginnings and goal setting
- teaching / seminar work in formation
- approaches to discernment

- ministry supervision
- evaluation and assessment of spiritual directors

Admission to a formation program

The first guideline of the Australian Ecumenical Council for Spiritual Direction is that *applicants should be suitably assessed.*[30] These are the recommendations:

> Applicants would normally complete a detailed application form and autobiography, submit two recommendation forms with referees who may be consulted, and participate in an assessment interview with two of the formation staff, who will assess the applicant's willingness and ability to engage in the process of formation.

Most formation programs for spiritual directors follow these recommendations. The following factors are normally considered when making judgments about readiness and suitability of applicants for admission into a program:

- the applicant's sense of call to the ministry of spiritual direction
- life experience and experience in helping ministries
- experience in receiving spiritual direction and supervision
- openness to and potential for personal growth
- faith life/prayer life

---

30 AECSD, "Guidelines for the Formation of Spiritual Directors," 1.2.

I emphasise a spiritual director's call to the ministry in my discussion of the relational norm for formation. In keeping with the transformative norm for formation, I emphasise now the need for openness and potential for personal growth in applicants to a formation program.

Formation programs do well to recognise the gift of inner freedom and yet the human experience of limited freedom, as discussed in my treatment of the realistic anthropology on which the *Siloam* program is based. Spiritual directors in a formation program live with some degree of *unfreedom* or unconscious self-interest in their relationships. The spiritual director's vulnerability to unconscious self-interest, however subtle, needs to be challenged consistently, especially in personal supervision, as described below. An experiential, contemplative approach to formation fosters participants' transformative growth as spiritual directors.

A psychological evaluation as part of the admission procedure is helpful, not so much to discover in advance someone with a psychological difficulty that would prohibit effective participation in the formation process, but more to help the individual's growth in self-awareness. Moreover, the evaluation clarifies for the supervisor the best approach to adopt with each participant, knowing the person's strengths, weaknesses and vulnerabilities.

Beginnings and goal setting

The invitation to spiritual directors in a formation program to be attentive to their own inner lives sets the scene from the very beginning of a program. A program's approach to the initial introduction of participants and the subsequent setting of goals for the year builds on the argued norms for formation.

Ideally, goal setting is approached contemplatively. Goals are not arbitrary and not chosen for their objective value. Rather, goals are personal and inspired by the Spirit of God. I give an example of possible guidelines for setting personal and ministerial goals in the appendix. I note that goals need to be quite specific and need to have a measurable outcome, not mere process towards some outcome. Usually goals are reviewed and adjusted from time to time during the program, particularly during mid-program and end-of-program evaluations. Goals give participants and supervisors a framework for the ongoing work of supervision.

Shared prayer, setting and reviewing of goals, and group interaction, all approached in a contemplative way, are concrete ways in which the norms for formation are expressed in practice. These approaches are integrated into each spiritual director's overall formation.

Teaching/seminar work in formation programs

As I discuss in the experiential norm for formation, I believe that spiritual directors' learning is most valuable when grounded in experience. For this reason, I recommend experiential seminar-style learning, involving participants' experience. The value of the experiential approach to seminar work is that it promotes integration and internalisation of learning. In that sense, learning in any one seminar permeates the whole program of formation. This approach differs markedly from the more academic teaching still favoured by some formation programs for spiritual directors. Also in the appendix, I list the seminars that are taught in the *Siloam* program of formation of spiritual directors.

Integration and internalisation of learnings in seminars is further promoted by a weekly tutorial. In a tutorial, participants are invited to present material to the group on topics emerging from the seminars, often treated from different stand-points in more than one seminar. Again with facilitation, all members of the group are invited to contribute to discussion and shared learning.

Approaches to discernment

I believe that processes of becoming discerning, as distinct from learning about discernment, need to be uppermost in a formation program. As in all teaching in a formation program (and all areas of practical theology), I recommend that in the seminar on discernment of spirits, the seminar leader begin with participants' experience of the spirits in their lives, move to reflection and interpretation of the movements noticed, and then apply this to decision making and action.

One learning in the *Siloam* program is that there are no short cuts to growth in self-knowledge and self-awareness towards inner freedom and discernment. Contemplative listening and sensitive discernment build on the directors' noticing movements in themselves – in their everyday experience and relationships, as much as in their ministry. Every interaction has the potential for some new awareness. The explicit focus on the work of the spirits in the seminar on discernment is supplemented by a habit of reflection on everyday experience. The prayer called the *Awareness Examen* is encouraged for this reason. This prayer was first developed by George Aschenbrenner.[31] My simplified version,[32] adapted from Aschenbrenner's writing and approved by him, is used with his permission.

Awareness Examen

The Awareness Examen prayer is a time of contemplative prayer focusing not on what I judge I have done well this day, but on what *God* has done in my life today. In practical terms, the prayer is best prayed at the end of each day, for maybe ten to fifteen minutes. It will involve:

- An expression of gratitude for the day and an openness and willingness to be led by God's Spirit right now

- A time of quiet relaxing and slowing down of body and mind, helped by slower and deeper breathing

- Then a conscious prayer, asking the Spirit to bring into my awareness whatever of the day – an event, a person, something that happened to me, a mood, a new insight – that God wants me to listen to again

- Having asked, I wait (*most people simply allow the experience of the day to flow back into awareness, quite freely, sometimes asking*

---

31 George Aschenbrenner, "Consciousness Examen," *Review for Religious* 31, no. 1 (1972): 14-21. and George Aschenbrenner, "Consciousness Examen: Becoming God's Heart for the World," *Religious Life Review* 47 (1988): 801-10.

32 Brian Gallagher, *Pray as You Are* (Sydney, NSW: Nelen Yubu, 1999). Appendix

> *questions of God – where were you most active in my life today? how have you been moving in my heart today? have you been calling me or challenging me in special ways today? Note that I do not review the day myself or make my own judgments about the day; I wait on God.*)

- God has ways of bringing to my attention whatever God wants me to listen to: sometimes via a memory, or a person who comes into my awareness, or some feeling that I notice in myself. I gradually become more sensitive to noticing God's ways in my life

- Whatever comes to me, I simply let myself stay with that: I re-live it, savour it, maybe more than I did during the day, I allow it to touch my heart, all the time asking for God's message to me, God's revelation to me right now

- At some point, quite spontaneously, I respond directly to what I have heard from God: maybe a prayer of gratitude, maybe sorrow for some lost opportunity, maybe a prayer of trusting surrender, or a plea for help. I trust whatever prayer comes

Most people then like to conclude with a verbal prayer of gratitude or praise of God, perhaps the Our Father

This Awareness Prayer is valuable in the actual ministry of spiritual direction, as director and directee together reflect contemplatively on the experience brought for spiritual direction. The spiritual director notices movements in themself, at the same time as noticing movements in the directee, trusting these movements as indicators of the spirits at work. It has also been found helpful as a preparation for a time of supervision, praying contemplatively over one's experience as a spiritual director.

Siloam's seminar on discernment also uses contemplative prayer exercises as a further help to noticing the ways of God's Spirit and spirits not-of-God in personal experience. Reflecting on their own experience in a contemplative way, waiting on God's revelation, participants are helped to name both the ways of the spirits and the fruits of following one or other spirit. These exercises are unique to *Siloam*. I list them in the appendix.

As mentioned, a strong learning from experience is that intellectual insight into one's inner dynamics, of itself, does not bring change. Only affective, emotional insight does that and only then is transformation possible. This is the background to my insistence that spiritual directors need to *become* discerning. For spiritual directors to become discerning people for whom awareness of the spirits is connatural, growth in inner freedom is essential. This invites inner conversion or transformation.

Ministry supervision in formation programs

Supervisors oversee the participants' ministry as spiritual directors and the personal growth flowing from their ministry. Spiritual Directors International describes supervision:

> The supervisory process invites the spiritual director to explore what is beneath the surface to better understand oneself, to discover best how

to accompany seekers, and to acknowledge how the Spirit is present and active in the spiritual direction relationship.[33]

Similarly, the Australian Ecumenical Council for Spiritual Direction names supervision as 'an essential component of a formation program':

> Supervision is a formal, collaborative process that monitors, develops, and supports student directors. Supervision provides the opportunity to assess and extend competencies, ensures adherence to standards and allows for the development of individual styles.[34]

To my knowledge, all formation programs respect the need for supervision. Programs differ, however, in their approach to the ministry of supervision. In keeping with the norms for formation that I have outlined, I recommend that the approach to both individual and group supervision also be contemplative and focus on the personal growth of the spiritual director.[35] Normally a spiritual director brings a concrete example of their ministry for supervision, ideally in a verbatim report. I include example guidelines for verbatim writing and evaluating the experience in the appendix.

I emphasise that the focus in a supervisory session is on the inner experience of the spiritual director being supervised, not on the experience of the person who comes for spiritual

---

[33] Spiritual Directors International: www.sdiworld.org/resources/spiritual direction/supervision

[34] AECSD, "Guidelines for the Formation of Spiritual Directors," 2.2.4.

[35] This focus on personal growth is followed also in the supervision of counsellors and therapists.

direction.[36] Director and supervisor listen to God's invitation in the inner movements they notice in themselves when reading a verbatim or recounting a spiritual direction session. As the supervisor notices and interprets movements in themself, trusting that these movements are indicators of the spirits at work in the director being supervised, the supervisor will ask the spiritual director to look again at some specific interchange in the verbatim. The supervisor may ask what motivated the response at that point, or what the director was listening to in themself at that point – all for the sake of growth in self-awareness and inner freedom. A parallel approach is taken in group supervision, the facilitator involving all members of the group. This is the contemplative, discerning approach.

This is a fictitious snippet from a meeting that Gus' spiritual director (chapter 4) had with his supervisor. The spiritual director had already given to the supervisor a verbatim account of part of his spiritual direction time with Gus:

> Supervisor: *It seems you had a couple of possible ways to go here – tell me what was going on in you at those times.*
>
> Spiritual Director: *You mean, when Gus talked about his difficulty in praying with Scripture and when he talked about his relationships in community that were suffering?*
>
> Supervisor: *Yes – I presume that you had noticed those two possibilities.*
>
> Spiritual Director: *When he was talking about relationships – I think he said that he had cut himself*

---

36   Barry and Connolly stress the value of this approach in supervision: Barry and Connolly, *The Practice of Spiritual Direction*, 175-7.

off from his brothers in community – I felt really uncomfortable, like this doesn't sound right to me; the other time when he talked about struggling with his morning prayer times, I can't say I noticed much in myself at all – almost like, what else is new?

Supervisor: *So you trusted your feeling uncomfortable at that point and took the conversation back to the relationships?*

Spiritual Director: *Yes, when I have a reaction like that, I've learned to trust that it's telling me something that needs to be followed up.*

Supervisor: *That's good – and it paid off for Gus. But can we look also at the other possible option you had. Would you believe, I had a similar reaction a moment ago when you said 'what else is new?' in response to Gus' prayer struggles. What's that about?*

Spiritual Director: *Oh, everyone has some struggles with prayer, don't they?*

Supervisor: *So we don't talk about them?! What does it do to you when you hear such frequent struggles with prayer?*

Spiritual Director: *I think I just get bored – I mean, I struggle in prayer myself.*

Supervisor: *And your struggles make you bored?*

Spiritual Director: *I try to ignore them. Surely there are plenty of other more interesting topics to talk about. I like things to be different, new things that are more exciting and keep me alive.*

> Supervisor: *And when things are no different and not very exciting?*
>
> Spiritual Director: *That's when I get bored. It's almost as though life's not worth living if that's all there is to talk about...*

In this example of supervision, the supervisor acted on her noticing her own discomfort at a specific point of the conversation with the spiritual director. This led to the director's awareness of his tendency to ignore anything apparently unexciting. The supervisor senses some unfree need ('a tendency to act in a certain way') in this spiritual director. It would take more time in supervision and in prayer before the director could name his inner need for change, novelty and excitement. This person imagines that meeting this need is essential for life to be 'worth living'.

The supervisor's listening to the invitation of God's Spirit in the experience of the one being supervised, and acting on that invitation, challenges the director to new depths of inner freedom. In this exchange, Gus' spiritual director is invited to such growth. Ultimately, his ministry of spiritual direction will benefit. Later, the supervisor may well ask this director to talk again about his avoidance of any conversation about difficulties in prayer, lest some other *unfreedom* is influencing his approach at that point of the conversation.

I encourage supervisors to resist telling a spiritual director what to say or how to respond to their directee, as happens in the more behaviourist approach adopted by some programs. Rather, the contemplative approach to supervision invites the director to deeper self-awareness and inner freedom, which then overflows into the director's ministry, precisely because the director then responds from a freer place in themself. This approach is well described by William Barry and Mary Guy, reflecting on their experience of supervision together.[37]

Some degree of self-supervision is possible and advisable, especially for spiritual directors who do not have easy access to competent supervisors during and after finishing their initial formation. Self-supervision happens when one is prepared to review critically concrete examples of one's ministry, asking oneself questions like 'what movements did I notice in the directee, and at what point in the interaction? What were the movements that I noticed in myself, and at what specific point? What do I know about these movements from past experience? What spirits were active – and when in the dialogue? At what points was I freely in touch with my own inner truth – what signs of that did I notice in myself? Did my vulnerable spot affect my responses at any point? How did this happen – what inner voices was I listening to? How have I been challenged personally in this ministerial encounter? What have I learned – about myself as a spiritual director, about the ministry of spiritual direction?'

Though the risk of self-deception limits the value of self-supervision, the consistent practice of reviewing one's ministry does sharpen one's sensitivity to the ways of the spirits, not unlike regular praying the Awareness Examen prayer, described above. As a preparation for a time of supervision, spiritual directors are encouraged to some degree of self-evaluation in writing their verbatim. This often becomes a point of supervision, especially when a supervisor finds themself evaluating the spiritual director's work quite differently.

---

37   William A. Barry and Mary C. Guy, "The Practice of Supervision in Spiritual Direction," *Religious Life Review* 37 (1978): 834-42.

Formation of Spiritual Directors

Growth in inner freedom and the gift of discernment become possible with good supervision and faithful contemplative prayer. The supervisor's role is pivotal in the overall formation of individual spiritual directors. Other aspects of the program complement the personal growth, the transformation that happens in supervision. For this reason, supervisors are challenged to the same inner freedom, the same contemplative listening, and the same ongoing growth in self-awareness that is asked of the spiritual directors participating in the formation program.

Supervisors should themselves be supervised, personally and/or with peers – for the sake of their ministry and for the sake of the participants in their formation programs. Interaction with a team, mutually supporting and challenging one another, working to keep the relationships open and honest, will ensure accountability.

Only an experiential, transformative approach on the part of the supervisor will ensure that the spiritual director being supervised becomes a discerning spiritual director. It bears repeating that only affective, emotional insight into one's inner dynamics brings change. Only then is transformation possible. This is the supervisor's responsibility towards the participants in the formation program.

I take for granted in all of the above that supervision is quite a different process from consultation. It can happen that a director needs to seek advice from a more experienced person to aid their understanding of what a directee brings to their times of spiritual direction. This is 'consultation'.[38] In consultation,

---

38 The use of consultation in ministry is described by May in his treatment of colleagueship: May, *Care of Mind, Care of Spirit*, 193-8.

the focus is more on the experience of the directee, whereas in supervision the focus is on the experience of the spiritual director being supervised. Consultation, then, requires some extension of the confidentiality agreed to by spiritual director and directee, in order to include the person being consulted. Normally, this would be discussed with the directee before the practice is adopted.

Evaluation and assessment of spiritual directors

Academic units normally set written assignments for assessment. Experiential work is more difficult to assess. Bringing the two together in order to assess a person's suitability to be a spiritual director has been a perennial and rather problematic question. The AECSD guidelines list *self-assessment, peer assessment, staff assessment, and assessment by external assessors,* all of which apply to both the academic and experiential requirements.

In relation to assessment for graduation and accreditation, ongoing assessment throughout the program is essential. Working regularly with a supervisor, each participant is encouraged to reflect on their call to the ministry of spiritual direction, their identity as a spiritual director, and their learnings in the program. Much of this assessment is a shared activity: the director and the supervisor work together all year, noting especially the spiritual director's personal growth and development in ministry.

This ongoing assessment is further helped by the mid-program and end-of-program self-evaluations that are asked of participants. I include possible guidelines for these evaluations in the appendix.

In summary, the contemplative approach, the approach to experiential learning and supervision, and the emphasis on holistic, spiritual and psychological formation – or transformation – illustrate how the argued norms for formation programs for spiritual directors are put into practice. This is the way of the *Siloam* program, offering and fostering an environment and an encouragement to *become* discerning spiritual directors.

Moreover, this approach emphasises that discernment involves a way of life as much as a way of ministry. *Siloam*'s contemplative/relational/experiential/transformative approach to formation encourages graduates to be people who live their whole lives in a discerning way.

Conclusion

Living a discerning way of life rests on growth in inner freedom in order to become a discerning person. In relation to the ministry of spiritual direction, I believe that living a discerning way of life is pre-requisite to becoming a discerning spiritual director. A spiritual director's accurate reading the signs of the spirits rests on their inner freedom.

The human species is essentially free. At the same time, the human experience is of a limited freedom. I understand this in terms of one's unconscious needs or compulsions, conflicting with one's professed values. I argue that such vulnerability in one's make-up is ripe ground for the temptations of spirits not-of-God in both the person who seeks spiritual direction, the directee, and the listening spiritual director. For this reason, growth in awareness of one's inner needs and growth in freedom from the compulsive tendencies of these needs become essential pre-requisites to growing in inner freedom and the process of becoming discerning.

This growth in inner freedom comes about in the faithful practice of contemplative prayer, self-reflection and professional supervision. Growth in inner freedom is gift of God's grace. The teachings of John of the Cross on the experience of 'dark night' and of Ignatius Loyola on contemplative prayer offer the commonly experienced ways in which people are gifted with growth in inner freedom. Inner freedom is both pre-requisite

Conclusion

for and fruit of discernment. A discerning heart is itself a gift of God's grace: one *becomes* discerning.

Discernment of spirits is integral to the ministry of spiritual direction. In the practice of spiritual direction, focusing on religious experience, director and directee listen together for the invitation of God's Spirit. As spiritual directors listen contemplatively, noticing inner movements in themselves, they come to recognise the signs of the activity of God's Spirit and the signs of the counter activity of spirits not-of-God in both the directee and in their own experience. The spiritual director learns to interpret and to trust these signs of the spirits by attending to the direction in which the different spirits lead. The fruit of following the Spirit of God is called consolation and the fruit of following spirits not-of-God is called desolation.

My conclusion that an effective spiritual director needs to be interiorly free in order to read the spirits truly implies that a program of formation of spiritual directors, while forming people *for ministry*, will necessarily place strong emphasis on *personal* formation. Such a formation program needs to be transformative to enable and promote growth in inner freedom and the possibility of contemplative discerning ministry in its participants. I conclude that only a formation program that is contemplative, relational, experiential, and transformative will effectively foster this inner freedom in its spiritual directors and prepare them for discerning ministry. Formation for the ministry of spiritual direction is to form discerning spiritual directors.

These norms are integrated in and permeate the formation program, *Siloam*. As detailed in chapter 10 and the appendix, what defines *Siloam* as a formation program for spiritual directors is the contemplative approach throughout, the unique approach to experiential learning, and the emphasis on holistic, spiritual and psychological, personal formation/transformation. In this way, the *Siloam* program offers and fosters an environment and an encouragement to spiritual directors to *become* discerning. Such an approach is recommended for all formation programs.

The anthropology on which *Siloam* is based makes possible and supports this approach. When one's human experience of freedom is limited, one risks believing and living as though one is not free, as though one has to set one's sights on and work towards some far-away goal called freedom. In fact, all people are essentially free, created free. The work of formation is cooperation with the gift already given, unearthing and transcending the *unfreedoms*, the unconscious inner attachments that block any response to the call to be free.

Effective formation will enable a spiritual director to transcend their *unfreedoms* in order to grow in inner freedom and to relate freely and less defensively with God and with other people. A free, more fully human spiritual director will be a discerning spiritual director. Discernment of spirits, then, is foundational in both the ministry of spiritual direction and the formation of spiritual directors.

Appendix
The Formation Program *Siloam*

Here is an astonishing thing:
You do not know where he comes from, yet he opened my eyes...
Never since the world began has it been heard that anyone opened
the eyes of a person born blind.[1]

John 9:30-32

Siloam's guidelines for **setting goals:**

After your prayer with Jesus' experience of his baptism and his temptations in the desert, you are invited to pray contemplatively with your own call and your own experience of being tempted away from your call. (This is your call to be yourself, to be true to who you are before God – not yet your call to be a spiritual director).

- In prayer, how/where do you sense you are being called right now? How might you respond to that call this year? What would help you? What might hinder you? How are you vulnerable to temptation to be untrue to your call?

- What would be a realistic aim/outcome as you continue to respond to this call this year? Be quite specific. This is your personal goal.

---

[1] Words of the blind man, healed by Jesus after washing in the pool of Siloam

- A key focus of your work this year is your ministry. Again in prayer, listen for how/where will your call find expression in your ministry? And how will your vulnerability to temptation show itself in your ministry? Once again, be specific in stating your ministerial goal.

- It might be useful to list some of the *means* you will use to help yourself to be true, and to name your awareness of *helps and obstacles* in your situation and *strengths and resistances* in yourself.

- What signs would you expect to notice in yourself when you are making 'progress' with your goals?

Experiential seminars (2 hours per week, some for 7 weeks, some for 14 weeks):

- **Personal grace:** Beginning with students' spiritual autobiographies, the seminar reflects on participants' personal experience of grace, developing a theology and a spirituality of grace. Some areas addressed are: grace in the ordinary events of our lives, grace through relationships, grace in joy and sorrow, grace in limitation and brokenness, etc.

- **The experience of conversion:** A guided contemplative reflection on the experience of conversion, from the perspectives of theology, human development theory, and personal experience. The seminar includes a study of true and false self, sinfulness, and the types of conversion – intellectual, moral, religious, affective.

- **Religious experience:** This seminar covers the varieties of religious experience, revelation, God's self-communication, relatedness to mystery, faith, guilt and forgiveness, and religious experience as the focus of spiritual direction.

- **Ethics for spiritual directors:** A seminar blending ethical teaching with experience in ministry: maintaining professional standards and facing ethical dilemmas in spiritual direction.

- **Discernment:** Learning from personal experience, the seminar studies the ways of God's Spirit and spirits not-of-God in human experience and in ministry: discernment of spirits and discernment of God's will.

- **Psychological aspects of spiritual direction:** This seminar presents an anthropological, psychological and pastoral framework for ministry, based on Luigi Rulla's theory of Theocentric Self-transcendence. The seminar includes a study of emotions and desires, needs, attitudes and values, defence mechanisms, and the spirituality of sexuality.

- **The human experience of God:** Through guided reflection on the human experience of God, the seminar studies participants' personal experience and the experience described in classical and contemporary writings in prayer and spirituality.

- **Ecological theology:** This seminar is based on the Trinitarian theology of Denis Edwards and its scriptural foundations. Focusing on God at the heart of the dynamic evolutionary universe, human relationships are situated within the inter-related and inter-dependent community of life, with implications for spiritual direction.

- **Story-telling and visual images in spiritual direction:** The seminar explores how stories from contemporary art, literature and cinema become part of one's religious experience and one's spiritual direction ministry.

Other optional seminars are available: The Art of Journal Writing, Art as Prayer, Mindfulness and Meditation, Dreams: God's Language, Mysticism: East and West.

To meet the requirements of the **Graduate Diploma in Spiritual Direction** offered by the University of Divinity (in 2013, the Melbourne College of Divinity), *Siloam's* seminars were restructured into academic units, but importantly without changing the overall content or the contemplative, experiential approach. Different combinations of seminars make up each unit. These are the study units:

Appendix

GRADUATE DIPLOMA IN SPIRITUAL DIRECTION

UNITS AND UNIT CODES

Full time Unit Name	Code	Part time Unit Name	Code
Foundational Concepts in Spiritual Direction I (FT) (Semester 1)	DS8701Y	Foundational Concepts in Spiritual Direction I (PT) (Year 1)	DS8711Y
Foundational Concepts in Spiritual Direction II (FT) (Semester 2)	DS8702Y	Foundational Concepts in Spiritual Direction II (PT) (Year 2)	DS8712Y
Interpersonal Dynamics in Spiritual Direction I (FT) (Semester 1)	DS8703Y	Interpersonal Dynamics in Spiritual Direction I (PT) (Year 1)	DS8713Y
Interpersonal Dynamics in Spiritual Direction II (FT) (Semester 2)	DS8704Y	Interpersonal Dynamics in Spiritual Direction II (PT) (Year 2)	DS8714Y
Spiritual Direction Practicum I (FT) (Semester 1)	DS8705Y	Spiritual Direction Practicum I (PT) (Year 1)	DS8715Y
Spiritual Direction Practicum II (FT) (Semester 2)	DS8706Y	Spiritual Direction Practicum II (PT) (Year 2)	DS8716Y

Examples of **prayer exercises** used in the seminar on discernment:

- Graced Moments: a 10-15 minute reflection on the graced moments of your life.

Ask God to bring to mind some concrete examples of times you have been surprisingly graced. Re-live these moments and touch again the inner movements: what did you notice in yourself at that time? What 'moved' in you, some emotion, some memory, some insight? These movements that you notice in yourself come from God's Spirit working in you. They will help you to recognise the same Spirit in later experiences.

- Images of your life: again a quiet reflection recalling some images of your life.

We express ourselves more dynamically in images than in abstractions: images are privileged doors to self-knowledge, for images contain and evoke our experience.[2] Once God brings into your awareness some image(s) of your life, sit quietly with each image and allow it to 'speak', to reveal itself, to put you in touch with whatever inner experience that image captures. Notice the inner movements in yourself as you do this, and then what happens in you when you stay with a particular movement: where does it lead you? With facilitation, you will learn more of the ways of God's Spirit (and possibly of other spirits, depending on your image) in your life experience.

- Good decisions: contemplatively, bring to mind (allow God to prompt your memory of) an example of a good decision, a decision of some importance that you have made in your life – 'good' because it bore good fruit.

Reflecting on the decision that God has brought to mind, there will be two learnings. What exactly is the good fruit of this decision, the fruit that enables you to call it a 'good decision'? This fruit is clear sign of God's Spirit at work in you.

---

2   Larkin, "Guidelines for Discernment," 43.

Appendix

> Then, how did you actually make this decision? What was the prompting that you 'heard' and responded to? This will help you to name one of the ways that God's Spirit works in you and invites you to life.

- 'Bad' decisions: some past decisions may not have borne good fruit, some you may even wish you could reverse, even though you made them sincerely at the time. See if examples of such decisions come to mind now, again praying contemplatively.

> Wait in prayer until an example of such a decision comes to mind, a decision that you made quite sincerely, but that has not turned out well. Sitting with such a past decision, name for yourself the fruits of this decision, the fruits that enable you to make the judgment that the initial decision has not been for the best (for example, maybe some relationships suffered or maybe you yourself became stressed). Then, look back on the time of making the decision: what was the inner voice that you listened to at the time, the message you were giving yourself, and that you acted upon? the message that you thought was true at the time, but that you can see now is quite false. A subsequent question for reflection is to ask how did it happen that you heard the message as true at the time? What was that message appealing to in you? This is often a way into awareness of your vulnerable spot – which will explain how a false message can be heard as true.

- Images of Jesus: ask God to remind you of some images of Jesus in your life.

  > As images of Jesus come to you, slowly savour each image. Different images will prompt different inner movements in you and suggest different ways of relating to Jesus from time to time in your experience (for example, Jesus as saviour, Jesus as healer, Jesus as brother, Jesus as companion). The seminar leader will help you to recognise in your experience the different ways in which God's Spirit attracts you at different stages of your growing relationship with Jesus.

Siloam's guidelines for **verbatim writing**:

- note in as much detail as you can remember the movements you noticed in your directee during the interview (reactions, feelings, new insights, desires), naming the specific point in the interview
- similarly note in detail the movements in yourself during the interview
- do any of these movements suggest to you the workings of good or bad spirits in yourself and/or your directee?
- do you recognise anything of your own agenda operating in this interview?

Siloam's guidelines for **evaluations**:

- Having completed your formation, where do you stand in relation to your goals?

- in relation to your ministerial goals, how would you describe your present 'growing edge' as a spiritual director?

- in relation to your personal goals, what personal learnings have there been for you in the program?

- Describe the development of your identity as a spiritual director. How do you see yourself now? How have your relationships – with your group, with your supervisor, and with your directees – contributed to this sense of identity?

As well, supervisors discuss with each spiritual director the director's own assessment of their eligibility to graduate. Assessment, then, includes all of the means listed by AECSD (external assessors for written assignments only):

- participation in seminars and open group
- weekly individual and group supervision, and verbatim reports on ministry
- mid-year and end-of-year evaluations (in light of goals set at beginning)
- an end-of-program statement of eligibility to graduate
- the supervisor's assessment at the conclusion of the program

Recommended Reading

On spiritual direction

Barry, William A. "The Contemplative Attitude in Spiritual Direction." *Review for Religious* 35, no. 6 (1976).

Barry, William A. *Spiritual Direction and the Encounter with God.* New York: Paulist, 2004.

Barry, William A. "What Is Spiritual Direction: A Retrospective Reflection." *Presence* 21, no. 2 (2015): 31-41.

Barry, William A. and William J. Connolly. *The Practice of Spiritual Direction.* San Francisco, CA: Harper & Row, 1982.

Barry, William A. and Mary C. Guy. "The Practice of Supervision in Spiritual Direction." *Religious Life Review* 37 (1978): 834-32.

Buckley, Suzanne M, ed. *Sacred Is the Call.* New York: Crossroad, 2005.

Castley, Paul F. "Supervision: A Contemplative Approach." *Presence* 5, no. 2 (1999): 25-30.

Culligan, Kevin G., ed. *Spiritual Direction: Contemporary Readings.* Locust Valley, NY: Living Flame Press, 1983.

Dyckman, Katherine Marie and L. Patrick Carroll. *Inviting the Mystic, Supporting the Prophet: An Introduction to Spiritual Direction.* New York: Paulist, 1981.

Dyckman, Katherine Marie, Mary Garvin, and Elizabeth Liebert. *The Spiritual Exercises Reclaimed: Uncovering Liberating Possibilities for Women.* New York: Paulist, 2001.

Edwards, Tilden. *Spiritual Director, Spiritual Companion: Guide to Tending the Soul.* New York: Paulist, 2001.

English, John J. *Spiritual Freedom.* Guelph, Ontario: Loyola House, 1973.

Gallagher, Brian. "Twenty-Five Years of Siloam." *Presence* 12, no. 4 (2006): 7-13.

Gratton, Carolyn. *The Art of Spiritual Guidance.* New York: Crossroad, 1992.

Guenther, Margaret. *Holy Listening: The Art of Spiritual Direction.* Boston, MA: Cowley Publications, 1992.

Haight, Roger. *Christian Spirituality for Seekers: Reflections on the Spiritual Exercises of Ignatius Loyola.* Maryknoll, NY: Orbis Books, 2012.

Leech, Kenneth. *Soul Friend.* London: Darton, Longmann & Todd, 1994.

May, Gerald G. *Care of Mind, Care of Spirit.* San Francisco, CA: Harper & Row, 1982.

May, Gerald G. *Will and Spirit: A Contemplative Psychology.* San Francisco, CA: Harper & Row, 1982.

Merton, Thomas. *Spiritual Direction and Meditation.* Collegeville, MN: Liturgical Press, 1960.

Prowse, Yvonne R. "Spiritual Direction and the Call to Ecological Conversion." *Presence* 22, no. 4 (2016): 17-23.

Ruffing, Janet. *Spiritual Direction: Beyond the Beginnings.* Malwah, NJ: Paulist Press, 2000.

Scofield, Mary Ann. "Waiting on God: Staying with Movements of God." In *Sacred Is the Call,* edited by Suzanne M. Buckley. New York: Crossroad, 2005.

On discernment

Alphonso, Herbert. *The Personal Vocation*. Rome: Centrum Ignatianum Spiritualitatis, 1990.

Arnold, Magda B. *Feelings and Emotions: The Loyola Symposium*. New York: Academic Press, 1970.

Arnold, Magda B. and Gasson John A. *The Human Person: An Approach to an Integrated Theory of Personality*. New York: The Ronald Press Company, 1954.

Aschenbrenner, George. "Consciousness Examen." *Review for Religious* 31, no. 1 (1972): 14-21.

Aschenbrenner, George. "Currents in Spirituality: The Past Decade." *Review for Religious* 39, no. 2 (1980): 196-218.

Aschenbrenner, George. "Consciousness Examen: Becoming God's Heart for the World." *Religious Life Review* 47 (1988): 801-10.

Au, Wilkie and Noreen Cannon Au. *The Discerning Heart: Exploring the Christian Path*. New York: Paulist Press, 2006.

Auer, John, Peter Bentley, Tess Milne, and Stephen Truscott. "Contemplatively Forming Tomorrow's Spiritual Directors." *Presence* 22, no. 4 (2016): 50-56.

Barry, William A. "Towards Communal Discernment." *The Way Supplement* 58, no. Spring (1987): 104-12

Barry, William A. "Towards a Theology of Discernment." *The Way Supplement* 64, no. Spring (1989): 129-40.

Barry, William A. *Paying Attention to God: Discernment in Prayer*. Notre Dame, IN: Ave Maria Press, 1990.

Barry, William A. "Communal Discernment as a Way to Reconciliation." *Human Development* 29 (2008): 10-14.

Buckley, Michael J. "The Structure of the Rules for Discernment of Spirits." *The Way Supplement* 20, no. Autumn (1973): 19-37.

Conroy, Maureen. *The Discerning Heart*. Chicago, IL: Loyola Press, 1993.

Dubay, Thomas. *Authenticity: A Biblical Theology of Discernment*. San Francisco, CA: Ignatius Press, 1977, updated 1997.

Edwards, Denis. "Discernment of the Holy Spirit." *Presence* 13, no. 4 (2007): 21-29.

Farrow, Jo. "Discernment in the Quaker Tradition." *The Way Supplement* 64, no. Spring (1989): 51-62.

Fitzgerald, Constance. "Impasse and Dark Night." In *Living with Apocalypse*, edited by Tilden H Edwards. San Francisco, CA: Harper & Row, 1984.

Futrell, John Carroll. "Ignatian Discernment." *Studies in the Spirituality of Jesuits* II, no. 2 (1970).

Futrell, John Carroll. "Communal Discernment." *Studies in the Spirituality of Jesuits* IV, no. 5 (1972).

Gallagher, Brian, *Communal Wisdom (revised edition),* Bayswater, Vic, Coventry Press, 2018.

Gallagher, Timothy M. *The Discernment of Spirits*. New York: Crossroad, 2005.

Guillet, Jacques. "Sacred Scripture in Discernment of Spirits." In *Discernment of Spirits*, 17-54. Collegeville, MN: The Liturgical Press, 1970.

Larkin, Ernest E. *Silent Presence*. Denville NJ: Dimension Books, 1981.

Larkin, Ernest E. "What to Know About Discernment." *Review for Religious* 60, no. 2 (2001): 162-70.

Liebert, Elizabeth. *The Way of Discernment*. Louisville, Ky: Westminster John Knox Press, 2008.

Liebert, Elizabeth. *The Soul of Discernment*. Louisville, Ky: Westminster John Knox Press, 2015.

Lonsdale, David. *Dance to the Music of the Spirit*. London: Darton, Longman & Todd, 1992.

Malatesta, Edward. "Introduction to Discernment of Spirits." In *Discernment of Spirits*. Collegeville, MN: The Liturgical Press, 1970.

O'Sullivan, Michael J. "Trust Your Feelings, but Use Your Head: Discernment and the Psychology of Decision Making." *Studies in the Spirituality of Jesuits* 22, no. 4 (1990).

Owen, Harrison. *The Power of Spirit*. San Francisco, CA: Berrett-Koehler Publishing Inc, 2000.

Silf, Margaret. *On Making Choices*. Oxford, UK: Lion Hudson, 2004.

Tetlow, Joseph A. *Always Discerning*. Chicago IL: Loyola Press, 2016.

Thibodeaux, Mark. *God's Voice Within*. Chicago, IL: Loyola Press, 2010.

Toner, Jules J. "A Method for Communal Discernment of God's Will." *Studies in the Spirituality of Jesuits* III, no. 4 (1971).

Toner, Jules J. *A Commentary on St. Ignatius' Rules for the Discernment of Spirits*. St. Louis, MO: Institute of Jesuit Sources, 1982.

Toner, Jules J. *Discerning God's Will*. St. Louis, MO: Institute of Jesuit Sources, 1991.

Ward, Benedicta. "Discernment: A Rare Bird." *The Way Supplement* 64 (1989): 10-18.

Recommended Reading

On formation of spiritual directors

AECSD. *Standards for the Formation of Spiritual Directors*. Edited by Australian Ecumenical Council for Spiritual Direction. Melbourne, Vic, 2005.

AECSD. *Guidelines for the Formation of Spiritual Directors*. Edited by Australian Ecumenical Council for Spiritual Direction. Melbourne, Vic., 2008.

AECSD. *Contemplatively Forming Tomorrow's Spiritual Directors*. Edited by Australian Ecumenical Council for Spiritual Direction. Melbourne, Vic., 2015.

Rulla, Luigi M. "The Discernment of Spirits and Christian Anthropology." *Gregorianum* 59, no. 3 (1978): 537-69.

Rulla, Luigi M. *Depth Psychology and Vocation*. Rome: Gregorian University Press, 1983.

Rulla, Luigi M. *Anthropology of the Christian Vocation*. Rome: Gregorian University Press, 1986.

On Prayer and Spirituality

Congar, Yves. *I Believe in the Holy Spirit*. New York: Crossroad Publishing Company, 1997.

Edwards, Denis. *Human Experience of God*. New York: Paulist, 1983.

Edwards, Denis. *Breath of Life: A Theology of the Creator Spirit*. Maryknoll, NY: Orbis Books, 2004.

Gallagher, Brian. *Taking God to Heart*. Strathfield, NSW: St Pauls, 2008.

Horney, Karen. *Neurosis and Human Growth*. New York: W. W. Norton & Co, 1950.

Ignatius Loyola. *The Spiritual Exercises of St. Ignatius*. Edited by Louis J. Puhl. Chicago, IL: Loyola University Press, 1951.

Ignatius Loyola. *The Autobiography of St. Ignatius Loyola*. Edited by John C. Olin. Translated by Joseph F. O'Callaghan. New York: Fordham University Press, 1992.

John of the Cross. "The Ascent of Mount Carmel." In *The Collected Works of St. John of the Cross*, edited by Kieran Kavanaugh and Otilio Rodriguez. Washington, DC: Institute of Carmelite Studies, 1973.

John of the Cross. "Censure and Opinion." In *The Collected Works of St. John of the Cross*, edited by Kieran Kavanaugh and Otilio Rodriguez, 683-84. Washington DC: Institute of Carmelite Studies, 1973.

John of the Cross. "Dark Night." In *The Collected Works of St. John of the Cross*, edited by Kieran Kavanaugh and Otilio Rodriguez. Washington DC: Institute of Carmelite Studies, 1973.

John of the Cross. "The Living Flame of Love." In *The Collected Works of St. John of the Cross*, edited by Kieran Kavanaugh and Otilio Rodriguez. Washington DC: Institute of Carmelite Studies, 1973.

John of the Cross. "Spiritual Canticle." In *The Collected Works of St. John of the Cross*, edited by Kieran Kavanaugh and Otilio Rodriguez. Washington DC: Institute of Carmelite Studies, 1973.

John of the Cross. *Centered on Love: The Poems of Saint John of the Cross*. Translated by Marjorie Flower. Varroville NSW: The Carmelite Nuns, 1983, reprinted 2002.

Johnson, Elizabeth A. *She Who Is: The Mystery of God in Feminist Theological Discourse*. New York: Crossroad, 1993.

Keating, Thomas. *The Human Condition*. New York: Paulist, 1999.

Matthew, Iain. *The Impact of God*. London: Hodder & Stoughton, 1995.

Merton, Thomas. *Contemplative Prayer*. New York: Herder & Herder, 1969.

Murphy-O'Connor, Jerome. *Becoming Human Together: The Pastoral Anthropology of St. Paul*. Wilmington, DL: Michael Glazier Inc, 1982.

Rahner, Karl. "Reflections on the Experience of Grace." In *Theological Investigations*, vol III. New York: Seabury, 1967.

Rahner, Karl. "Experience of the Holy Spirit." In *Theological Investigations*, vol XVIII. New York: Seabury, 1983.

Rahner, Karl. *Ignatius of Loyola Speaks*. Translated by Annemarie S. Kidder. South Bend, IN: St. Augustine's Press, 2013.

Teresa of Avila. "The Book of Her Life." In *The Collected Works of St. Teresa of Avila*, edited by Kieran Kavanaugh and Otilio Rodriguez. Washington DC: Institute of Carmelite Studies, 1963.

Teresa of Avila. "The Way of Perfection." In *The Collected Works of St. Teresa of Avila*, edited by Kieran Kavanaugh and Otilio Rodriguez. Washington, DC: Institute of Carmelite Studies, 1963.

www.ingramcontent.com/pod-product-compliance
Lightning Source LLC
Chambersburg PA
CBHW052012290426
44112CB00014B/2215